Studio Visual Steps

Interesting Online Applications for SENIORS

Get aquainted with thirteen free Internet applications

www.visualsteps.com

This book has been written by Yvette Huijsman, Sietse Kuipers, Alex Wit, Emma Schipper and Henk Mol using the Visual Steps™ method.
Translated by Yvette Huijsman and Chris Hollingsworth.
Edited by Jolanda Ligthart, Ria Beentjes and Rilana Groot.
Copyright 2008 by Visual Steps B.V.
Cover design by Studio Willemien Haagsma bNO

First printing: November 2008
ISBN 978 90 5905 285 7

Would you like more information?
www.visualsteps.com

Do you have questions or suggestions?
E-mail: info@visualsteps.com

Website for this book:
www.visualsteps.com/online
Here you can register your book.

Register your book
We will keep you aware of any important changes that are necessary to you as a user of the book. You can also take advantage of our periodic newsletter informing you of our product releases, company news, tips & tricks, special offers, etcetera.
www.visualsteps.com/online

Table of Contents

Foreword

The World Wide Web (WWW) is quickly becoming a treasure trove of interesting online applications. With these programs, services and tools you have new methods of communicating with your loved ones, friends and family and easier ways to look up information. Or perhaps you want to organize, maintain and share your photo collection. You can use one of the many free services to create your own online web album. This is a great way to show your photos to friends and family who live far away.

Buying and selling on the Internet is steadily becoming more and more popular. You may have spent years trying to find that one final addition to your collection, and now there is *eBay*, an online auction site with tens of thousands of items from all over the world.

There are also many websites that allow you to create your own blog or personal webpage. Many users post a new message on their page every day and visit the pages of their friends and acquaintances. A blog is a very convenient way of letting others know about your activities, for example when you are travelling. You can update these blogs or webpages from any computer as long as it is connected to the Internet.

In addition to these applications, there are many more interesting things. Take *Google Earth* for example, a spectacular application about the planet we live on. Or *Google Maps*, a useful tool when you want to plan a trip, whether it be across town or on the other side of the globe! In short: there is plenty enough to discover on the Internet!

All of the online applications and programs described in this book are easy to download and available for free. So what are you waiting for?

We wish you a lot of fun with these interesting online applications!

The Studio Visual Steps authors

Your comments and suggestions are most welcome.
Our e-mail address is mail@visualsteps.com

Introduction to Visual Steps™

The Visual Steps handbooks and manuals are the best instructional materials available for learning how to work with computers. Nowhere else can you find better support for getting to know the computer, the Internet, *Windows* and related software programs.

Properties of the Visual Steps books:

- **Comprehensible contents**
  Addresses the needs of the beginner or intermediate computer user for a manual written in simple, straight-forward language.
- **Clear structure**
  Precise, easy to follow instructions. The material is broken down into small enough segments to allow for easy absorption.
- **Screenshots of every step**
  Quickly compare what you see on your screen with the screenshots in the book. Pointers and tips guide you when new windows are opened so you always know what to do next.
- **Get started right away**
  All you have to do is turn on your computer, place the book next to your keyboard, and begin at once.
- **Format**
  The text is formatted to allow easy readability.

In short, I believe these manuals will be excellent guides for you.

dr. H. van der Meij

Faculty of Applied Education, Department of Instruction Technology, University of Twente, the Netherlands

What You Will Need

In order to work through this book, you will need a few things on your computer:

The primary requirement is that you have **Windows Vista** or **Windows XP** installed on your computer.

The screenshots in this book have been made on a computer running *Vista*. This book is also perfectly suitable for a computer running *XP*. If any difference may occur in a window or a particular set of instructions, it will be noted.

To be able to work with the Internet you also need to have these two programs installed on your computer:
- *Internet Explorer* 7
- *Windows Mail* or *Outlook Express*

These programs are included in *Windows*.

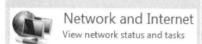

To work the most effectively with the online applications discussed, a fast **Internet connection** (DSL or cable) is necessary.

⇨ **Please note:**

Be sure you are logged in to *Windows* with a user account that has administrator rights. If you are logged in as a user without administrator rights, *Windows* will ask for the administrator password before you can install a program or notify you that you are not entitled to perform a particular action.
In case you do not have any experience in using user accounts, you can find more information in these Visual Steps books:

- **More Windows Vista for SENIORS** - ISBN 978 90 5905 055 6
- **More Windows XP for SENIORS** - ISBN 978 90 5905 114 0

How to Use This Book

This book has been written using the Visual Steps™- method. The method is simple: have the book near you as you work on your computer, read the relevant section and perform the tasks as described. The concise instructions with screenshots to visualize each step tell you exactly what to do. By performing the tasks right away, you will quickly learn how to work with the applications described in this book.

In this Visual Steps™ book you will see various icons. This is what they mean:

Techniques
These icons indicate an action to be carried out:

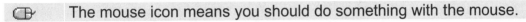   The mouse icon means you should do something with the mouse.

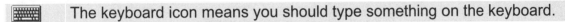   The keyboard icon means you should type something on the keyboard.

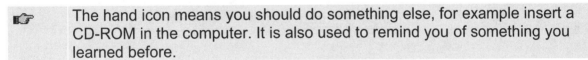   The hand icon means you should do something else, for example insert a CD-ROM in the computer. It is also used to remind you of something you learned before.

In addition to these techniques, sometimes **extra help** is given to assist you in working through this book more effectively.

Help
These icons indicate that extra help is available:

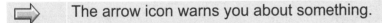   The arrow icon warns you about something.

   The bandage icon will help you if something has gone wrong.

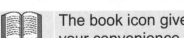   Have you forgotten how to do something? The number next to the footsteps tells you where to look it up in *Appendix B How Do I Do That Again?*

In separate boxes you find tips or additional, background information.

Extra information
Information boxes are denoted by these icons:

   The book icon gives you extra background information that you can read at your convenience. This extra information is not necessary for working through the book.

   The light bulb icon indicates an extra tip for using the program.

The Reading Order

This book is set up in such a way that you do not necessarily need to work through the book from beginning to end. Work through the chapters at your own pace and in the order you want, depending on your interests.

The Screenshots

The screenshots in this book were made on a computer running *Windows Vista Ultimate*. Depending on the *Vista* edition you have on your computer, the screenshots may look a little bit different from what you see on your screen. This makes no difference however in performing the requested actions. In the text it will be noted where a difference may occur.

The screenshots used in this book indicate which button, folder, file or hyperlink you need to click on your computer screen. In sections with bold text you will see a cut-out of the exact portion of the window where you should click. Heavy black lines point to the location of the item in the window on your computer screen. Please be aware that some of the smaller screenshots may contain some text that is not legible, but this is not important. Each window depicted in the book appears in actual size on your computer screen and is easy to read. It is not necessary for you to read the textual information shown in the screenshots.

 Help! Other windows.

The program windows and the various options available for each application described in this book may be updated or otherwise modified by their creators after this book is published. If this happens, the screenshots in this book may no longer be (completely) the same as what you see on your screen. In most cases you can still perform the described actions, because these applications are not radically changed. You may have to search a little while for the right button or the location of a hyperlink. As soon as an application is changed radically, the differences will be explained on the website of this book. If you notice that the screenshots in your book look totally different from what you see on your screen, you can visit this book's website to see if the revised chapter is available.

Please refer to webpage **www.visualsteps.com/online**

Newsletter

All Visual Steps books follow the same methodology: each new concept is carefully explained in small steps and richly illustrated with screenshots.

A listing of all available books can be found on **www.visualsteps.com**
Visit our website and subscribe to the **free Visual Steps Newsletter** sent by e-mail.

The Visual Steps Newsletter provides periodic information about:
- the latest titles and previously released books;
- special offers, free guides;
- news about recent updates that may apply to a Visual Steps book.

Our Newsletter subscribers have access to free information booklets, handy tips and guides which are listed on the webpages **www.visualsteps.com/info_downloads** and the tips on **www.visualsteps.com/tips**

Test Your Knowledge

When you have completed this book, you can test your knowledge by taking one of the free tests available on the website **www.ccforseniors.com**
These multiple choice tests will show you how much you know about the computer, *Windows* and related programs.
If you pass the test, you are eligible to receive a Free Computer Certificate by e-mail.
There are **no costs** involved in taking part in these tests. The test website is a free service provided to subscribers of the free Visual Steps Newsletter.

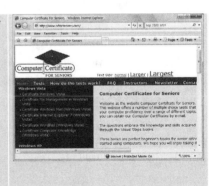

For Teachers

Visual Steps books are designed as self-study guides for individual use. These books are also well-suited for use in a group or a classroom setting. For some titles, a free teacher's manual (PDF file) is available. The teacher's manuals and other additional materials can be found on the website: **www.visualsteps.com/instructor**
You can use this free service after registering on this website.

1. Plan Your Trip with Google Maps

It has become increasingly popular to plan a trip or find a location with a special kind of planning application known as a road trip planner or route planner. In addition to in-car navigation systems (like the well known TomTom and Garmin systems), there are many trip planners and map services available on the Internet. The advantage of these online applications is the ability to display additional information. With so much information available from the Internet along with satellite imagery, it is more easier than ever to plan a trip across town or look up a friend's address on the other side of the world.

Google Maps is an excellent example of a free Internet application that lets you view maps and satellite imagery. *Google* is the company that offers the well known search engine application. Trip planners are not only useful for preparing a long trip; you can use *Google Maps* to find places of interest right in your own neighbourhood.

In this chapter you will learn how to use the most important features of *Google Maps*.

In this chapter you learn how to:

- find a location;
- zoom in and out on the map;
- move the map;
- set a default location;
- view satellite imagery of a location;
- find businesses and organizations;
- plan a trip;
- view detailed maps;
- print directions;
- change a route.

1.1 Finding a Location

You do not need to install anything on your computer to be able to use *Google Maps.* The maps can be accessed from the *Google Maps* website.

☞ **Open *Internet Explorer*** ¹

You see the home page that is set on your computer.

Click in the Address bar

The web address in the Address bar is now selected.

Type:
`maps.google.com`

Press Enter ↵

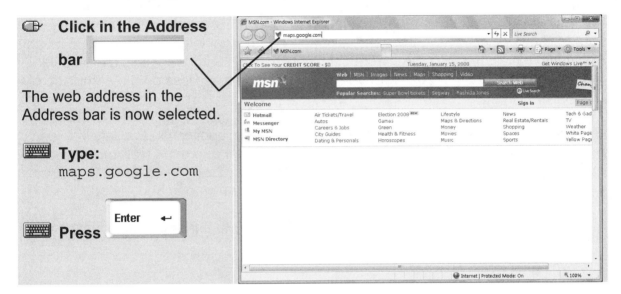

➡ **Please note:**

You do not need to type **www** in front of the web address maps.google.com

You see the *Google Maps* window:

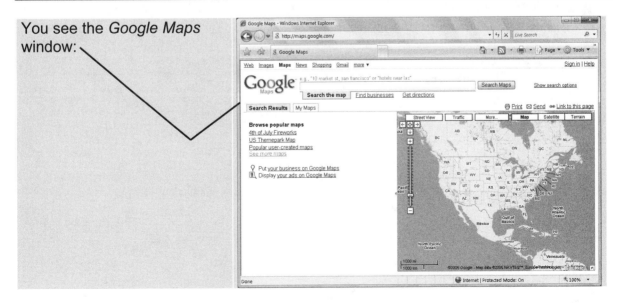

You can start using this application right away. The first step is to find a location. For example when planning a trip, you could enter a city that you plan to visit. Or simply look up any address that you would like to see on the map.

The cursor is already in the box where you can type an address:

 Type:

1600 pennsylvania ave nw 20500

 Press Enter ⏎

💡 Tip

It is not necessary to use caps when you type an address.

The address is indicated on the map:

You see that information is added even if you have not typed the full address:

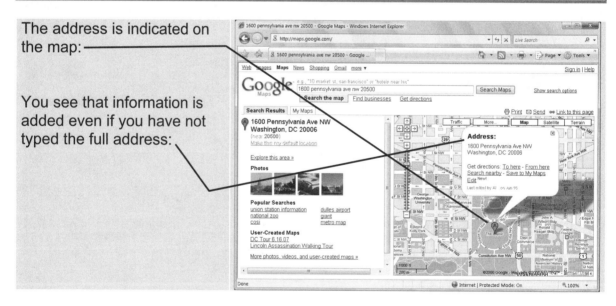

In this example you typed a street name, a house number and a ZIP code to determine the exact location of an address. If you just type a street name and a city, the general area of the street you typed is indicated on the map.

You can close the information window with the address details to get a better look at the map:

Click ⊠

The information window is hidden now.

To display the information window again:

Click

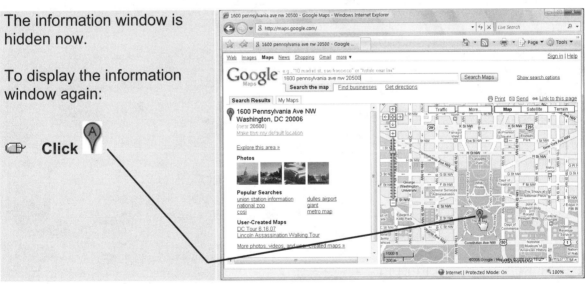

1.2 Zooming In and Out

You see the White House and its surroundings. You can zoom out to see more of the local area:

Click ⊟ three times

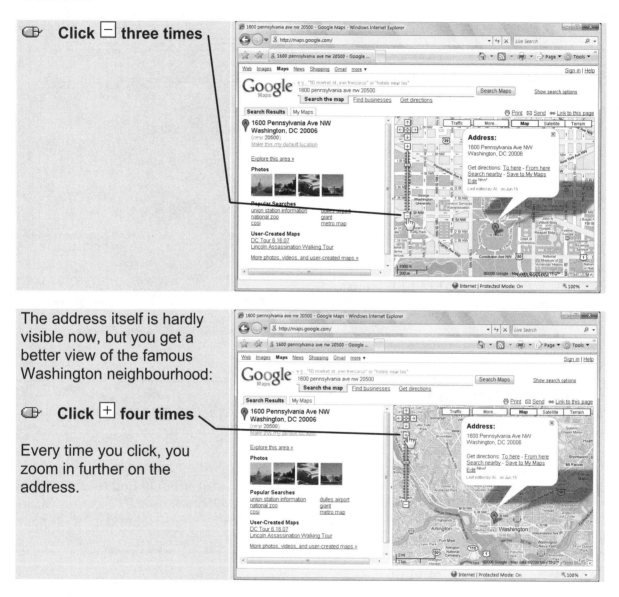

The address itself is hardly visible now, but you get a better view of the famous Washington neighbourhood:

Click ⊞ four times

Every time you click, you zoom in further on the address.

You can also show a small map that shows the location of the current map view within the context of a larger geographical area:

Click ◹

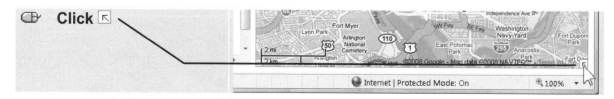

Tip

Zooming in and out by dragging
You can also zoom in and out by dragging the slider ⊟ in the zoom bar:

To zoom in:

 Drag the slider ⊟ up

To zoom out:

 Drag the slider ⊟ down

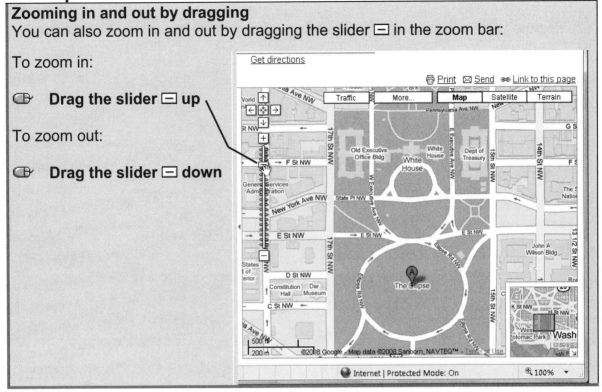

 Tip

Zooming in and out by double-clicking
When you double-click a spot on the map, you zoom in on that location. When you double-click using your right mouse button, you zoom out again.

You can work even faster when your mouse has a scroll wheel:
- when you roll the wheel forward (away from you), you zoom in and everything is enlarged;
- when you turn the wheel backward (toward you), you zoom out and everything becomes smaller.

1.3 Moving the Map

When you zoom in, you see the location you searched for and part of the surrounding area. If you want to see another part of the adjacent area you can move the map:

☞ **Place the mouse pointer on the map**

The mouse pointer changes into ✋:

☞ **Click the map and hold the mouse button down**

The mouse pointer changes into ✊. Now you can drag:

☞ **Drag the mouse pointer a little bit upward**

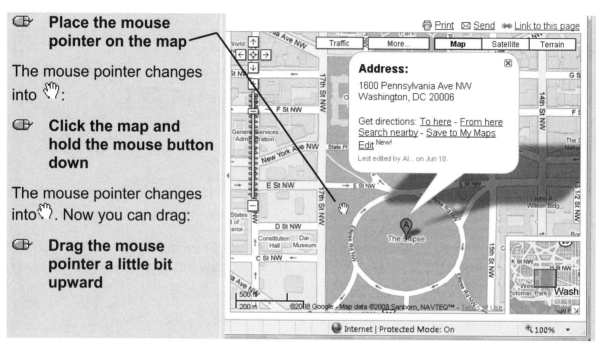

The map moves upward and you see a larger area below the location:

You can also use a different method to move the map:

☞ **Click ← three times**

The map moves to the left.

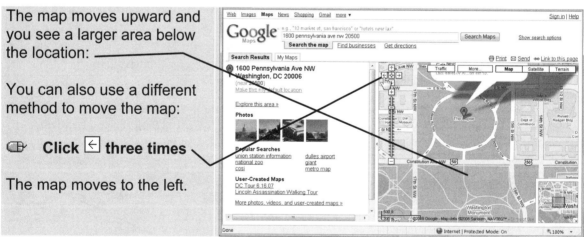

Using the buttons ←, ↑, ↓ and →, you move the map in the direction of the arrow.

 Tip

You can also move the map using your keyboard. Use the buttons Page Up (up), Page Down (down), Home (left) and End (right).

You can quickly return to your original view of the map like this:

👉 **Click** ⊞

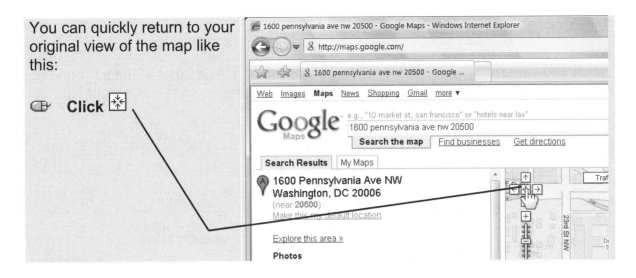

1.4 Setting a Default Location

You can set your own address or another address as the default location. Then you do not need to type the address every time. To show how this works, you can make the White House your default location:

👉 **Click**
Make this my default location

You see the default address:

To see the result of this action, close the program *Internet Explorer*:

👉 **Click** [X]

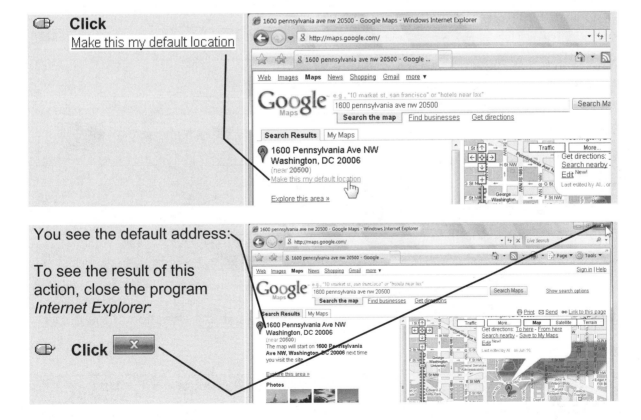

Now you open *Internet Explorer* again:

☞ **Open *Internet Explorer***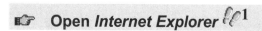

☞ **Go to the web address maps.google.com**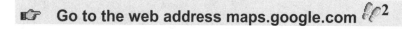

Your default location appears when the program opens: —

The default location is no longer indicated with a green arrow.

If you want to change the default location, you can click Change default location.

Then you can type a new address and save it.

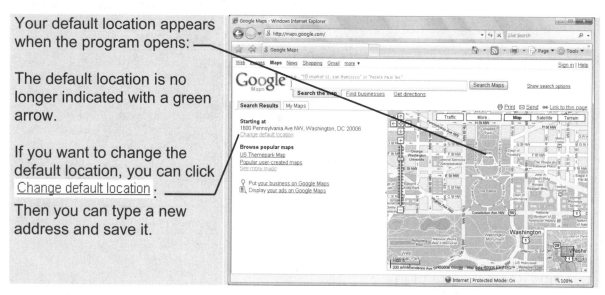

1.5 Using Satellite Images

Even though *Google Maps* is meant to be used with maps, you can also view satellite images of the locations.

☞ **Click** Satellite

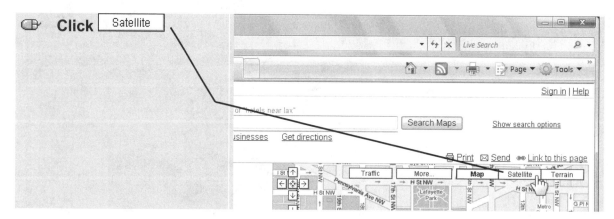

Now you see the satellite imagery of the same area.

By default, the street names are displayed in the satellite imagery:

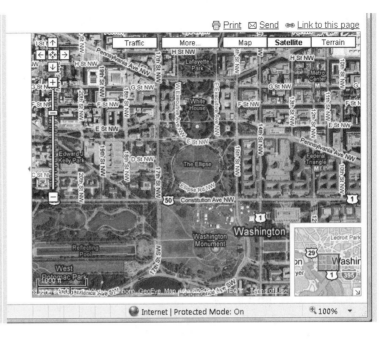

Tip

Hiding the street names

If you want to see the satellite image without the street names, you can hide them like this:

👆 **Point to** | Satellite |

A small menu appears:

In *Google Maps*, the street names are called *labels*.

👆 **Click to remove the check mark for**

☑ Show labels

The street names are removed from the image.

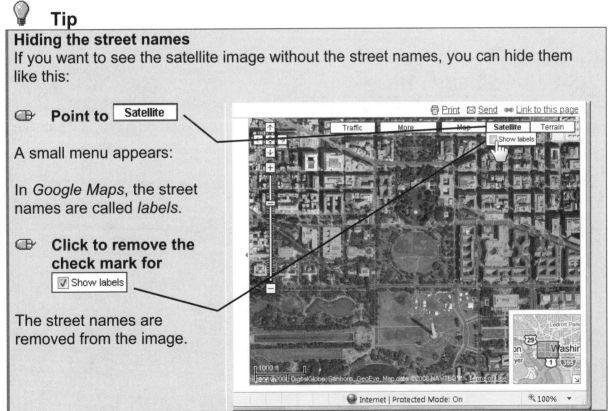

Just like you did with the regular map, you can move the map and zoom in or out:

Click ⊞ twice

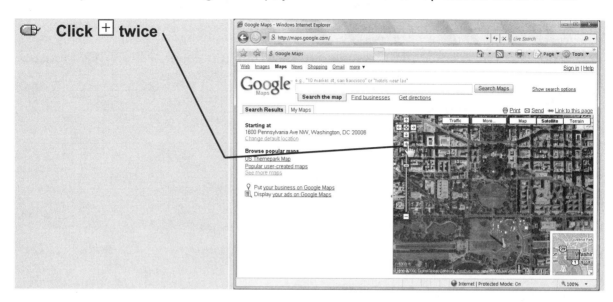

The satellite imagery is enlarged, just like the map earlier.

⇨ Please note:

The quality of the satellite images may be different for each area. When you zoom in too far, the image often becomes blurry and it is difficult to see details.
Strategic objects, like military airfields and bases are always blurred on the satellite images.

To return to the regular map:

Click [Map]

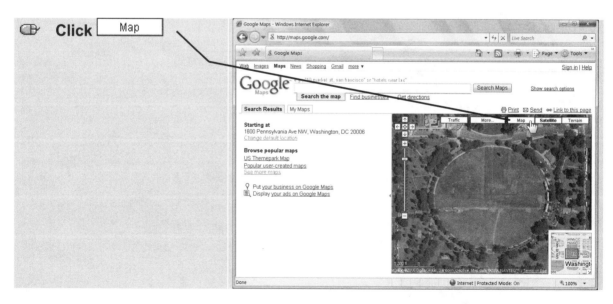

1.6 Finding Businesses and Organizations

In addition to cities and streets, you can also search for businesses and organizations. To demonstrate this, you can try to find a hotel near the White House:

Click Find businesses

Type:
hotel

Click   Search Businesses

Google Maps searches for a hotel in the area of your current location. When more than one location is found, you can select one from the list:

If necessary, drag the vertical scroll bar down

For example, click

More information is available for this hotel. This is indicated on the map by the

placemarker :

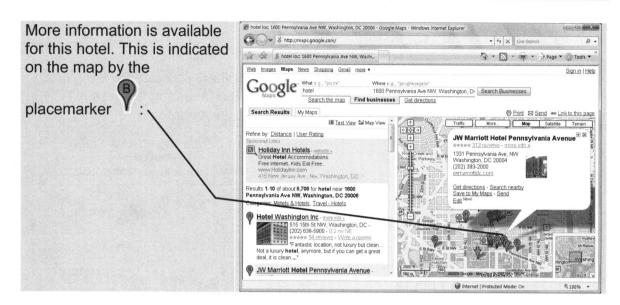

💡 **Tip**

When you look for a hotel in another city, enter the city name and either the state or ZIP code:

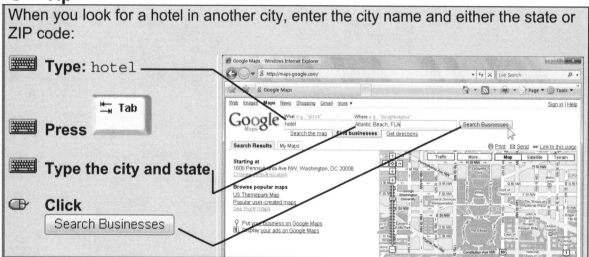

⌨ **Type:** `hotel`

⌨ **Press** [⇥ Tab]

⌨ **Type the city and state**

🖱 **Click** [Search Businesses]

➡ **Please note:**

Google Maps gathers business information from numerous websites, Yellow Pages directories, and other sources to populate the search results. This information may not always be current or correct. If you cannot find what you are looking for, you can try searching for the address of the business or organization.

1.7 Getting Directions

It is very easy to get directions from one location to another. You can get the exact route to the nearest pizza parlor or the closest post office for example. Here is how to get directions from Washington Dulles Airport to the hotel you found previously:

Click Get directions

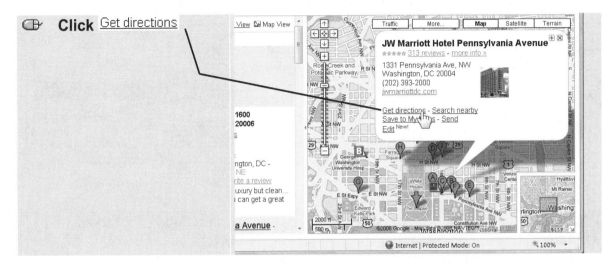

By default, the current location is listed in the blue box under Start address . You can now enter a different starting point:

Type:
washington dulles
airport

Click Go

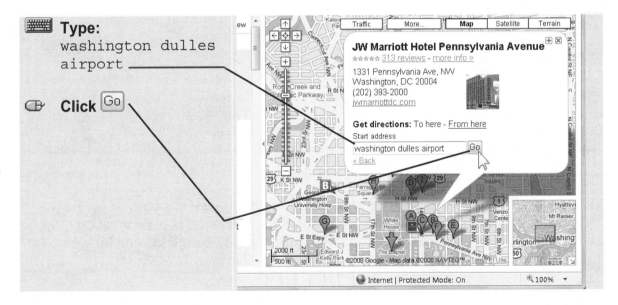

 Tip

From here
When you click From here, the current location becomes the start address (the *from*) and you can enter the end address yourself (the *to*).

Google Maps shows the directions on the map. On the left side of the window the directions are displayed as text. If necessary, you can zoom in on the map, move the map or hide the overview map to get a better view of the route:

If necessary, click ⌄ **to hide the overview map**

If necessary, move the map to see the whole route 👣⁸

The distance and travelling time by car are indicated here

30.8 mi – about 43 mins
up to 1 hour 0 mins in traffic

In the text the directions are described step by step:

To read the last part of the directions:

Drag the vertical scroll bar down

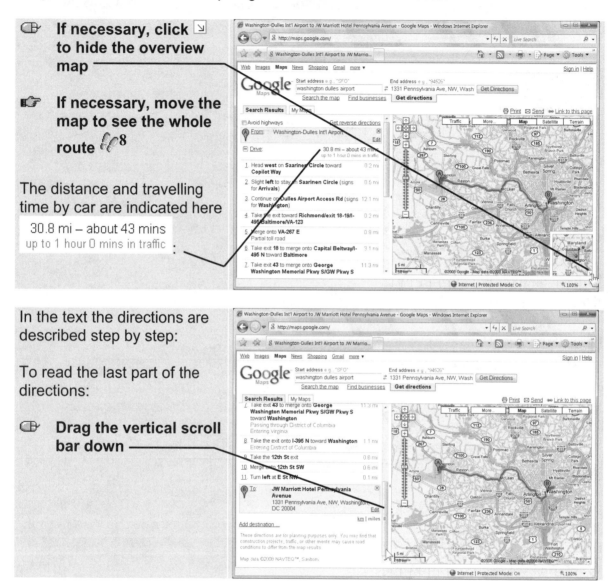

Tip

Detailed map

You can view detailed maps of the destination and of each step along the route:

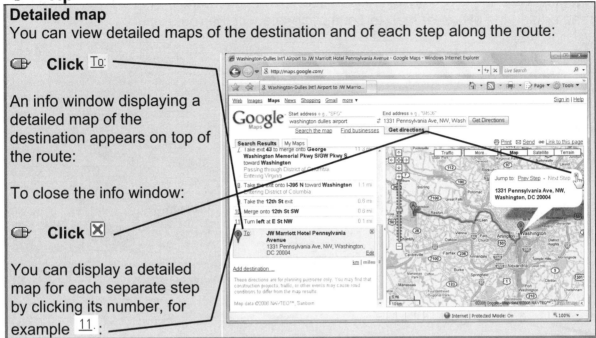

Click To:

An info window displaying a detailed map of the destination appears on top of the route:

To close the info window:

Click ☒

You can display a detailed map for each separate step by clicking its number, for example 11:

 Tip

Traffic information

Another useful feature in *Google Maps* is the ability to obtain traffic information. To see the current traffic conditions for a route you planned, do the following:

Click [Traffic]

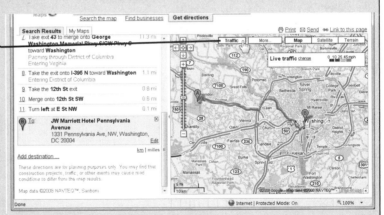

Now the map also shows the traffic conditions.

Red depicts heavy traffic, yellow depicts slow traffic and green depicts normal speed. Gray indicates that no traffic information is currently available.

Traffic data is available in over 30 major US metropolitan areas (including Los Angeles, New York and Chicago), with partial coverage available in many more.

To hide the traffic information:

Click [Traffic]

1.8 Printing the Directions

If you want to take the directions along in your car, you can print them:

☞ **Click** 🖶 <u>Print</u>

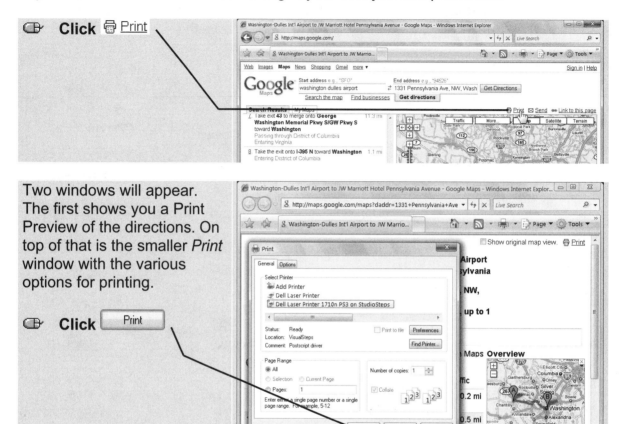

Two windows will appear. The first shows you a Print Preview of the directions. On top of that is the smaller *Print* window with the various options for printing.

☞ **Click** ⟦ Print ⟧

The directions are printed with three small maps containing:
- an overview of the route
- the start location
- the end location

You can close the Print Preview window:

☞ **Click** ⟦ X ⟧

1.9 Changing the Route

You can also change very easily the route you just planned. Let's say for example, you want to figure out how to get back to your hotel after visiting the US Thomas Jefferson Memorial. You can enter a new start address like this:

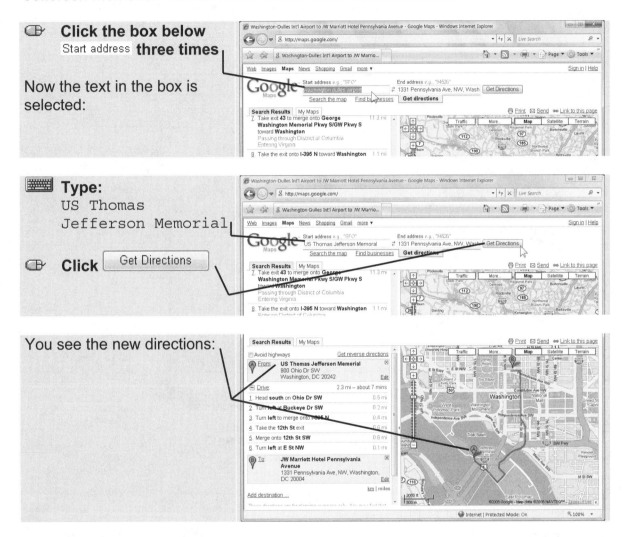

Click the box below `Start address` **three times**

Now the text in the box is selected:

Type:
US Thomas
Jefferson Memorial

Click `Get Directions`

You see the new directions:

 Tip

Dragging the start or end markers
You can also edit the start or end address by dragging the markers for the start address Ⓐ or end address Ⓑ on the map. Using this method however makes it a bit more difficult pinpointing an exact location.

1.10 Adding Destinations

If you want to travel to the National Zoo from the hotel, you can add a destination. The hotel will then become a stop on the route from the US Thomas Jefferson Memorial to the National Zoo:

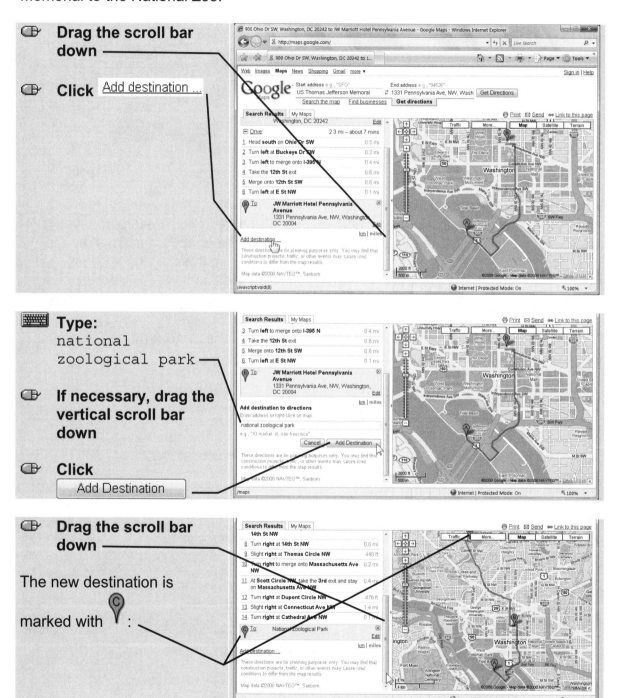

Drag the scroll bar down

Click Add destination ...

Type:
national
zoological park

If necessary, drag the vertical scroll bar down

Click Add Destination

Drag the scroll bar down

The new destination is marked with :

☞ **Drag the scroll bar up**

You see the total travelling
distance and time:

Here you see the travelling
distance and time for each
stretch of the route:

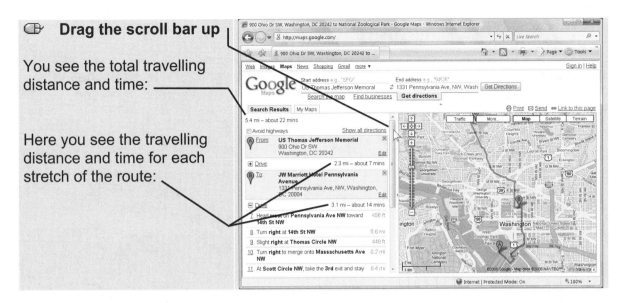

⇨ **Please note:**

If you want to make one or more stops on your way to your final destination, you
need to enter the stops and your final destination in the correct order. This means
you have to build up your route step by step from start address to end address.
Many other route planners work differently: you add the start and end address first
and then you add the stops you want to make along the way.

The directions are only displayed for the last stretch of the route. You can display the
directions for the first stretch like this:

☞ **Click** ⊞

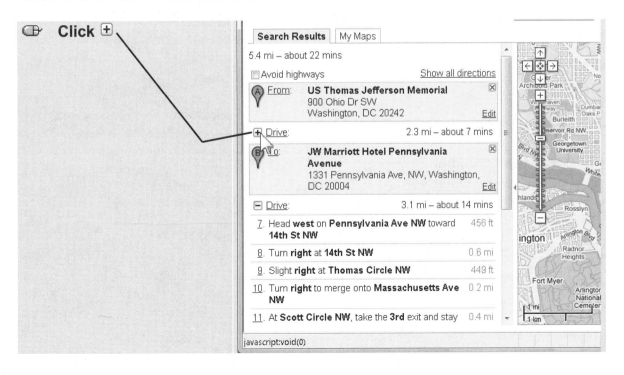

Tip

Adding destinations by dragging
In *Google Maps* you can add destinations between the start and end address of a route by dragging part of the route on the map. Using this method it is more difficult to pinpoint an exact location:

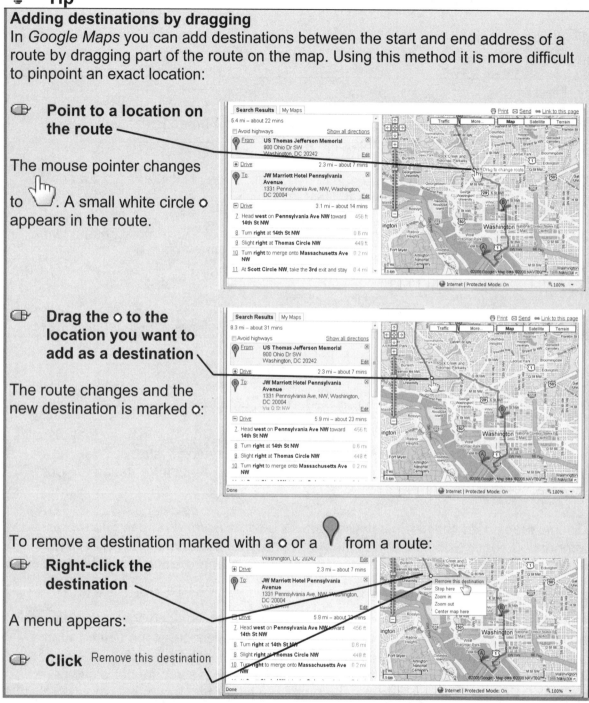

☞ **Point to a location on the route**

The mouse pointer changes to 🖑. A small white circle ○ appears in the route.

☞ **Drag the ○ to the location you want to add as a destination**

The route changes and the new destination is marked ○:

To remove a destination marked with a ○ or a 📍 from a route:

☞ **Right-click the destination**

A menu appears:

☞ **Click** Remove this destination

In this chapter you have learned how to find locations, businesses and routes using the maps and satellite imagery in *Google Maps*.

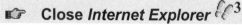 **Close** *Internet Explorer* ³

1.11 Background Information

Glossary	
Blurring	Making parts of an image or object unrecognizable in the satellite imagery.
Default location	Location you can set yourself, to be displayed as the first map when you open *Google Maps*.
Zoom in	Enlarging part of a map or image, allows a more detailed view.
Zooming (in / out)	Making part of a map larger or smaller.
Zoom out	Reducing part of a map or image, allows a less detailed view.

Reliability

The map data found in *Google Maps* is sourced largely from companies that also provide map data to manufacturers of automotive navigation systems. By using these maps on the Internet, you always have the most recent information at your disposal.

Google Maps uses the same satellite data as *Google Earth*. You can find more information about *Google Earth* in the next chapter of this book. *Google Earth* acquires the best imagery available, most of which is approximately one to three years old.

Not all cities are covered in high resolution detail (where you can see individual buildings and cars). Currently there is more imagery available of the United States than of other countries. And because the imagery comes from a variety of sources, and is meshed together, it is difficult to specify the date the imagery of a city or region was taken. A single city may be built from imagery taken in different months.

Source: Google Help Center

1.12 Tips

 Tip

Get reverse directions
To get directions for your way back, you can swap the start and end address:

 Click Get reverse directions

or:

Click ⇄

Click Get Directions

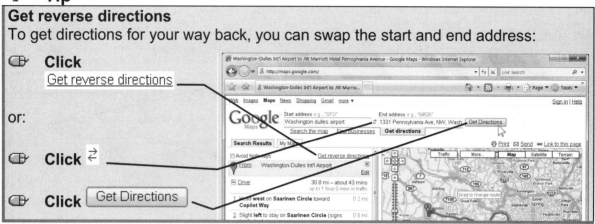

 Tip

More information
When you have found a place of interest, you can access more information directly:

Click more info »

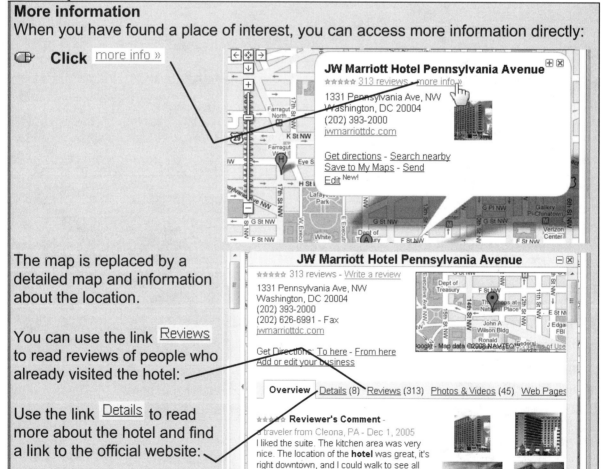

The map is replaced by a detailed map and information about the location.

You can use the link Reviews to read reviews of people who already visited the hotel:

Use the link Details to read more about the hotel and find a link to the official website:

Tip

Terrain view

The terrain view allows you to see physical features on the map, such as buildings, mountains and vegetation, with elevation shading.

To switch to terrain view:

⊂▷ **Click** | Terrain |

To return from terrain view to map view:

⊂▷ **Click** | Map |

Please note: terrain view is only available for selected areas.

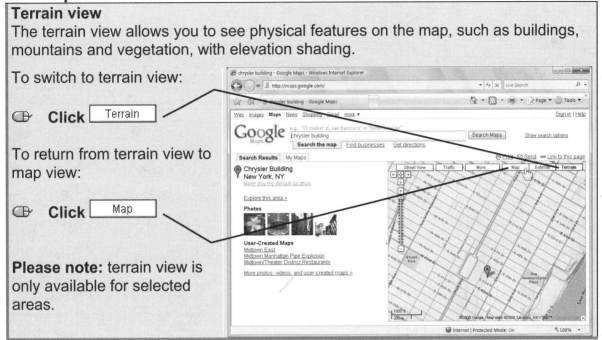

 Tip

Street view

In certain locations, you can view and navigate within street level imagery.

⊂▷ **Click** | Street View |

A human icon appears. The streets for which street level imagery is available now have a blue outline:

⊂▷ **Click**

An information window containing the street level imagery appears:

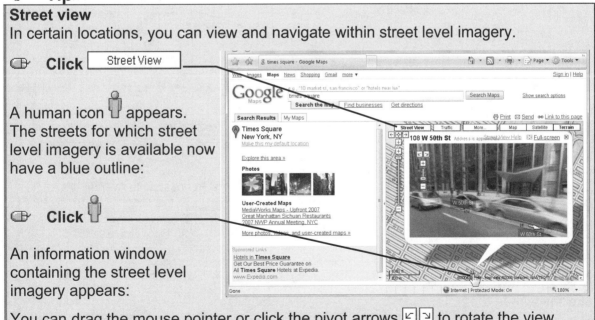

You can drag the mouse pointer or click the pivot arrows to rotate the view 360°. In some locations, you can drag the imagery up to look skyward.

To navigate along a blue outlined street, click one of the white arrows overlaid on the street to move in that direction. You can also use the arrow keys.

Tip

Saving locations

Google Maps allows you to save locations you look up regularly and to create your own personalized maps. You can add annotations and mark your favorite locations on your maps, and share the maps with your friends and family. You can also overlay information from other sources such as photos, weather and public transit maps on your map. To be able to use these features, you need to sign in to *Google Maps* first:

👆 **Click Sign in**

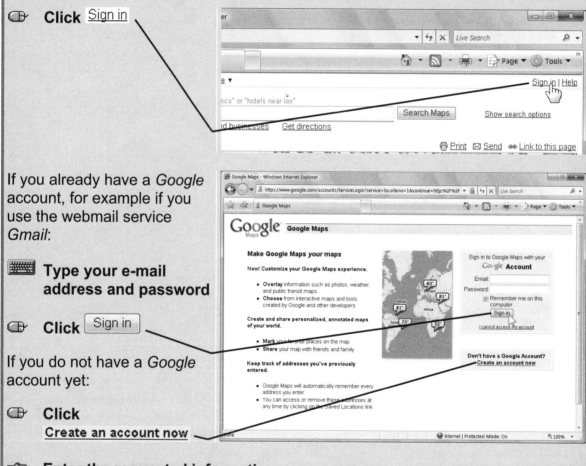

If you already have a *Google* account, for example if you use the webmail service *Gmail*:

⌨ **Type your e-mail address and password**

👆 **Click Sign in**

If you do not have a *Google* account yet:

👆 **Click**
Create an account now

☞ **Enter the requested information**

If you need any help, please check *Chapter 6.1 Creating a Google Account*.

👆 **Click I accept. Create my account.**

You will receive an e-mail containing a hyperlink that you need to click to confirm you signed up for a *Google* account. After that, you can use the features Saved locations and My maps.

Notes

Write down your notes here.

2. Explore the World with Google Earth

Every place on earth is regularly photographed from satellites in space. You can use *Google Earth* to show this satellite imagery on your computer and take a look at your hometown or other interesting places from the air.

Google is the company that offers the well known search engine application: www.google.com.

Google Earth is not only fun, but also very useful. Before you book a hotel, you can check if the hotel is really close to the beach, if the promised woods are larger than just five trees, and if the city dump is not located next to the hotel. Before you sign a lease on a house, it may be a good idea to take a look at its surroundings from the air.

The quality of the satellite imagery has increased so much, that even smaller details have become easily recognizable. Sometimes you can even see your own car standing in the driveway! Not all areas are covered in high resolution detail at this time, but there is continuous improvement. *Google Earth* acquires the best imagery available, most of which is approximately one to three years old.

In this chapter you learn how to use the most important features of the free version. You can find more information about the more extensive paid versions in the background information at the end of this chapter.

In this chapter you learn how to:

- install *Google Earth*;
- find locations;
- navigate and use the joystick;
- zoom in and out;
- look up photos and find information about a location;
- use layers;
- plan and fly a route;
- display a 3D model of a building;
- tilt a 3D model;
- mark locations.

2.1 Installing Google Earth

To be able to use *Google Earth*, you must first install the program on your computer. You use the program to view maps and other information that is found on the Internet. You can install *Google Earth* as follows:

☞ **Open *Internet Explorer*** 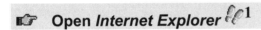¹

Now you see the home page that is set on your computer.

☞ **Surf to the web address earth.google.com**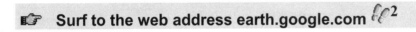

⇨ **Please note:**

You do not need to type **www** in front of the web address earth.google.com

You see this window:

☞ **Click**

Download Google Earth 4

There will be some extra options possible. To be able to see how you will normally start the program, turn off these options for now:

☞ **Click to remove all check marks**

☞ **Click**

Agree and Download

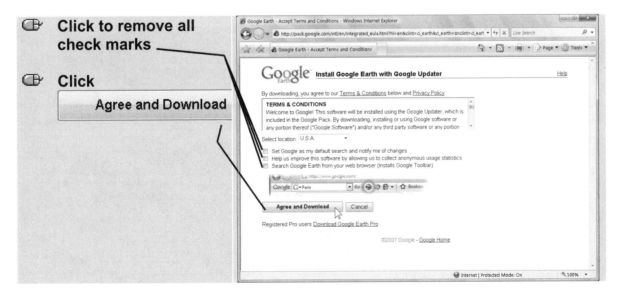

Please note:

Depending on the security settings of your computer and the version of *Windows* you use, some windows may not appear or you will get additional questions instead. In that case follow the directions in the window.

First the necessary files are downloaded from the Internet, and then they are installed. You see a couple of windows with information and questions:

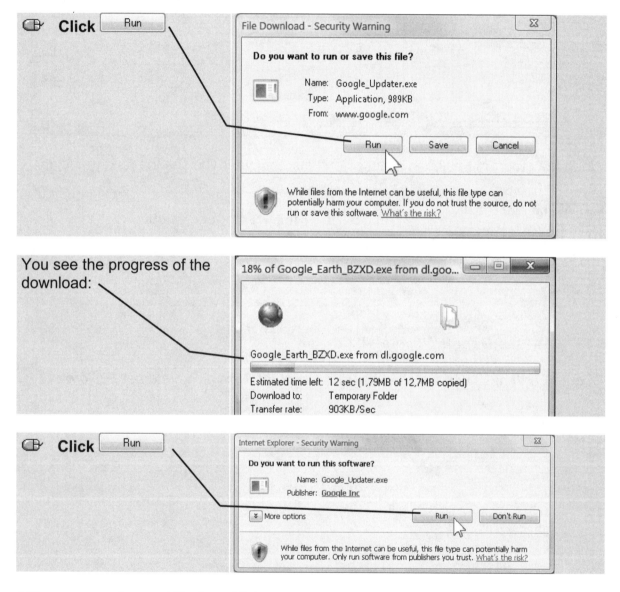

When you work on a *Windows Vista* computer, your screen goes dark and you need to give your permission to continue:

In the next window you see the progress of the installation procedure:

When the program has been installed on your computer you see the next window.

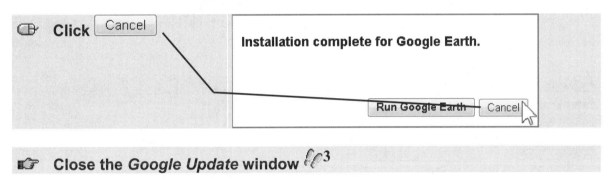

☞ **Close the *Google Update* window** 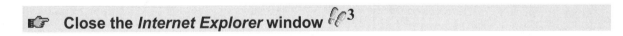³

Google Earth has been installed on your computer. Now close *Internet Explorer*.

☞ **Close the *Internet Explorer* window** ℓℓ³

2.2 Finding Locations

During the installation a shortcut to *Google Earth* was placed on your desktop. You use this shortcut to open the program:

☞ **Double-click**

Every time you open the program you see a tip:

☞ **Click** Close

You see a satellite image of the earth in the window.

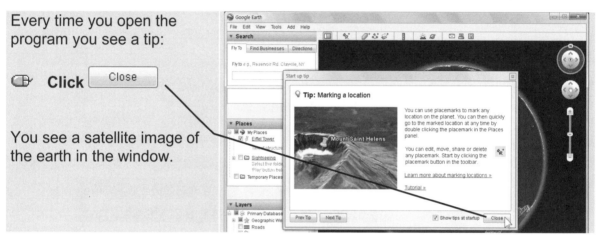

 HELP! I do not see the whole globe.

Depending on the settings of your computer, you will see the entire globe or only the middle portion. The North and South Pole may not be in view. This does not make a difference for the actions you are going to perform.

Now you can enter the location you want to view.

⌨ **Type:**
    eiffel tower,
    paris, france

☞ **Click** 🔍

 Tip

You do not need to use caps when you type an address.

Now you see a spectacular zoom sequence that takes you to the location you entered: the Eiffel Tower in Paris, France.

To hold overview in the sidebar.

☞ **Click** ⊟

2.3 Navigating

You can display a location by typing its address. Another way to view the satellite imagery is to navigate using the navigation controls.

You see the navigation controls in the top right corner of the window: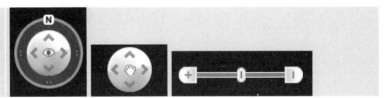

These navigation controls automatically disappear after a few moments and reappear when you place your mouse pointer on them. You are going to change this setting so the navigation controls are always visible:

☞ **Click** View

☞ **Click** Show Navigation

☞ **Click** Always

You can use the navigation arrows to move the photo.

Click ◄

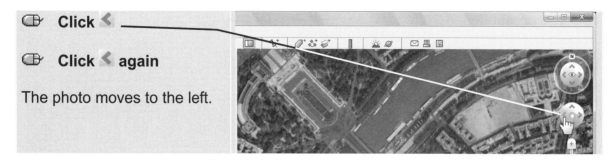

 Click ◄ **again**

The photo moves to the left.

🩹 HELP! The image keeps moving.

When you quickly click ◄ or another arrow a couple of times, the photo keeps moving. You can stop that by clicking the arrow or the photo once.

By clicking the arrow, you move the image. You can also use the *little hand* 🖐. The little hand is located in between the navigation arrows.

 Place the mouse pointer on 🖐

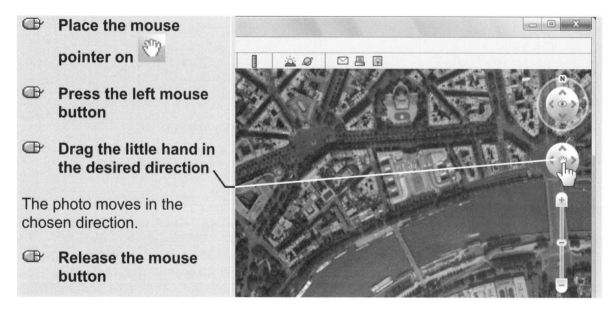

 Press the left mouse button

 Drag the little hand in the desired direction

The photo moves in the chosen direction.

 Release the mouse button

💡 Tip

In the *Google Earth* help windows you find an overview of the keyboard shortcuts you can use for navigation. Click Help , Keyboard Shortcuts and wait until the information is downloaded from the Internet.

To quickly return to the Eiffel Tower, you search for it again:

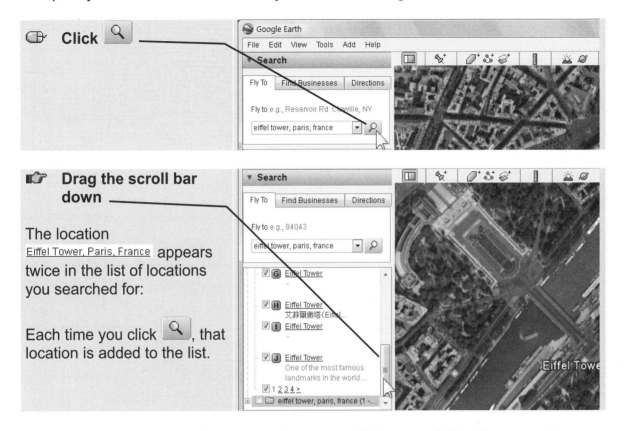

Click 🔍

☞ **Drag the scroll bar down**

The location Eiffel Tower, Paris, France appears twice in the list of locations you searched for:

Each time you click 🔍, that location is added to the list.

You can remove the locations you no longer need. You can delete the second location Eiffel Tower, Paris, France like this:

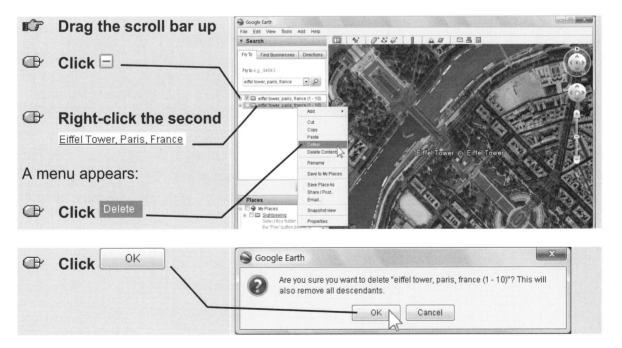

☞ **Drag the scroll bar up**

Click ⊟

Right-click the second Eiffel Tower, Paris, France

A menu appears:

Click Delete

Click OK

2.4 Zooming In and Out

You can zoom in to take a better look at the location:

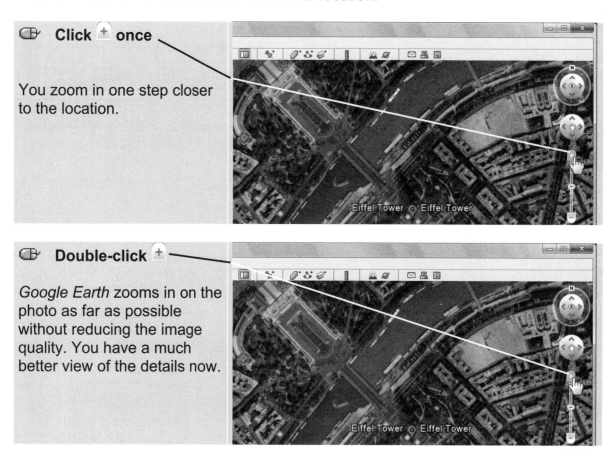

Click ⊕ once

You zoom in one step closer to the location.

Double-click ⊕

Google Earth zooms in on the photo as far as possible without reducing the image quality. You have a much better view of the details now.

To zoom out, you use the button ⊟.

2.5 Viewing Photos and Information

On the satellite image you see various symbols that when clicked can be used to view photos or additional information:

☞ **Click ⊞ until you see cameras**

☞ **Click a camera 📷**

💥 HELP! I do not see any cameras.

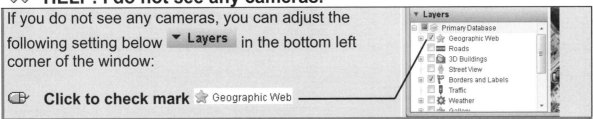

If you do not see any cameras, you can adjust the following setting below ▼ **Layers** in the bottom left corner of the window:

☞ **Click to check mark** ⭐ Geographic Web

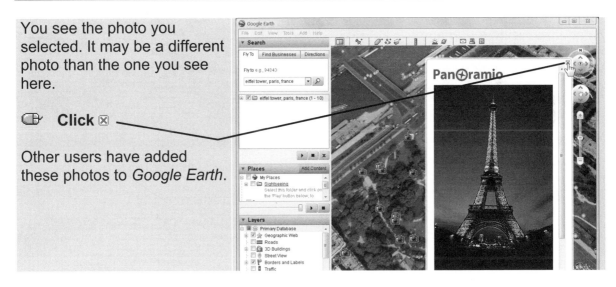

You see the photo you selected. It may be a different photo than the one you see here.

☞ **Click** ☒

Other users have added these photos to *Google Earth*.

You can check out more information that is added to this location.

The icons 📄 and 🔵 on the satellite image indicate that information has been added:

☞ **Click** 📄

A window is opened with information about the selected location:

This piece of background information was added by members of the *Google Earth Community*:

☞ **Click** ☒

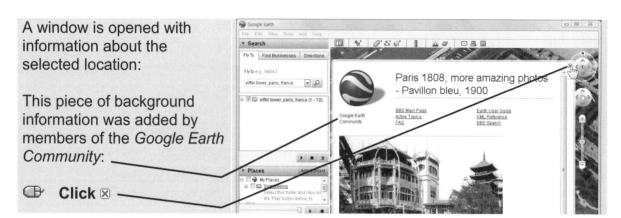

⇨ **Please note:**

If you do not see the icon ⬤ :

☞ **Click a couple of times** ±

☞ **Click** ⬤

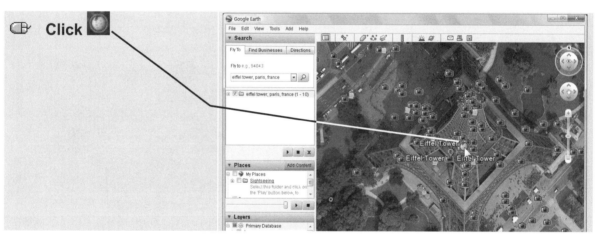

Now you see an article from the Internet encyclopedia *Wikipedia*:

☞ **Click** ☒

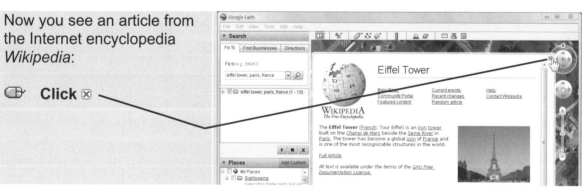

Tip

Hyperlinks

The text usually contains one or more hyperlinks that you can use to look up more information about that subject on the Internet.
These hyperlinks are blue and underlined, like Paris:

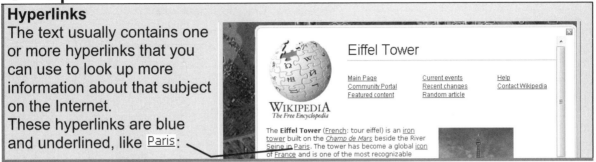

2.6 Measuring Using the Ruler

It is possible to measure distances on the satellite image. For example, you can use the ruler tool to measure the diameter of the Eiffel Tower.

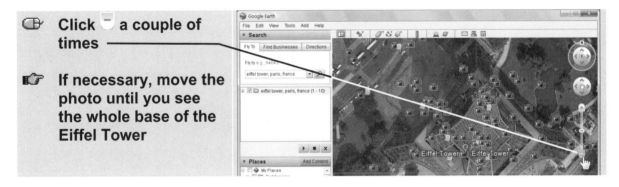

☞ **Click** ⊖ **a couple of times**

☞ **If necessary, move the photo until you see the whole base of the Eiffel Tower**

Note that when you zoom out further, the cameras change into blue dots ▣. You can still click these blue dots to display photos.

⚕ HELP! Google Earth keeps zooming out.

When you quickly click ⊖ a couple of times, *Google Earth* zooms out automatically. You can stop that by clicking the photo once. You can zoom in by clicking ⊕ again.

Now you can adjust the settings of the ruler:

 Click Tools

☞ **Click** Ruler

First set the measuring unit to yards.

☞ **Click** ▾

☞ **Click** Yards

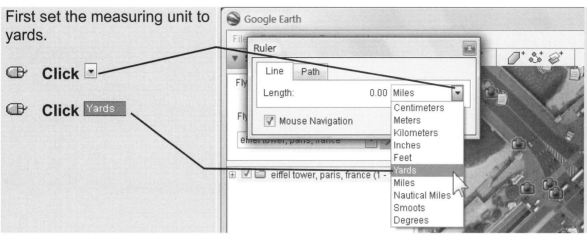

The mouse pointer changes into ⊡ :

☞ **Click one end of the base**

A small green dot appears at that spot.

☞ **Slide gently to the opposite end of the base**

A white line appears:

☞ **Click the end of the base**

You see the measured distance:

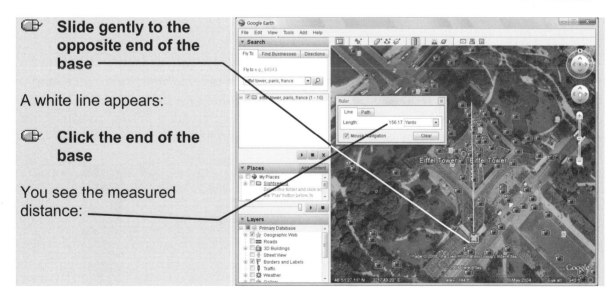

Click [Clear]

The line disappears.

You can close the ruler:

 Click ⊠

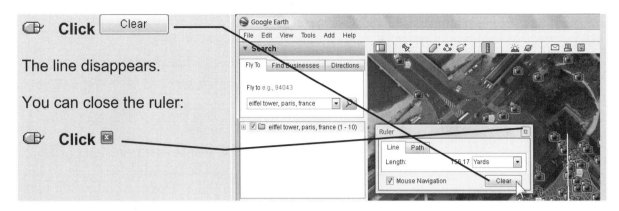

💡 **Tip**

The more you zoom in on the image, the more accurate the measurement will be.

💡 **Tip**

Length of a route
You can also measure the total distance of a route by clicking [Path]. You can click at each corner. You can also drag the line that is added. At the end you can view the total distance.

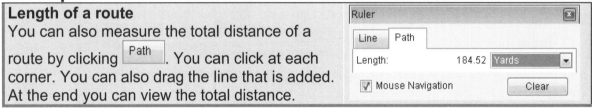

2.7 Adding Layers

On every satellite image additional information is displayed, such as the photos and the information windows. You can decide for yourself which items you want to display or hide in *Google Earth*. The additional information is displayed in layers on top of the image. You can hide the layer with the photo information like this:

At the left side of the window:

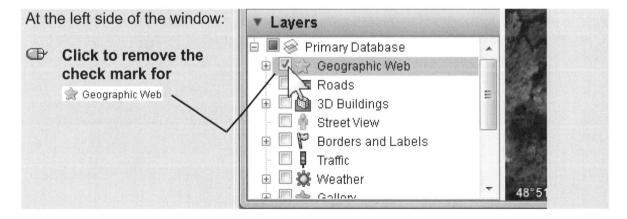

 Click to remove the check mark for

⭐ Geographic Web

The cameras or blue dots have disappeared.

On the satellite images you can also display the public transportation services. To display the train, bus and subway stations, select the layer ✈ Transportation :

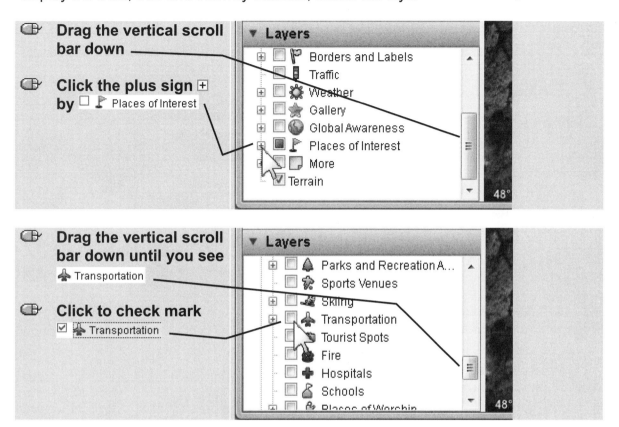

You probably do not see any public transportation icons on the satellite image yet. This is because the current image is zoomed in too far on the Eiffel Tower. First you need to zoom out:

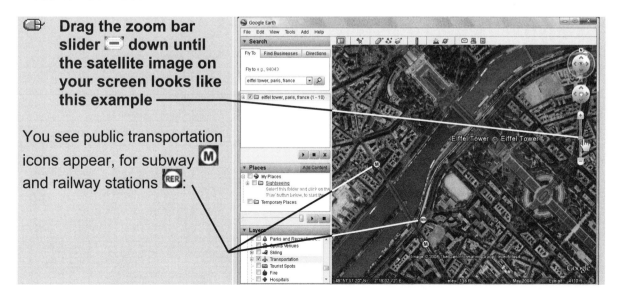

HELP! I do not see these icons.

It is possible there are no stations in the area you are currently viewing. You can try moving the image, or zooming out some more. Make sure you do not zoom out too far, as that will make the icons disappear altogether.

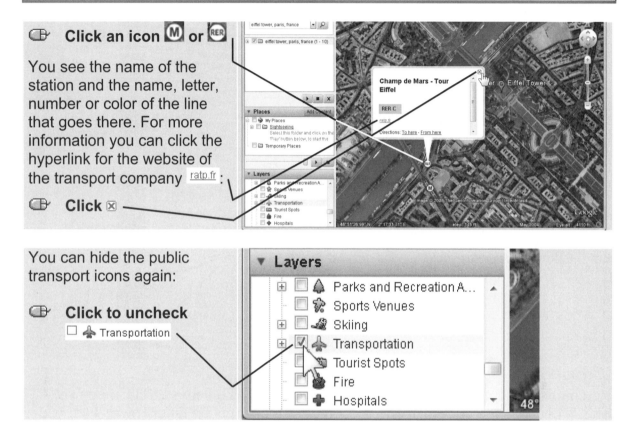

☞ **Click an icon Ⓜ or RER**

You see the name of the station and the name, letter, number or color of the line that goes there. For more information you can click the hyperlink for the website of the transport company ratp.fr :

☞ **Click ⊠**

You can hide the public transport icons again:

☞ **Click to uncheck**

☐ ✈ Transportation

2.8 Flying a Route

You can also use *Google Earth* to plan a route. For example, if you want to visit the Eiffel Tower after you visit the Arc de Triomphe monument, you can 'fly' the route on your screen:

☞ **Click**

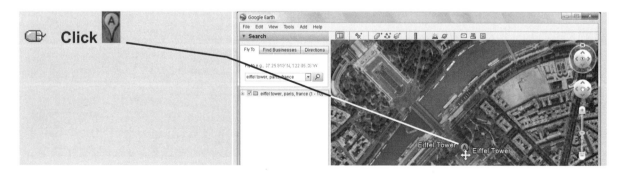

Right-click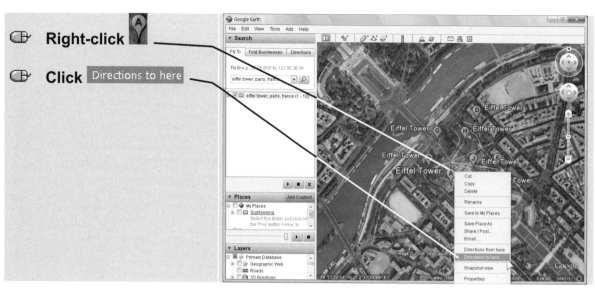

Click Directions to here

Click the box below

From

Type:
arc de triomphe

Press Enter ←

Google Earth will zoom out
until the entire route is in
view: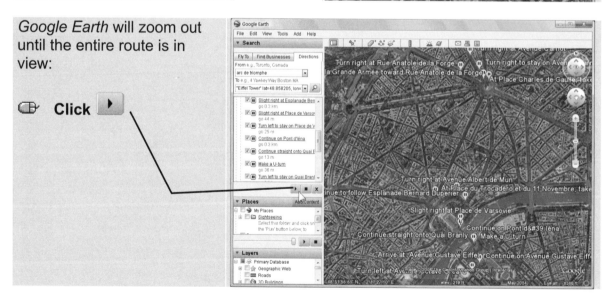

Click ▶

Now you get a flying tour to the Eiffel Tower:

You can stop the tour by clicking ▪ :

You can use ‖ to pause the tour.

You stop at the end of the route.
To delete a route, simply click ✕ :

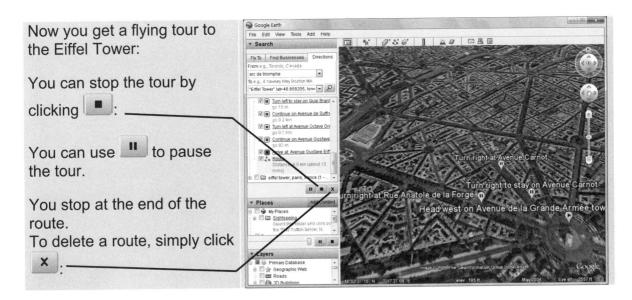

2.9 Viewing a 3D Display

Even though the satellite images have been made to look like there is an effect of depth and elevation, they are not real 3D images. However, users can add their own 3D images to *Google Earth*. This is mostly done for important buildings and structures. Sometimes architects create a 3D rendering of a house they designed, to allow customers to view the building and its surroundings. You can take a look at a 3D image of the Eiffel Tower:

Click ▲ until you see
   3D Buildings

Click to check mark
   ☑ 3D Buildings

You see the Eiffel Tower appear in 3D:

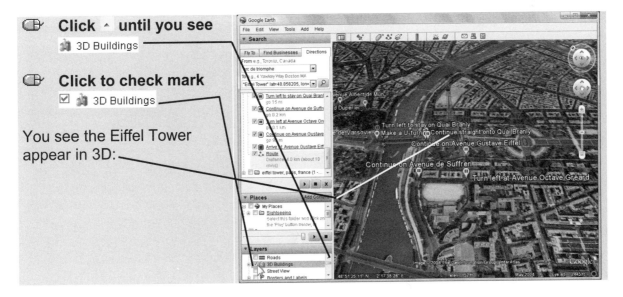

Please note:

Because the information is downloaded from the Internet, it may take a few moments before the 3D image appears.

Now you delete the route:

☞ **Click** X

You can quickly zoom in on the Eiffel Tower like this:

☞ **Double-click the Eiffel Tower**

You zoom in on the Eiffel Tower automatically.

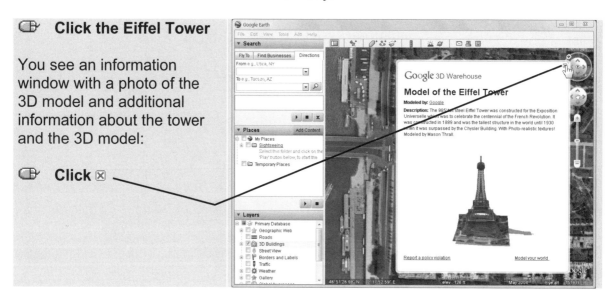

☞ **Click the Eiffel Tower**

You see an information window with a photo of the 3D model and additional information about the tower and the 3D model:

☞ **Click** ⊠

Tip

Downloading 3D images
You can download 3D images to your computer and edit them in the program *Google SketchUp*.

To download the model of the Eiffel Tower:

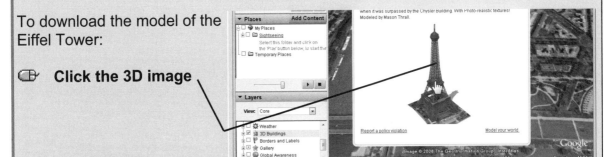

👉 **Click the 3D image**

A separate *Internet Explorer* window opens containing the model and additional information.

👉 **Click**

A list of downloadable files appears. To download the model:

👉 **Click** Download 699 kb **next to** Google SketchUp 5 (.skp)

2.10 Tilting

So far you have looked at the *Google Earth* satellite images from the air. But you can also tilt the view and look at them as if you are standing on the ground. This is especially interesting with 3D buildings and hilly or mountainous terrain. To illustrate this option, we continue with the Eiffel Tower.

You can use this part of the navigation controls to tilt the

view :

☞ **Click** ⊞

The image tilts a little.

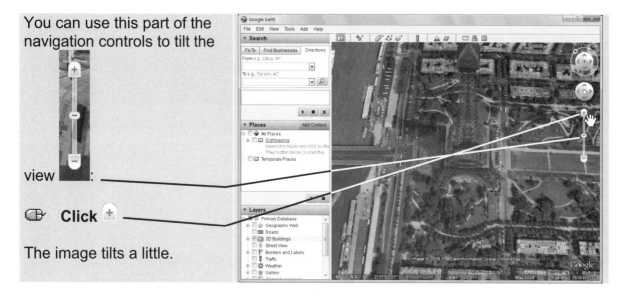

⇨ **Please note:**

The image you see on your screen may look different from what you see in this example. When you are looking at the Eiffel Tower from a different position, you see the structure at a different angle. This does not make a difference for the actions you need to perform.

☞ **Double-click** ⊞

The image tilts until you are looking at the building from a position on the ground.

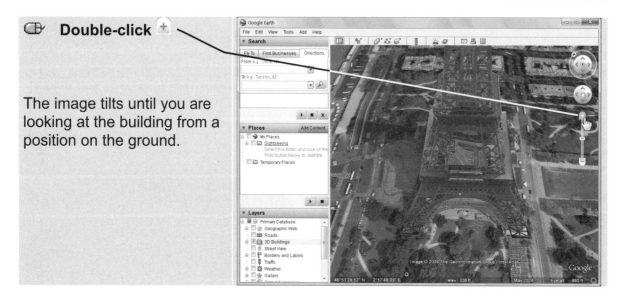

You can take a walk around the 3D model from that position:

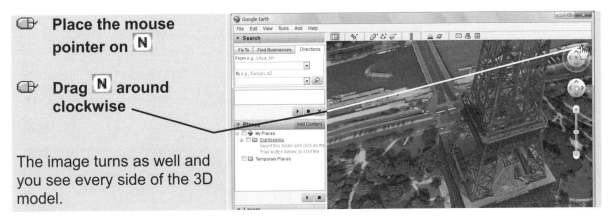

☞ **Place the mouse pointer on**

☞ **Drag** **around clockwise**

The image turns as well and you see every side of the 3D model.

Tilting and rotating gives you a good view of the 3D model. But its potential is still being developed. There are only a limited number of 3D buildings available in *Google Earth* at this time. But more will be added in the future. In the case of the Eiffel Tower there are no adjacent buildings with the same 3D rendering. To get a good view of Paris, it is better to return to the view from the air:

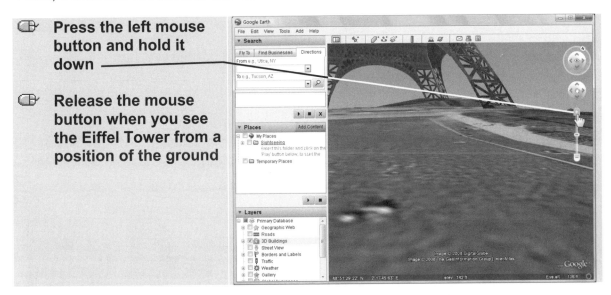

☞ **Press the left mouse button and hold it down**

☞ **Release the mouse button when you see the Eiffel Tower from a position of the ground**

You can easily rotate the photo to have the top of the image face north:

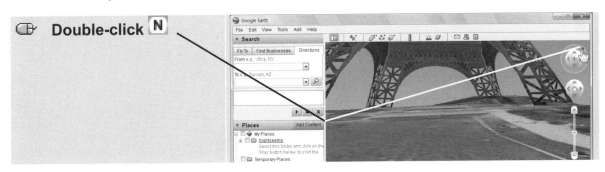

☞ **Double-click**

2.11 Marking

You can mark important locations, so you can quickly retrieve them when you need them. To be able to place the marker accurately, turn off the 3D Buildings first:

☞ **Click to uncheck**
   ☐ 🏛 3D Buildings

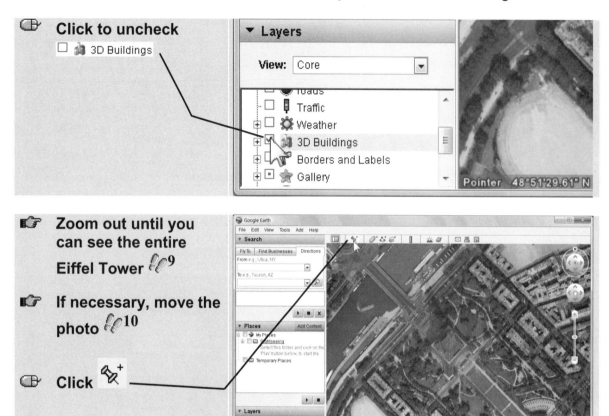

☞ **Zoom out until you can see the entire Eiffel Tower** 👣⁹

☞ **If necessary, move the photo** 👣¹⁰

☞ **Click** 📌⁺

The placemark icon 📌 appears on the satellite image. You can drag this icon to the location you want to mark:

☞ **Drag** 📌 **to the Eiffel Tower**

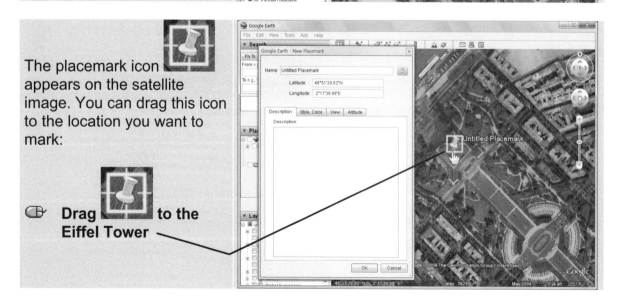

Type next to Name: **:**
Eiffel Tower

Type below Description: **:**
Tallest structure
in Paris

Click OK

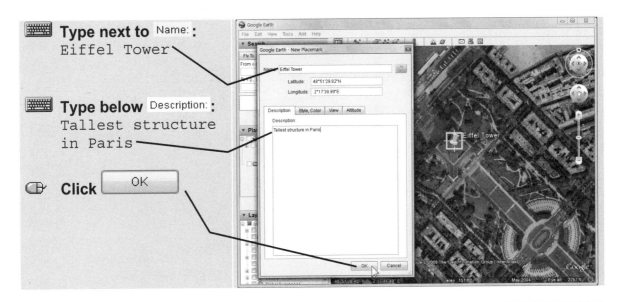

☞ **Move the satellite image so you no longer see the Eiffel Tower** 🐾¹⁰

Double-click Eiffel Tower
below ▼ **Places**

You will fly directly to the
Eiffel Tower.

Click

An information window
appears with the information
you entered:

Click ⊠

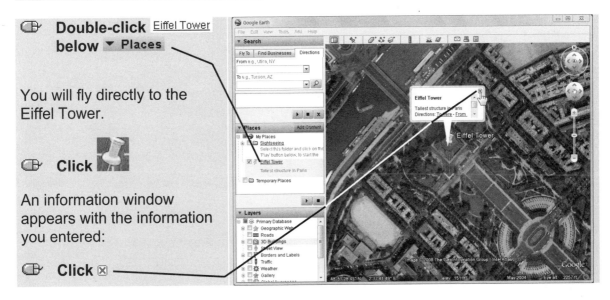

You have seen that you can use *Google Earth* to take a look at almost every location from space. The image quality should steadily improve over the next few years. However, some locations will remain blurry. This is done expressly for example with military bases and other strategic objects.

☞ **Close *Google Earth*** 🐾³

2.12 Background Information

Glossary

Blurring	Making parts of an image or object unrecognizable in the satellite imagery.
Layers	Extra information that can be displayed on the area you are viewing.
Marking	Adding a placemark to a location on a map or image, so you can quickly find it again later.
Navigating	Moving the viewpoint on a map or photo.
Tilting	Changing the angle that is used to view an object.
Zoom in	Enlarging part of a map or image, to get a more detailed view of that part.
Zoom out	Making part of a map or image smaller, to get a less detailed view of that part.

Source: Google Earth User Guide

Versions

In addition to this free version of *Google Earth* there are three other versions: *Google Earth Plus*, *Google Earth Pro* and *Google Earth Enterprise*.

Google Earth Plus offers extra features, such as:
- Higher resolution for making larger and clearer prints;
- Spreadsheet importer, to import a maximum of 100 locations from .CSV files;
- Real-time GPS tracking and track/waypoint import for uploading data from select GPS devices.

Google Earth Pro is the edition for business and commercial use. This edition contains among others:
- Additional measurement tools (square feet, mile, acreage, radius and so on);
- A feature that allows you to transfer up to 2,500 locations by address or geospatial coordinates from a spreadsheet;
- The highest resolution for printing and saving data, to create larger and clearer prints (up to 4,800 pixels);
- A feature you can use to export movies of zooms and tours.

You can read more at Help , Help Center Website , Product Tour , Products .

Source: Google Earth Help Center

2.13 Tips

 Tip

Switching to Google Maps

You can switch from *Google Earth* to *Google Maps* to see a map of your route or location:

🖱 **Click**

A new window is opened, displaying a satellite image of your location in *Google Maps*. The street names are added to the image.

To switch to map view:

🖱 **Click** | Map |

To return to *Google Earth*:

🖱 **Click** [X]

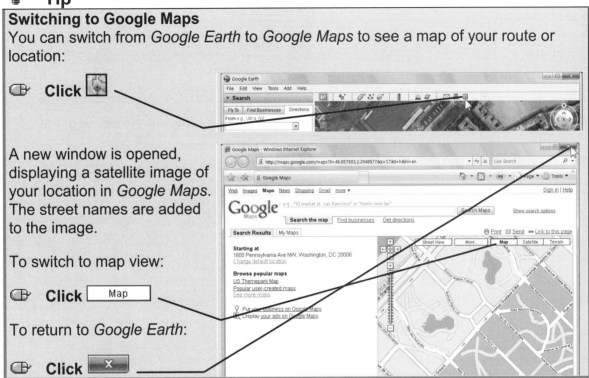

 Tip

Stars and planets

You can also use *Google Earth* to look at the stars and planets in outer space:

🖱 **Click**

You see a layer with links to information about solar systems and constellations.

In the Search box you can type the name of a star or planet:

To return to earth:

🖱 **Click** again

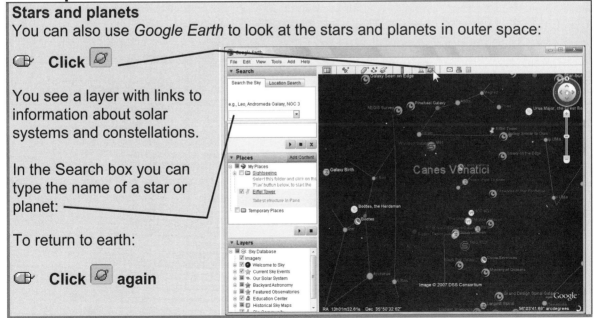

Tip

Sightseeing

You can also take a flying tour to well known locations on earth, like Saint Peter's Basilica, the Grand Canyon, the Red Square etcetera. These locations are already marked in *Google Earth*:

⊙ **Click** Sightseeing **below**

▼ **Places**

⊙ **Click** ▶

 Tip

Displaying layers

The basic version of *Google Earth* is distributed free of charge by *Google*. The costs of this enormous investment are recovered by commercial activities.
For example, businesses pay to be displayed in *Google Earth*.

Below the header ▼ **Layers** you can choose to display shopping malls, hotels, restaurants etcetera. These are arranged under the header ▶ Places of Interest . To display the list:

⊙ **Click** ⊞ **in front** ☐ ▶ Places of Interest

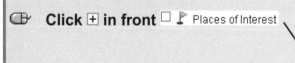

Notes

Write down your notes here.

3. Making Internet Phone Calls with Skype

Making phone calls over the Internet is rapidly becoming a popular activity among PC users. It is no wonder when these calls can be made free of charge. *Skype* is a program that lets you make free calls over the Internet.
Skype comes in two varieties. The first enables free telephone calls from one PC to another PC. It does not matter what country the computer is in, you can make free calls to anyone who has the *Skype* program installed. The second enables phone calls at a substantially lower rate than regular landlines and cell phone subscriptions used throughout the world. This is called *SkypeOut*. It works as a prepaid system. You have to buy *Skype Credit* before you can start making phone calls.

Before you decide to cancel your regular phone subscription, you should be aware that there are some limitations when using the Internet to make phone calls. It is not possible to support or carry emergency calls using the *Skype* services. For example, you cannot use *Skype* to call 911.

In this chapter you are introduced to both the free and the prepaid version of *Skype*. If you do not want to use the prepaid version, you can just read through that section.

In this chapter you learn how to:

- install the program *Skype*;
- create an account;
- perform a sound test;
- add contacts;
- call from PC to PC and call to landlines;
- buy *Skype Credit*.

➭ **Please note:**

You need a microphone and speakers to make phone calls using *Skype*. It is even more convenient to use a *headset*, a combination of earphones and a microphone. You can buy a good headset for under twenty dollars.

In this chapter you will learn how to add a contact. Start by asking around among friends or family if anybody uses *Skype* and write down their *Skype* name. If you cannot find other *Skype* users yet, you can just read through these sections.

3.1 Installing Skype

You can install *Skype* directly from the Internet. First you surf to the *Skype* website:

☞ **Open *Internet Explorer* 📖¹ and go to the website www.skype.com 📖²**

You see the *Skype* website. It may look different on your computer. This website is frequently updated.

🖱 **Click**

⑤ Download Skype

If you do not see this exact button, look around on the webpage until you find the link to download *Skype*.

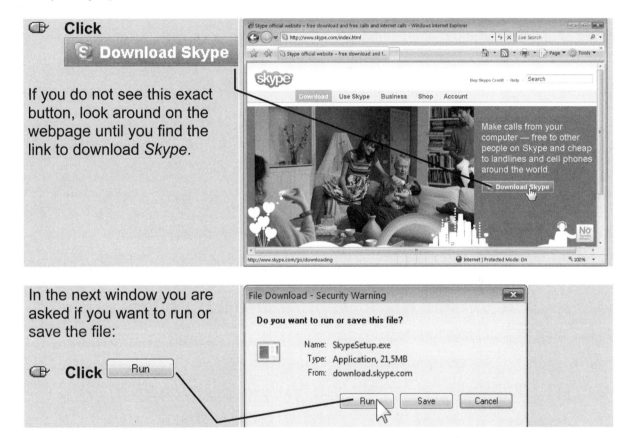

In the next window you are asked if you want to run or save the file:

🖱 **Click** [Run]

In most cases a window appears with a *Windows* security warning. *Skype* is a reliable program that is used by millions of people. You can safely install the program:

🖱 **Click** [Run]

The installation file *SkypeSetup.exe* is copied to the computer first:

You can follow the progress of the download in the window.

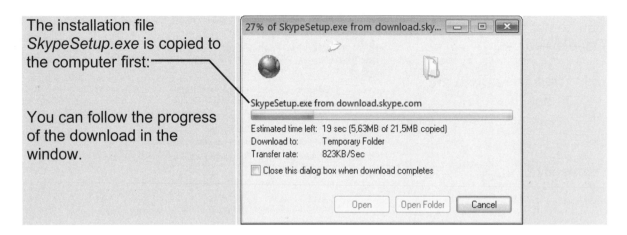

When you work on a *Windows Vista* computer, your screen goes dark and you see the window *User Account Control*. You need to give your permission to continue:

☞ **Click** Continue

☞ **Click** Skype™ - Install **on the taskbar**

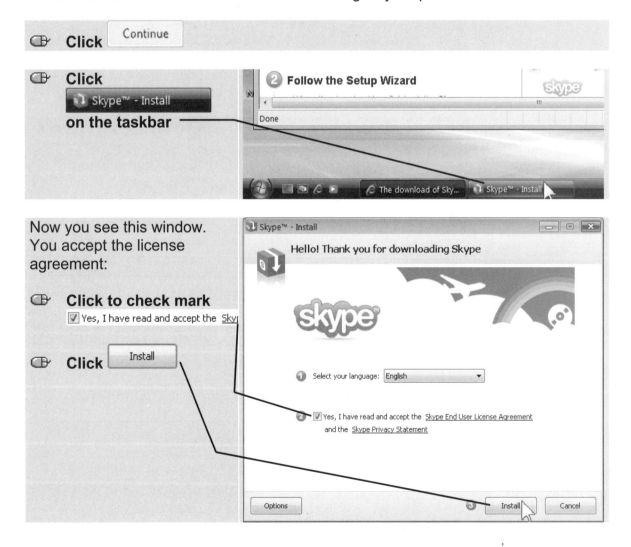

Now you see this window. You accept the license agreement:

☞ **Click to check mark**
☑ Yes, I have read and accept the Skyp

☞ **Click** Install

You do not need to install the *Google Toolbar*:

☞ **Click to remove the check mark for**

☐ **Install the free Google Toolbar**

☞ **Click** [Next >]

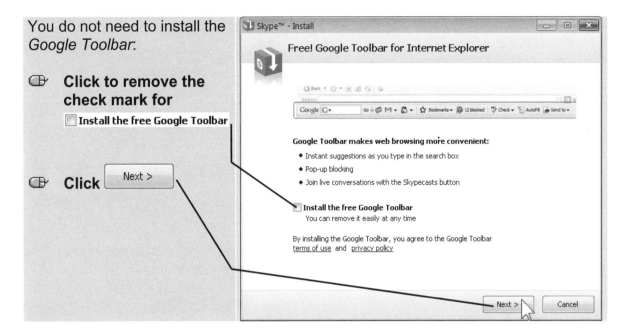

The program is installed on your computer. You can follow the installation process in the window.

After a few moments you see the final window of the installation process:

☞ **Click** [Finish]

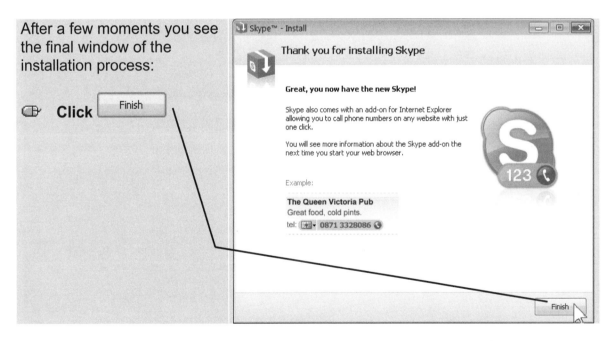

Skype is now installed on your computer.

☞ **Close the *Internet Explorer* window** $\ell\ell^3$

3.2 Creating an Account

Before you can make phone calls using *Skype*, you need to create an account. Your account consists of a user name, a password and some information about your location. Make sure you have pen and paper at hand so you can write down the password right away. You also need an e-mail address.

A shortcut to *Skype* has been placed on your desktop:

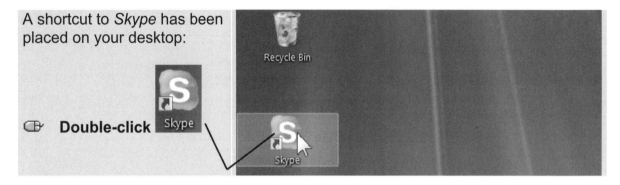

☞ **Double-click** Skype

On your desktop two windows appear:

The first window is the *Skype* main window. You need this window to use *Skype*:

You can use the second window to create your new *Skype* account:

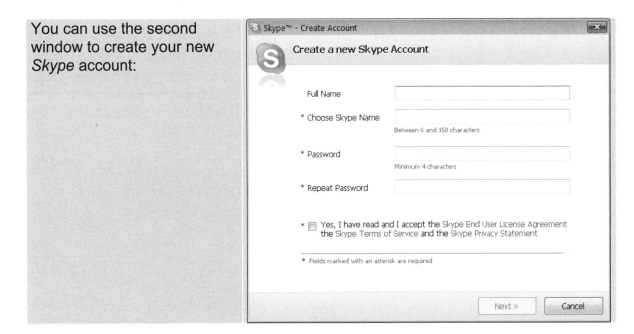

You start by creating an account in the second window. You need an account to be able to make phone calls. In the first box you type your name, in the second box you type another name that you create for yourself. This will be your *Skype* name, and will be seen by other *Skype* users. A *Skype* name cannot contain caps and spaces. You can also make up your own password.

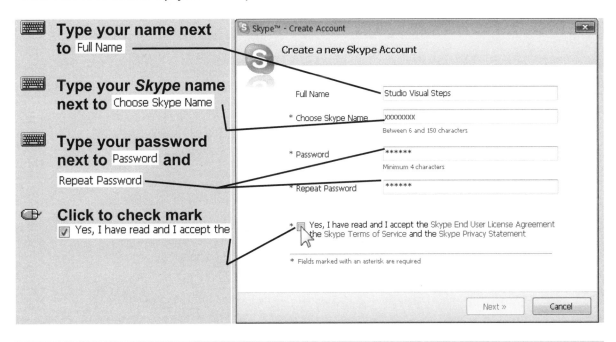

Type your name next to Full Name

Type your *Skype* name next to Choose Skype Name

Type your password next to Password **and** Repeat Password

Click to check mark ☑ Yes, I have read and I accept the

☞ **Write down your name, your *Skype* name and your password**

☞ **Click** Next »

In the next window you enter more information:

Type your e-mail address next to E-mail

Click to remove the check mark for
Yes, send me Skype news

Select your country next to Country/Region

Type your city next to City

Click Sign In

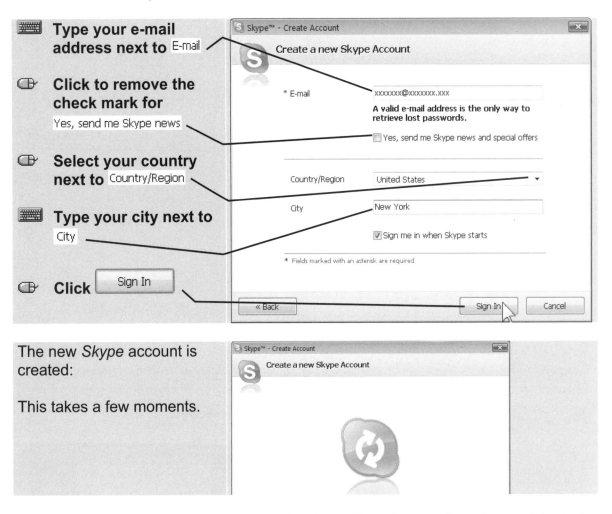

The new *Skype* account is created:

This takes a few moments.

When your account is created, you can begin making phone calls. It is possible that you see a security warning first. In that case *Windows Firewall* or your own firewall blocks the Internet connection. When you see this message, you need to unblock the program, otherwise you cannot use *Skype*.

Click Unblock

On a *Vista* computer, your screen goes dark and you need to give your permission to continue:

☞ **Click** [Continue]

You see the window *Getting started*:

You can close this window:

☞ **Click to check mark**
    ☑ Do not show this guide at startu

☞ **Click** [✕]

Now you only see the second *Skype* window on your desktop:

If you need to, you can make the window wider to display the tabs at the top in a single row:

☞ **Place the mouse pointer on the left edge of the window**

The mouse pointer changes into ⟺:

☞ **Drag ⟺ to the left**

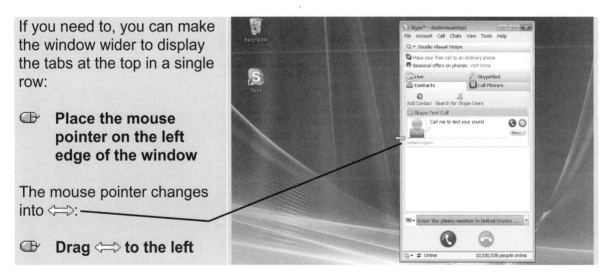

3.3 Connecting the Headset

You can use a headset to make *Skype* calls. A headset is a set of earphones with a microphone attached. A simple model, costing under twenty dollars will work just fine.

Headsets

Headsets are available in different price ranges. Here you see an example of a headset:
You plug the two plugs of the headset into the small round outlets for the microphone and earphones on the computer. Usually these are found at the back of the system case. Outlets on a laptop could be on the side, back or front. On each plug you see an icon that shows in which outlet the plug should go. Sometimes color codes are used: a pink plug for the microphone and a green plug for the earphones. Often the outlets on the PC have the same colors as the plugs, so you cannot go wrong. The cable of this headset has a built-in volume control. More expensive headsets often have a USB connection that you connect to the USB port of the computer. Wireless models are also available.

☞ **Connect your headset to the PC and set the volume control in the cable to the maximum level**

3.4 Sound Test

The sound test is very simple. When you click the green calling button, you hear some instructions. Then you hear a beep. You say a few words into the microphone and after a few moments you hear your own voice.
When the headset is connected, you can perform the sound test:

☞ **Click**

☞ **Listen to the voice and wait for the beep**

☞ **Say a few words into the microphone**

☞ **Listen to your own voice**

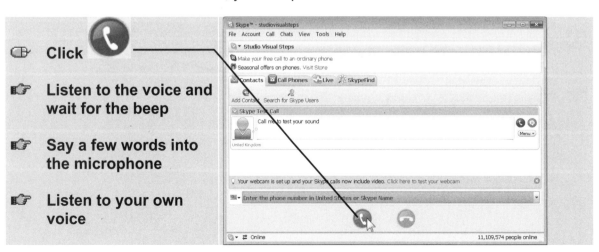

When you hear your own voice, the sound test has succeeded.

 HELP! The sound test has not succeeded.

When you do not hear any sound, there may be an incorrect setting on your computer. On the webpage of the book, you find the PDF file **Checking the Sound**. This document describes step by step how to check the *Windows* sound settings.

3.5 Adding a Contact

Skype needs to be installed on each person's computer before you try to establish a connection. In addition, the person you want to call must have his or her own *Skype* account. You can search for a *Skype* user by entering a *Skype* name, a full name or an e-mail address.

If you do not know anybody who uses *Skype*, you can just read through this section:

You see the window *Add a contact*:

When you entered the correct information for the other *Skype* user, he or she is found. When a list of users that match the criteria you entered is found, you choose your contact from this list. You can add the new contact like this:

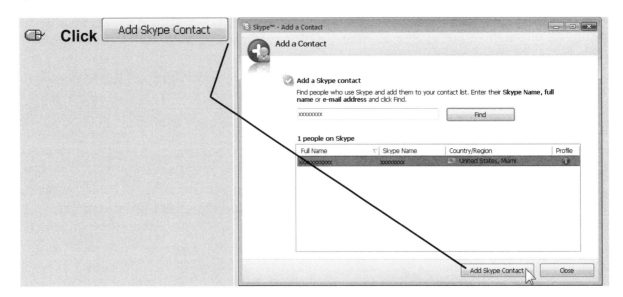

In the window *Say hello to* you can type a message for your contact to let him or her know that you added him or her to your contact list. Then your contact knows you can be reached by *Skype* from now on:

The message is sent to your contact and this person is added to your contacts list. When you have more friends with a *Skype* account:

☞ **Find and add other** *Skype* **users the same way**

When you have finished adding contacts, you can close this window:

👆 **Click** [Close]

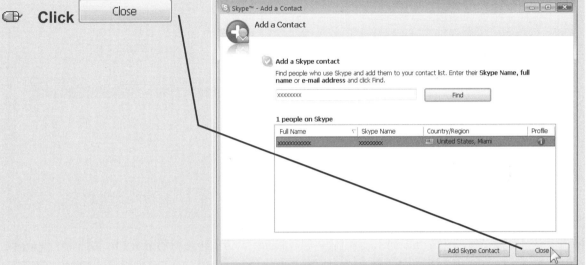

Your contact sees this window, where he or she can choose to accept or decline you as a contact:

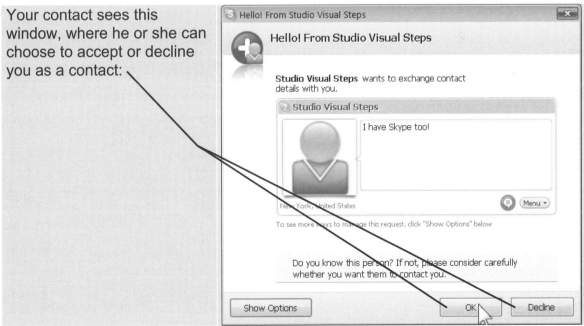

3.6 Calling a Contact

As soon as you have added a contact, you can try to establish a connection. Of course a call can only be made if your contact is online.

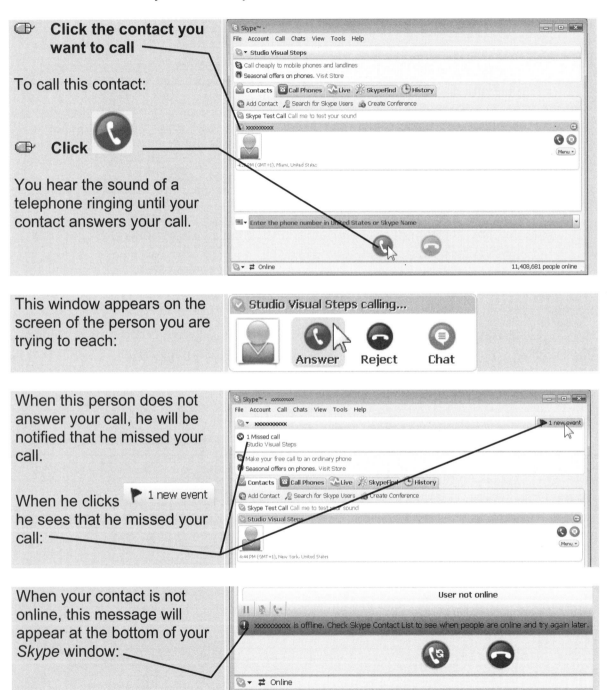

Click the contact you want to call

To call this contact:

Click

You hear the sound of a telephone ringing until your contact answers your call.

This window appears on the screen of the person you are trying to reach:

When this person does not answer your call, he will be notified that he missed your call.

When he clicks ▶ 1 new event he sees that he missed your call:

When your contact is not online, this message will appear at the bottom of your *Skype* window:

When you are connected to your contact, you can talk as long as you want, for free!

☞ **Finish your phone call**

When you are ready to end
the call:

☞ **Click**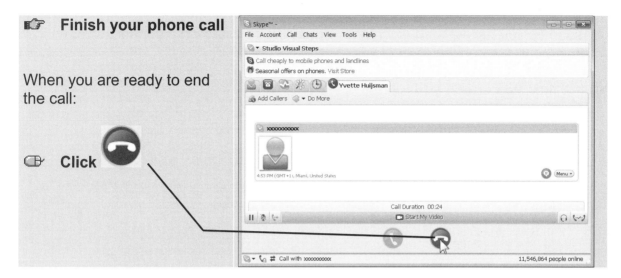

You see how easy it is to make free Internet phone calls to other online *Skype* users.

3.7 Buying Skype Credit for SkypeOut

You can also make phone calls to landlines and cell phones using *Skype*. In *Skype* this is called *SkypeOut*. You pay for these calls in advance using *Skype Credit*. In this section you can read how to purchase *Skype Credit*.

If you are not interested in *SkypeOut*, you can skip the following sections.

☞ **Click** Account

☞ **Click** Buy Skype Credit...

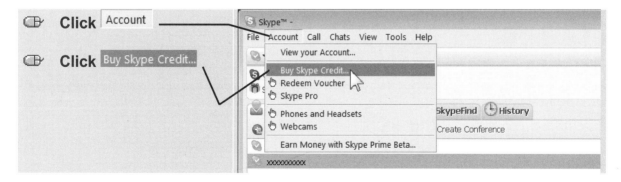

💡 **Tip**

In the *Tips* at the end of *Chapter 5 Trading on eBay* you can read more about Internet payments.

You can buy a maximum of $10 of *Skype Credit*. In this window you enter your first name, last name, address, city, state, ZIP code and country. Please note: these items are all mandatory:

You can get up to date information about the rates for *SkypeOut* calls by clicking Check rates :

☞ **Enter the correct data below**
Enter your billing name and add

🖱 **Click** Next

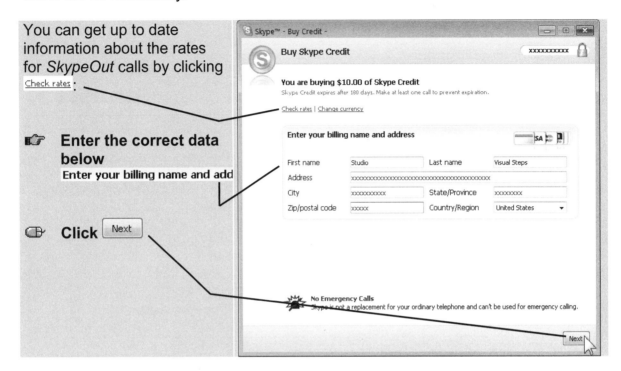

In the next step you can select your payment method. You need to decide for yourself which payment method you want to use. You can pay directly using a credit or debit card, or you can use the safe and convenient method offered by *PayPal*, or use a bank transfer.

💡 **Tip**

PayPal
PayPal is a service that allows payments and money transfers to be made through the Internet. It serves as an electronic alternative to traditional paper methods such as cheques and money orders. Your financial details are not shared with the seller, so you can pay online with confidence. *PayPal* performs payment processing for many online vendors and auction sites. This means you can use your *PayPal* account for a lot more than just buying *Skype Credit*.
PayPal is owned by *eBay*, the online auction site you can read about in *Chapter 5 Trading on eBay*.

PayPal

In this example a new *PayPal* account is created and used for this payment of $ 11.50 (including VAT):

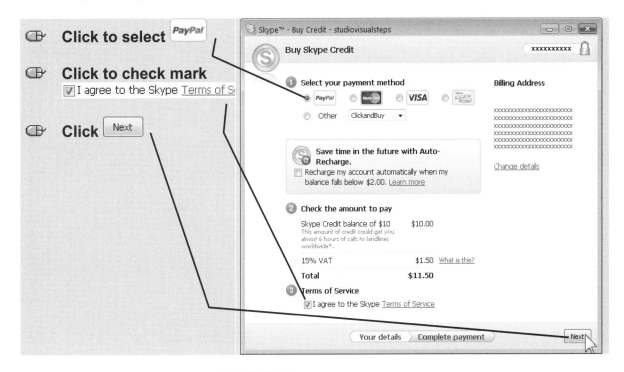

Click to select PayPal

Click to check mark
☑ I agree to the Skype Terms of S

Click Next

In the next window you can **Log In** and pay directly if you already have a *PayPal* account. In the following example the debit or credit card details for the new *PayPal* account are entered instead:

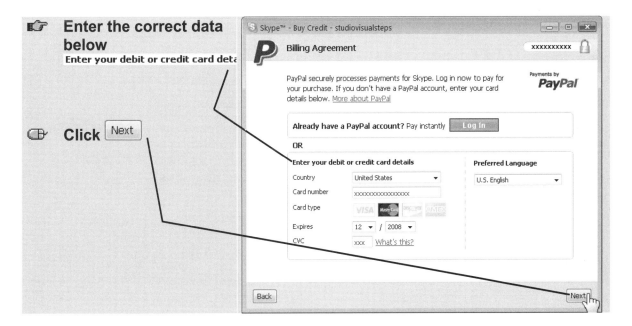

Enter the correct data below
Enter your debit or credit card det

Click Next

In the next window you enter your correct billing address as it appears on your bank or credit card statement:

☞ **Enter the correct data below**

Please enter your address as it appe

☞ **Click** `Next`

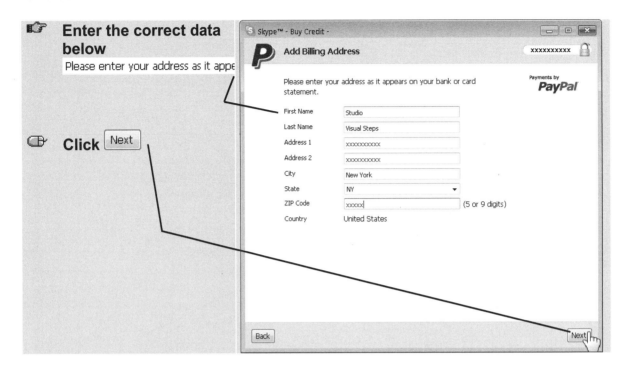

Finally, you enter your e-mail address and the new *PayPal* password you create yourself. Your e-mail address is your *PayPal* login ID. You have to enter your password twice:

☞ **Enter your e-mail address and password**

It is a good idea to write this information down and keep it in a safe place:

☞ **Write down the e-mail address and the password you entered**

☞ **Click** `Agree & Continue`

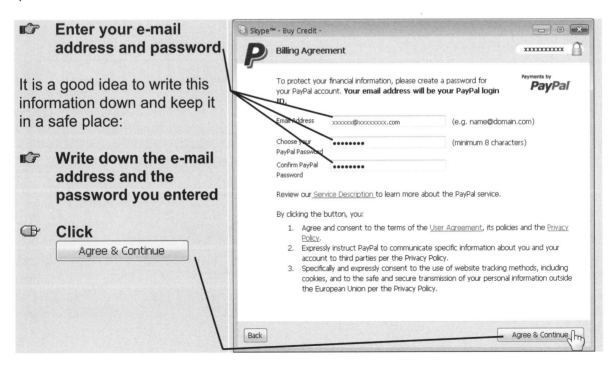

You have created a *PayPal* account. Now you can agree to the billing agreement and authorize *Skype* to debit payments from your funding source:

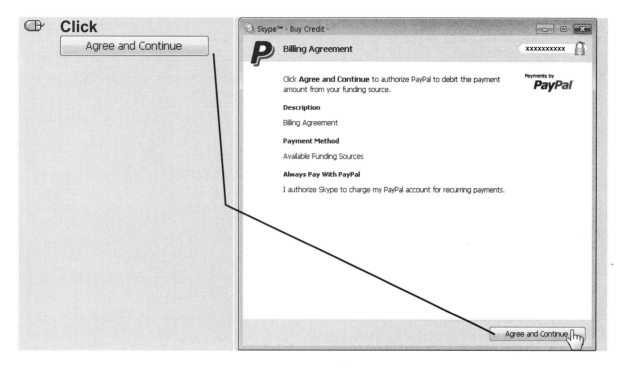

Now you can pay for the *Skype Credit* balance of $11.50:

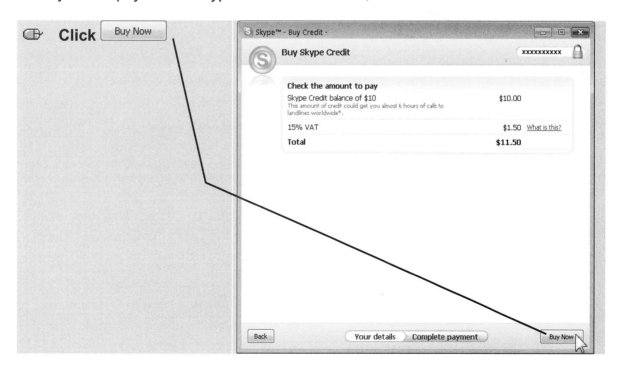

You see a confirmation and an order summary:

☞ **Click** Close

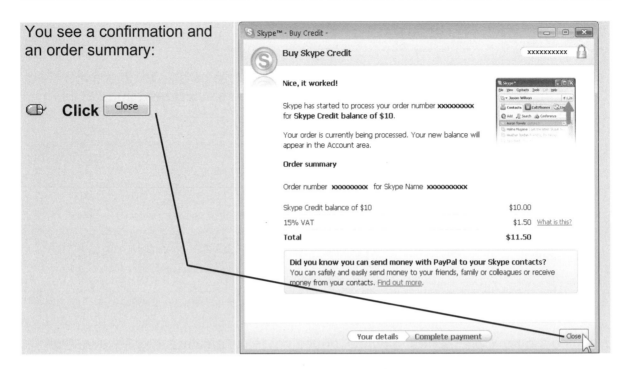

Now that you have created a *PayPal* account and used it to make a payment, you will receive a number of confirmation e-mails from both *PayPal* and *Skype*. You can open and read these e-mails in your e-mail program yourself.

Please note that it may take up to half an hour for your payment to be processed. As soon as your payment has been received, you can use *SkypeOut* to call landlines and cell phones. It is also possible you have to log out and log in again before you see your *Skype Credit*.

Your remaining *Skype Credit* is displayed in the *Skype* main window:

3.8 Calling with SkypeOut

You can use *SkypeOut* to call a landline or cell phone. To be able to do so, you need *Skype Credit*. If you did not purchase *Skype Credit* you can just read through this section.

Click the tab
🖲 Call Phones

You see the tab *Call Phones*. *SkypeOut* does not make a difference between local and long distance phone calls. This means you have to enter both the phone number and the area code:

☞ **Select the country below**
① Select the country/region

⌨ **Type the phone number below**
② Enter the phone number

🖲 **Click**

☞ **Make the phone call**

To end the phone call:

🖲 **Click**

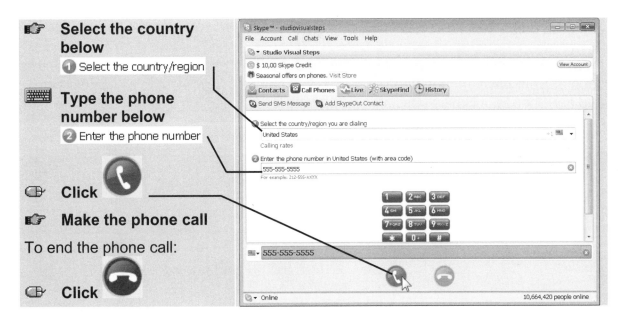

You see how simple it is to call a landline or cell phone using *SkypeOut*.

3.9 Adding SkypeOut Contacts

Your contacts list contains the people you want to call using *Skype*. You can extend this list by adding *SkypeOut* contacts and their phone numbers. Then you do not have to type the phone number every time you want to call a contact:

Click the tab
☐ Call Phones

Click
☐ Add SkypeOut Contact

You see the window *Add a Contact*:

Enter the name and phone number of the new contact

Next to Phone Number ▦ you see the flag of the selected country: ————

You can click the flag to select another country.

Click Add SkypeOut Contact

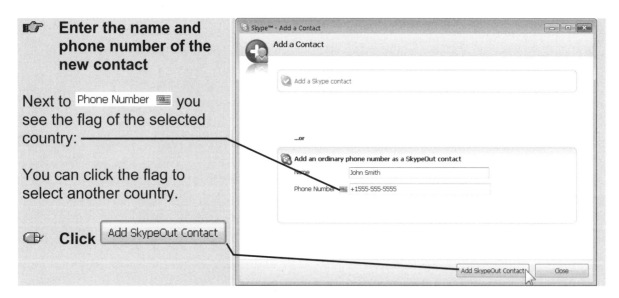

The contact has been added. *Skype* has added the correct country code automatically. For the United States that is +1.

You can call a contact using *SkypeOut* the same way you call your regular contacts:

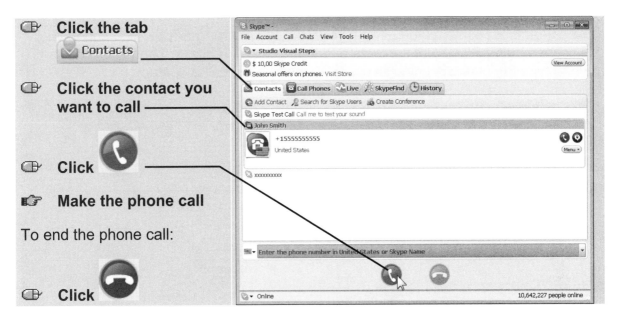

⟳ **Click the tab**

      Contacts

⟳ **Click the contact you
want to call**

⟳ **Click** 📞

☞ **Make the phone call**

To end the phone call:

⟳ **Click** 📞

In this chapter you have learned how to make *Skype* Internet phone calls to other *Skype* users. You have been introduced to *SkypeOut* for making calls to landlines and cell phones.

3.10 Background Information

Glossary	
Account	An account gives its user access to a service. It consists of a user name and a password. You need an account to be able to use *Skype*.
Headset	Combination of earphones and a microphone.
Internet phone call	Calling someone over the Internet.
Local call	Calling someone using a landline; the area codes of the caller and the person that is called are the same.
Long distance call	Calling someone using a landline; the area codes of the caller and the person that is called are different.
Skype Credit	Balance or time remaining for making phone calls.
SkypeOut	*Skype* service you can use to call landlines and cell phones from the computer. *SkypeOut* does not require a subscription, but you need to buy *Skype Credit* in advance.

Source: Skype Help; Wikipedia

SkypeOut Rates

SkypeOut is the service you can use to call landlines and cell phones from your computer. This is not a free service, because part of the connection is not made over the Internet, but over connections that *Skype* has to pay for as well. *Skype* charges you for these costs.

The cost of a *SkypeOut* call has two parts: a connection fee and a rate per minute. At the moment this book was written, the connection fee was $ 0.045 (incl. VAT). The rate per minute for calls within the USA and to common international destinations was $ 0.024 (incl. VAT). For example, an eight minute phone call from the US to a landline in London or Sydney costs $ 0.045 plus 8 x $ 0.024 = $ 0.237 (incl. VAT). Some destinations are incredibly expensive. For example, you can call the atoll Diego Garcia in the Indian Ocean for $ 2.142 (incl. VAT) per minute. Before you decide to call an exotic destination, always check the rate list first. It is a good idea to do that regularly, because *Skype* can change its rates from day to day.

- Continue reading on the next page -

Examples of *SkypeOut* rates for some popular destinations (January 2008):

Destination	Rate/minute	USD excl. VAT	USD incl. VAT
USA incl. Hawaii		$ 0.021	$ 0.024
USA - Alaska		$ 0.056	$ 0.064
UK, Ireland, Italy, Greece, Germany		$ 0.021	$ 0.024
Cuba		$ 1.025	$ 1.179
Mexico		$ 0.099	$ 0.114

For more destinations and a list of current rates, you can check:
www.skype.com/prices/callrates

Utilization of your computer by Skype

Many people accept a license agreement for software without reading its content. That is understandable, because these documents are usually quite boring.

However, a license agreement may contain very important information.
It does here: *Skype* is a program that works differently than regular software. It operates on a huge network of millions of computers, of which yours is one.

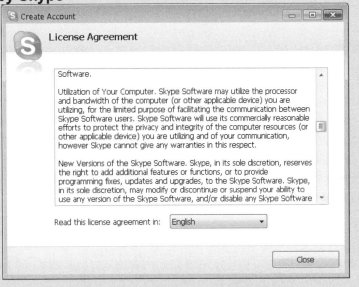

To put it differently: when you use *Skype*, *Skype* uses your computer. In this case you do not have a choice, since you cannot install *Skype* without accepting the license agreement.

When you do not like the idea of your computer being used by *Skype*, you can always remove the program from your computer. You can read how to do that in *Appendix A. Removing a Program.*

3.11 Tips

 Tip

Starting automatically
Skype works best when you start the program automatically:

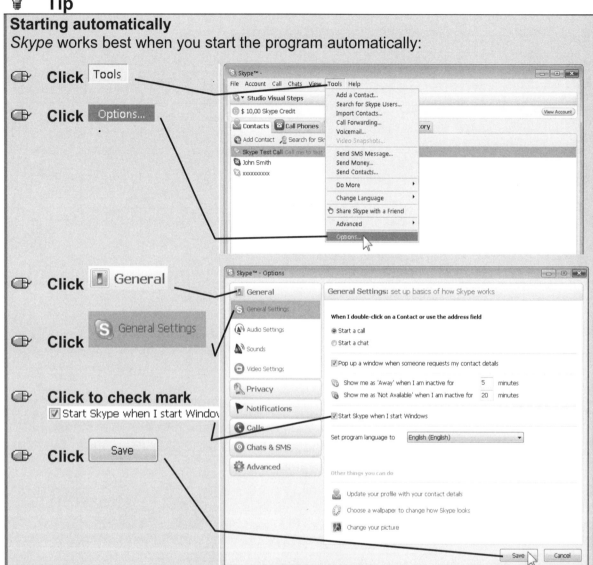

 Tip

Skype Help
Skype has an extensive help feature that you can use to learn more about the program features:

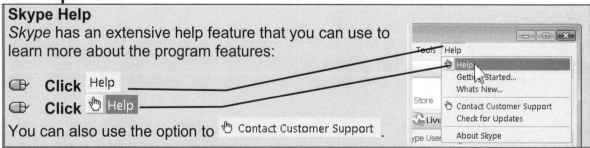

Tip

Contacts only
By default, the settings of *Skype* allow anyone to contact you.
To protect yourself from unwanted calls or chats, you can change this setting so that only people from your contacts list can contact you:

Click `Tools` , `Options...`

Click 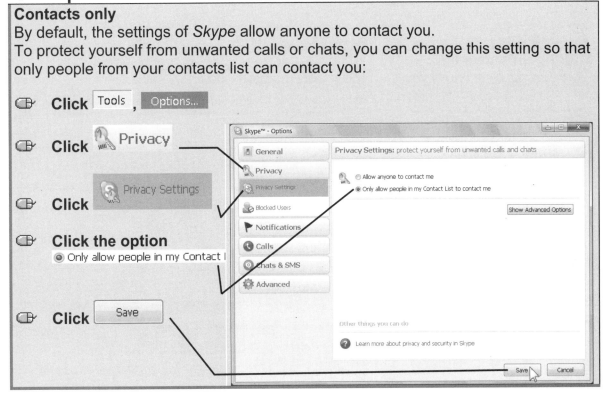 **Privacy**

Click `Privacy Settings`

Click the option
○ Only allow people in my Contact I

Click `Save`

 Tip

Changing your status
Just like in the program *Windows Live Messenger*, you can change your status in *Skype*. For example, you can let your contacts know that you do not want to receive any calls for a while. You can do that like this:

Click in the bottom left corner of the window

A menu appears:

You can change your status by clicking one of these options.

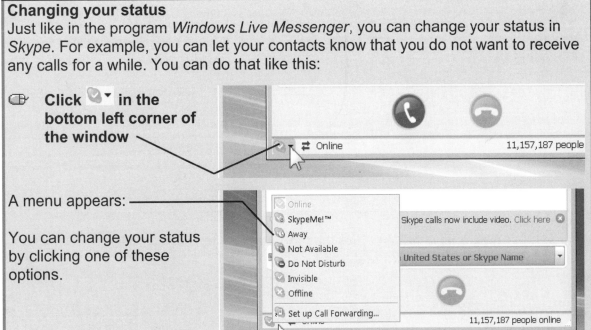

4. Subscribing to RSS feeds: Podcasts, Computer Tips and News

News agencies like CNN and other dynamic websites offer a service called *RSS feeds*, also called *web feeds*. The acronym *RSS* stands for *Really Simple Syndication*, a format used to publish frequently updated digital content. *Internet Explorer 7* has a built-in feed reader that can display these feeds.

Feeds are often used to publish news updates or sports scores. But feeds can also be used to publish other types of digital content, like images and audio or video files.

Publishing audio files this way is called *podcasting*. The word *podcasting* is made up from the words *iPod* - the well known audio player created by *Apple* - and broad*casting*. Each separate broadcast or episode is called a *podcast*.
The content of a podcast can be as rich and varied as any regular radio broadcast: music, documentaries, radio plays, talk shows, interviews and news are just some of the many possible subjects. The audio files used are usually in the MP3 file format which can be played on your computer or MP3 player.

Podcasts and other RSS feed applications are usually offered for free. When you subscribe to a news agency feed for example, the latest headlines are automatically sent to your computer when you connect to the Internet.

This chapter will show you how to:

- find and play a podcast;
- subscribe to a podcast;
- subscribe to the free Computer tips feed from Visual Steps;
- display RSS feeds in the *Vista* gadget *Feed Headlines*;
- find and sort feeds.

⇨ **Please note:**

The creators of websites are constantly adding new information. The sreenshots used in this chapter may look different from what you see on your screen. This should not pose any problems; the basic features will not be removed. However, it is possible that certain features will be moved to a different location on the website.

4.1 Podcasts

You are going to look for a free podcast on the Internet and then play it:

☞ **Open *Internet Explorer*** 🦶¹

☞ **Surf to the web address cnn.podcast.com** 🦶²

➡ **Please note:**

You do not need to type **www** in front of the web address cnn.podcast.com

You see the CNN podcast home page. Here you can play podcasts from CNN, as well as other podcasts from around the world. You are going to listen to an audio podcast from the *Audio* folder first:

👆 **Drag the vertical scroll bar down a little** ───

👆 **Click ▢ Audio**

A list of CNN audio podcasts appears. You can take a look at the news update podcasts:

👆 **Click 📶 CNN News Update**

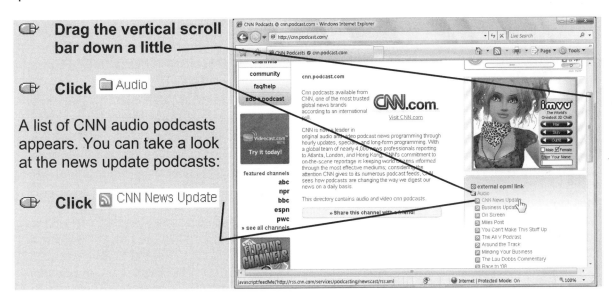

The CNN News Updates are updated regularly, usually every hour. The latest podcasts appear in a list in the middle section of the webpage.

Listening to a podcast is very easy. The audio file is downloaded first and then played automatically. The speed of this process depends largely on the size of the audio file and the speed of your Internet connection.

☞ **Check if the speakers of your computer are turned on**

👆 **If necessary, drag the vertical scroll bar down**

You are going to listen to the latest News Update:

👆 **Click**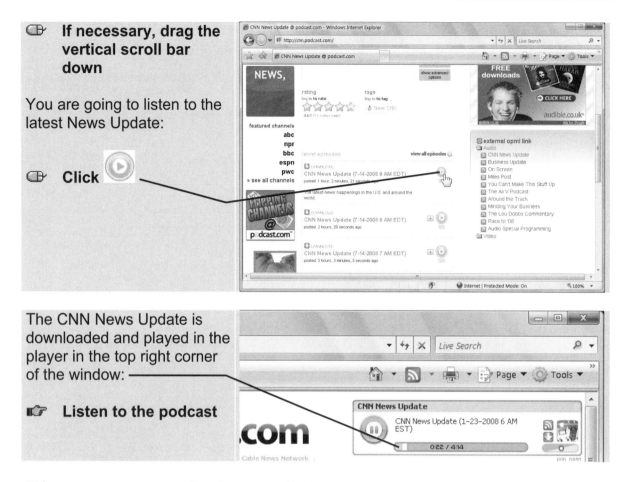

The CNN News Update is downloaded and played in the player in the top right corner of the window:

👉 **Listen to the podcast**

There are many types of podcasts available and there are different ways to find the ones you are interested in. For example, you can display a list of podcast categories like this:

👆 **If necessary, drag the vertical scroll bar down**

👆 **Click** **load the main podcast.com fo**

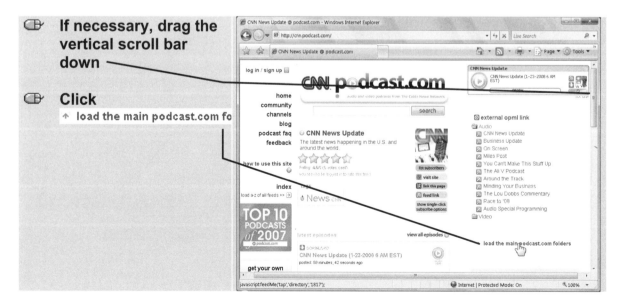

You see a list of podcast categories. Each category has its sub categories. For example, take a look at a podcast in one of the *Food* subcategories:

☞ **If necessary, drag the vertical scroll bar down**

☞ **Click** 🗀 FOOD

☞ **Click** Munchcast

If this podcast is no longer available, you can select another podcast.

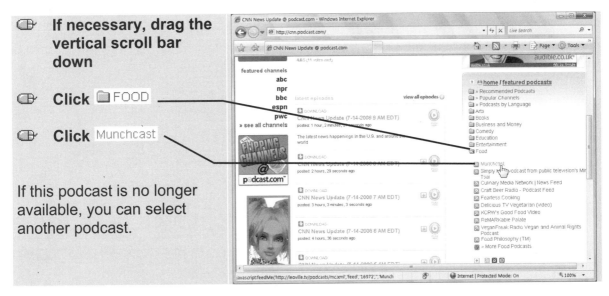

☞ **Drag the vertical scroll bar down**

The episodes of this podcast are displayed in the middle section of the window:

You do not need to listen to these podcasts now.

☞ **Drag the vertical scroll bar all the way up again**

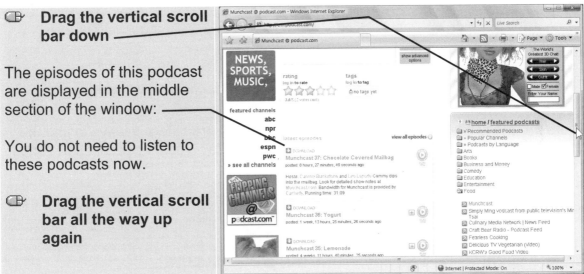

You can also use the search feature on this webpage to find a podcast:

☞ **Click the Search box**

⌨ **Type:**
msnbc headlines

☞ **Click** search

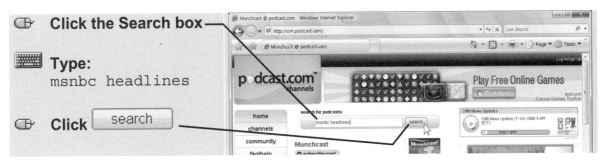

At the top of the search results, you see the link to MSNBC Headlines:

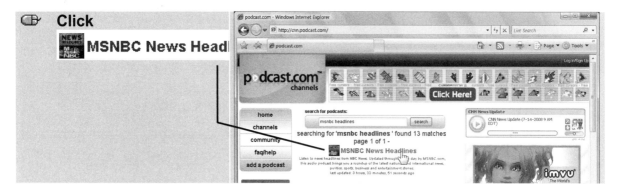

In the next section you are going to subscribe to this podcast.

4.2 Subscribing to a Podcast

You can subscribe to the MSNBC Headlines podcast. To do so, you need to display its feed page in *Internet Explorer*:

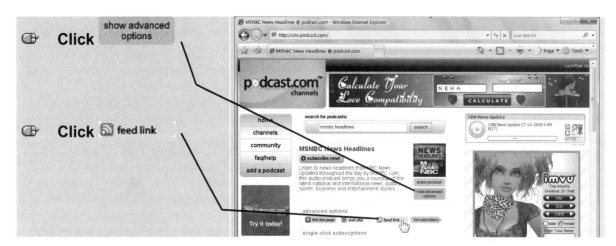

On this page you can subscribe to the feed containing this podcast:

The name of the feed is
already entered: —

☞ **Click** [Subscribe]

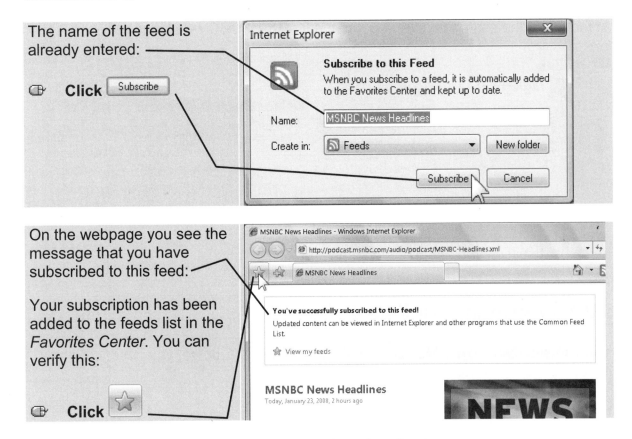

On the webpage you see the
message that you have
subscribed to this feed:—

Your subscription has been
added to the feeds list in the
Favorites Center. You can
verify this:

☞ **Click** [☆]

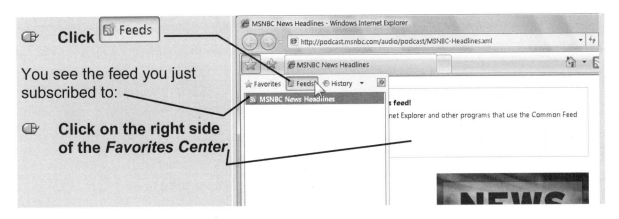

The RSS feeds are listed separately in the *Favorites Center*.

☞ **Click** [Feeds]

You see the feed you just
subscribed to: —

☞ **Click on the right side**
   of the *Favorites Center*

The *Favorites Center* closes. Now you can view and adjust the properties of the feed:

Click `View feed properties...`

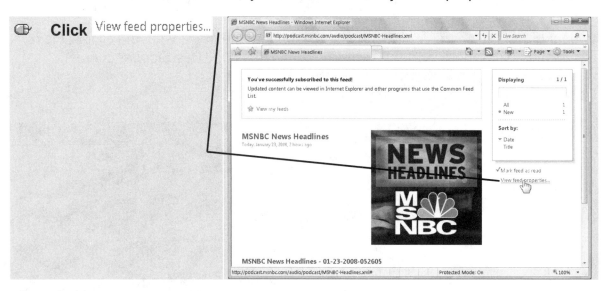

Here you can select how often your computer should check for feed updates:

For example, you can check for a new podcast every hour:

Click the option
◉ Use custom schedule

Click `1 day`

Click `1 hour`

You can also choose how many feeds you want to keep. In this example only the 200 most recent items are kept:

Click `OK`

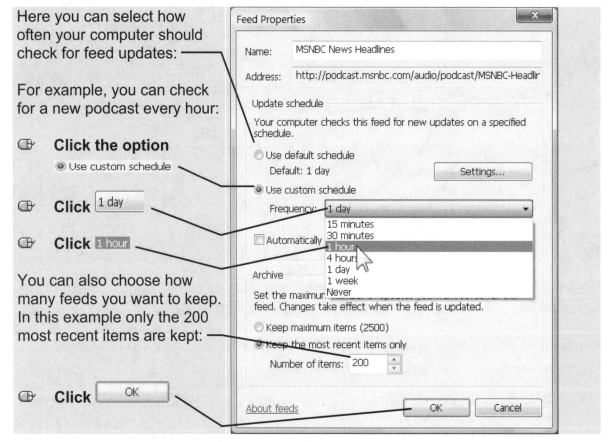

Now the feed is checked for updates every hour.

☞ **Close both *Internet Explorer* windows** $\ell\ell^3$

4.3 Adding RSS Feeds to Windows Vista Sidebar

Windows Vista users have the *Windows Sidebar* at their disposal. The *Sidebar* is a remarkable extra toolbar on the right side of the desktop. This *Sidebar* contains various mini-programs also known as *gadgets*.
Do you use *Windows XP*? Then you can just skip this section.

In this example you see three gadgets:

The third gadget in this example is called *Feed Headlines*:

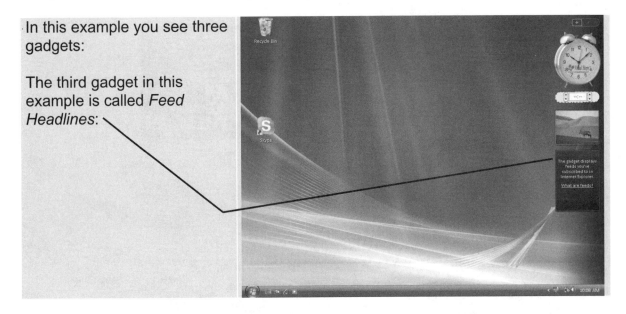

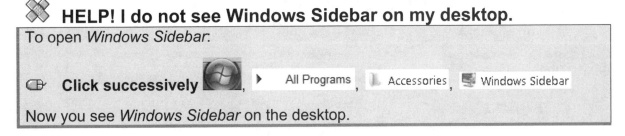

HELP! I do not see Windows Sidebar on my desktop.

To open *Windows Sidebar*:

Click successively ⊞ , ▶ All Programs , Accessories , Windows Sidebar

Now you see *Windows Sidebar* on the desktop.

When you have a broadband Internet connection (DSL or cable), you can display the feed you just subscribed to in the gadget *Feed Headlines*.

In case you do not see the gadget *Feed Headlines* in your *Sidebar*, you can add it like this:

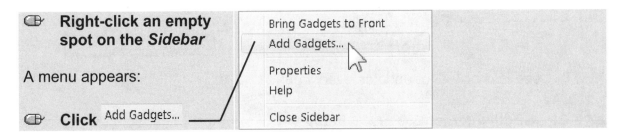

Right-click an empty spot on the *Sidebar*

A menu appears:

Bring Gadgets to Front
Add Gadgets...
Properties
Help
Close Sidebar

Click Add Gadgets...

You see a window containing the available gadgets. You can add a gadget to *Windows Sidebar* by double-clicking it.

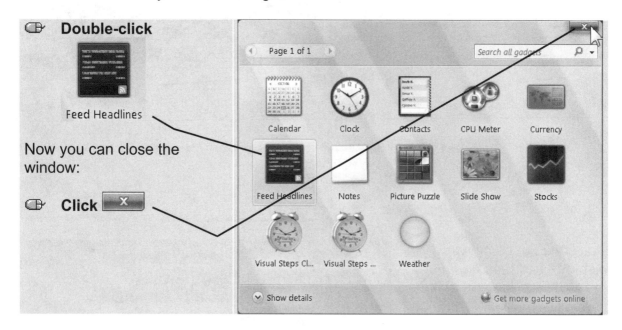

☞ **Double-click**

Feed Headlines

Now you can close the window:

☞ **Click** [X]

The *Feed Headlines* gadget has been added to *Windows Sidebar*.
Usually the RSS feeds you have subscribed to are displayed automatically in this gadget. You need a broadband Internet connection for that, like cable or DSL.

If you do not see the feeds in the gadget yet, you can check the settings like this:

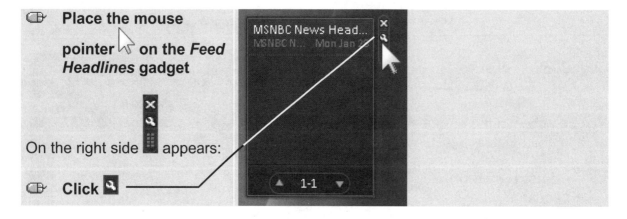

☞ **Place the mouse**

pointer on the *Feed Headlines* gadget

On the right side appears:

☞ **Click**

A window appears. Here you can choose which feeds to display:

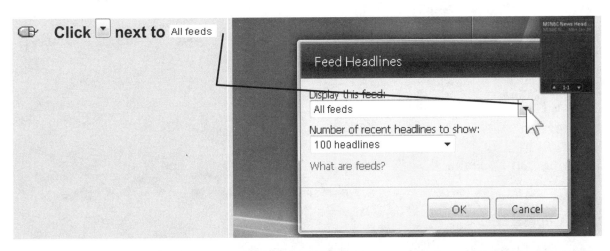

☞ **Click** ▾ **next to** All feeds

You can choose between displaying all feeds, or just the MSNBC News Headlines podcast.

You choose the second option:

☞ **Click** MSNBC News Headlines

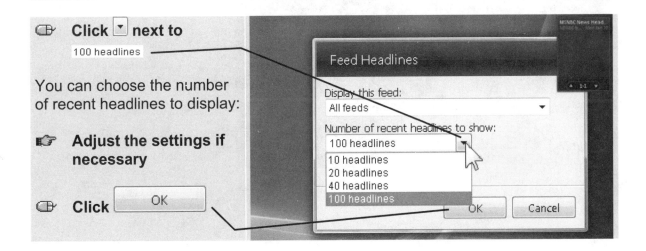

☞ **Click** ▾ **next to**

100 headlines

You can choose the number of recent headlines to display:

☞ **Adjust the settings if necessary**

☞ **Click** OK

In this example only one feed is displayed in the *Feed Headlines* gadget. You can read a few words from the headline.

You can open a feed like this:

☞ **Click a feed headline**

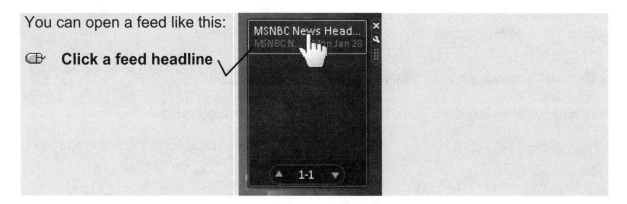

A small window appears displaying the contents of the feed.

☞ **Click**

MSNBC News Headlines

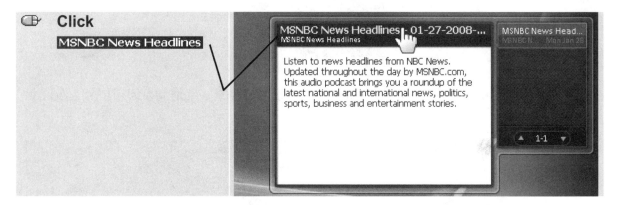

When you click MSNBC News Headlines, the podcast is automatically downloaded and played in *Windows Media Player,* so you can listen to it right away. Please note: it is possible that on your computer another program is set to play MP3 files.

When you have finished listening to the podcast you can close *Windows Media Player.*

☞ **Click** [X]

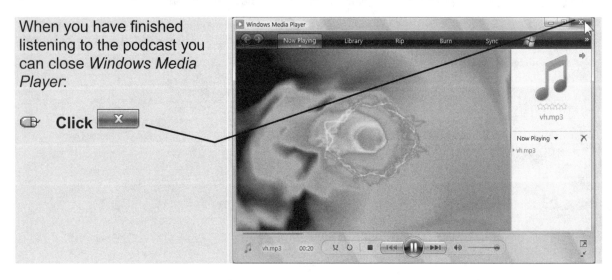

4.4 Computer Tips from Visual Steps

In this section you are going to take a look at the free Computer tips feed from Visual Steps. Two new computer tips are added to this feed weekly.

☞   **Surf to the web address www.visualsteps.com** 𝓁𝓁²

Internet Explorer looks for RSS feeds on every webpage you visit.

When a RSS feed is detected, the RSS feed button will change from grey to orange :

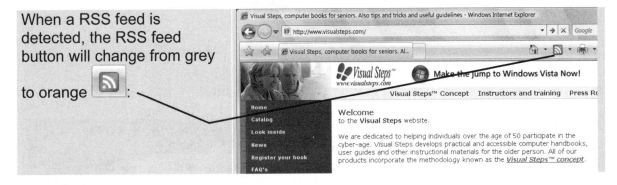

Some websites offer more than one feed. You can check which feeds are offered by this website:

The RSS feed button is orange:

☞   **Click** ▼ **next to**

You see a menu with the title of the available RSS feed:

☞   **Click**
Computer tips from Visual Steps

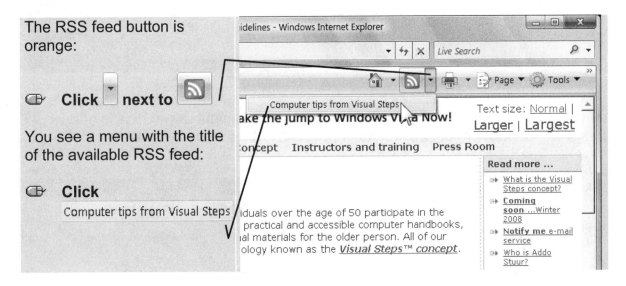

On the webpage you see the list of computer tips that have been published so far:

This feed page looks the same as the feed page with the MSNBC podcasts you saw earlier.

All feed pages in *Internet Explorer* look and behave the same. On each feed page you can decide which category of feeds you want to display on the page. In this example there are three categories of computer tips: tips about *Internet Explorer*, *Outlook Express* and *Windows Mail*.

To display the tips about *Windows Mail* and hide the other tips:

☞ **Click** Windows Mail **below** Filter by category:

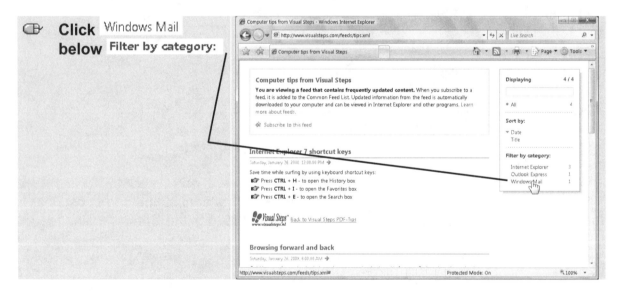

Now you see the tips in the `Windows Mail` category:

To display all tips:

☞ **Click** `All`

Now you see all tips again.

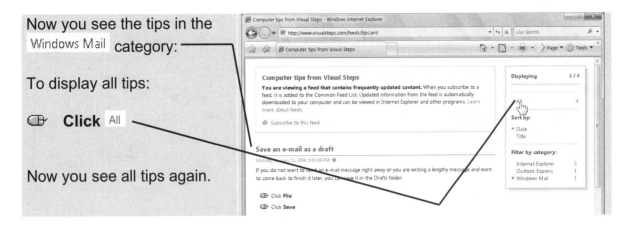

You can also search by keyword to quickly find a tip:

☞ **Click the box below** `Displaying`

⌨ **Type:** cursor

As you type, the tips are immediately filtered to display only the tip(s) containing the word *cursor*:

To display all tips again:

☞ **Click** `All`

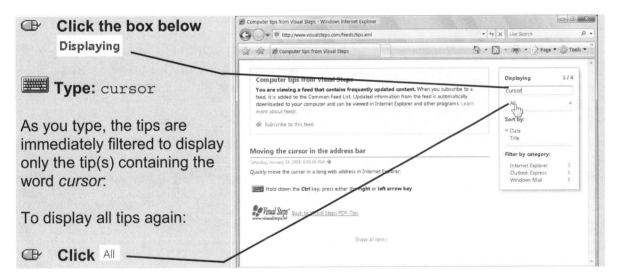

4.5 Subscribing to Computer Tips

To ensure that you keep up to date with the latest computer tips, you can subscribe to this feed. Every week two new computer tips are added to the Computer tips feed.

☞ **Click**
   ⭐ `Subscribe to this feed`

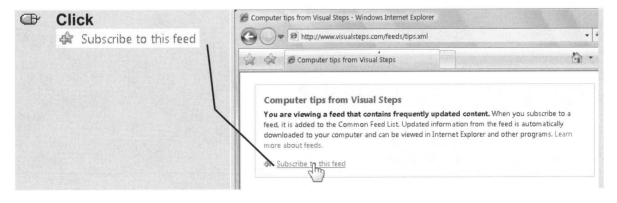

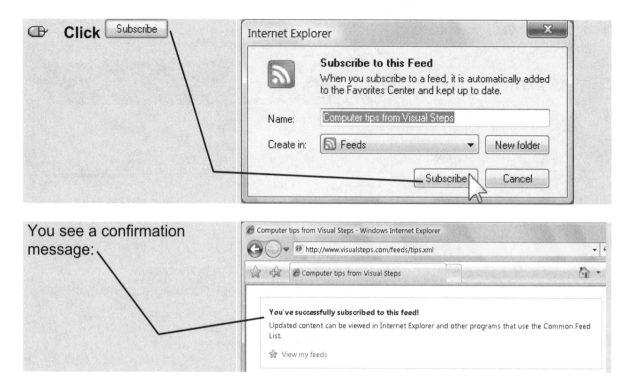

So far you have subscribed to two feeds: the MSNBC Headline News podcast and the Visual Steps computer tips. In the next section you are going to add one more feed.

4.6 Subscribing to More Feeds

Now that you have learned how to use RSS feeds, you can add another feed from a website you are interested in. Many websites offer feeds. When the RSS feed button on your favorite website turns orange, there is a feed available. You can also check these pages for interesting RSS feeds:

www.cnn.com	latest news and headlines
news.yahoo.com/rss	directory of feeds about various topics
www.nfl.com/rss/rsslanding	find feeds about your favorite football team
www.nba.com/rss	find feeds about your favorite basketball team

In this example you are going to subscribe to a feed containing sports news:

☞ **Surf to the webpage sports.espn.go.com/espn/rss/index** $\ell\ell^2$

You see the list of sport feeds offered by ESPN:

☞ **For example, click**

• NFL Headlines

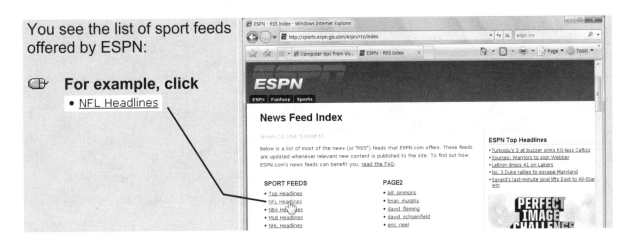

✖ HELP! I see a message about the information bar.

Internet Exporer can alert you when a pop-up is blocked. You can show it like this:

☞ **Click** [Close]

☞ **Right-click the information bar**

☞ **Click**

Temporarily Allow Pop-ups

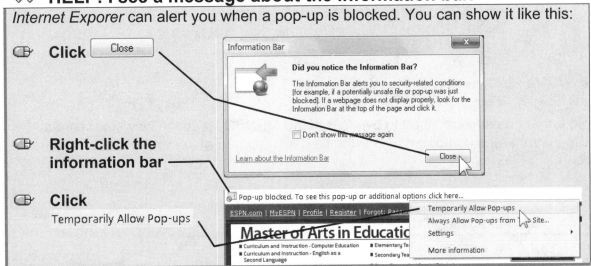

☞ **Click**

⭐ Subscribe to this feed

The subscriptions to the feeds containing computer tips and NFL news have been added to the feed list in the *Favorites Center*.

4.7 The Feed List in the Favorites Center

All feed subscriptions are listed in the feed list in the *Internet Explorer Favorites Center*. You can verify that:

You can open the accompanying webpage by clicking the title of the feed:

You see the page with the
RSS feed Computer tips from
Visual Steps again:

You can print the tips on this
page and create your own
Computer tips folder.

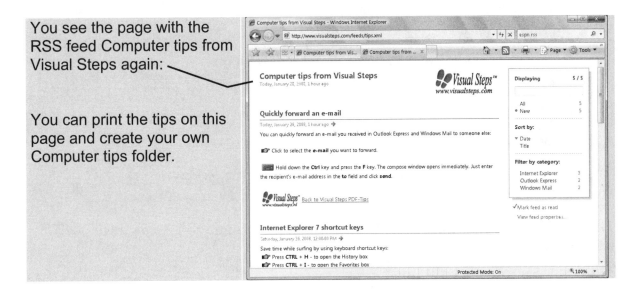

☞ **Open the feed page ESPN.com - NFL** ℰℰ⁴

You see the page containing the ESPN.com NFL news feeds:

When you click a headline,
you can read the full story:

☞ **Click a headline**

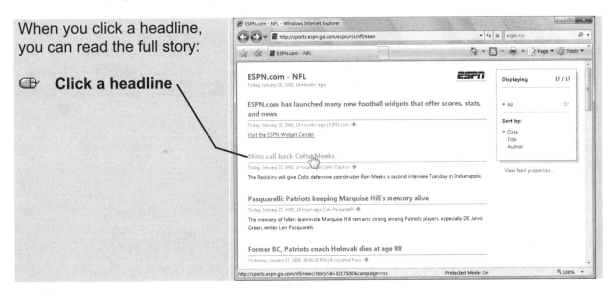

You see the full story behind the feed headline:

Now you can close *Internet Explorer*:

⊂⊐ **Click** X

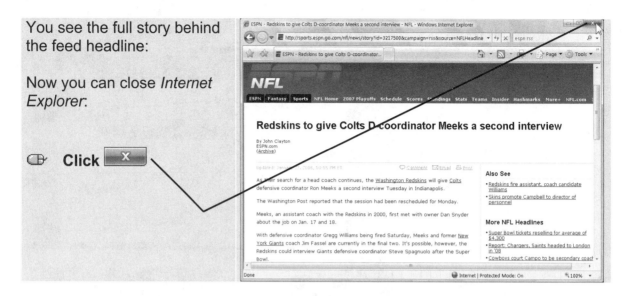

You have seen how you can open the feeds you have subscribed to in the feed list in the *Internet Explorer Favorites Center*.

4.8 Displaying All Feeds in the Feed Headlines Gadget

When you subscribed to the MSNBC News Headlines podcast earlier, you adjusted the settings of the *Vista* gadget *Feed Headlines*. Only the podcast feed is displayed in the gadget. You can change the settings to show more feeds.

If you do not use *Windows Vista*, you can skip this section.

⊂⊐ **Right-click the gadget** *Feed Headlines*

A menu appears:

⊂⊐ **Click** Options

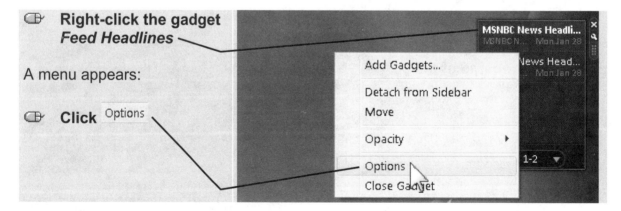

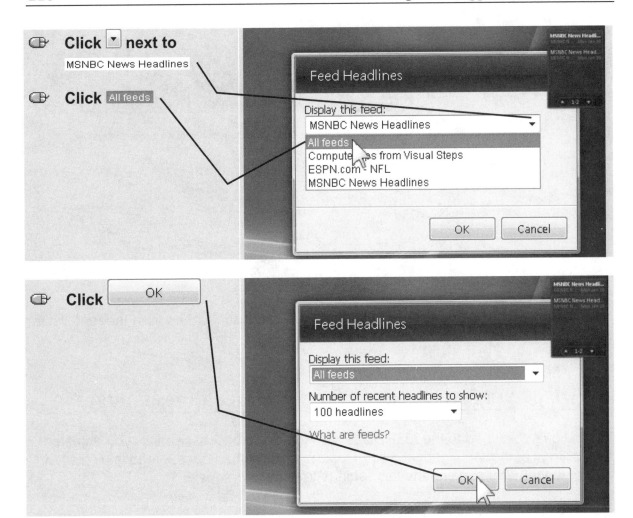

☞ **Click ▼ next to**
MSNBC News Headlines

☞ **Click** All feeds

☞ **Click** OK

Now all feeds are displayed in the *Feed Headlines* gadget.

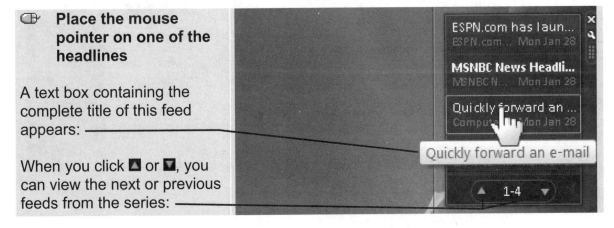

☞ **Place the mouse pointer on one of the headlines**

A text box containing the complete title of this feed appears: —————

When you click ▲ or ▼, you can view the next or previous feeds from the series: —————

In this chapter you have learned how to subscribe to free RSS feeds. There are literally thousands of RSS feeds available on the Internet to choose from. You can subscribe to any new feed that interests you in the same way you have learned here.

4.9 Background Information

Glossary	
Audio file	Sound file.
Downloading	Copying and transferring files from the Internet to your computer.
Favorites Center	The *Internet Explorer* area that contains a list of saved favorite websites, the feed list and the browsing history.
Feed, Web feed	Summary of content from an associated website.
Feed Headlines	One of the default gadgets in *Windows Vista* that is displayed in *Windows Sidebar*. This gadget displays RSS feeds.
Feed list	List of feeds you have subscribed to, visible in the *Internet Explorer Favorites Center*.
Feed reader	(Part of a) program that can be used to display feeds. *Internet Explorer 7* has a built-in feed reader.
File format	The format of a file, indicated by the file name extension (the last three or four letters of a file name – that follow a dot). The file format decides in which program the file can be opened.
Gadget	Small program that runs in *Windows Sidebar*.
MP3	File format used to compress audio, allowing a relatively high sound quality.
Podcast	Audio file distributed on the Internet.
RSS	Abbreviation of Really Simple Syndication. File format that can be read by a special *feed reader* (also called RSS reader).
Windows Media Player	Program used to play audio and video files, comes packaged with *Windows*.
Windows Sidebar	Part of the *Windows Vista* desktop where you can install and run small programs called *gadgets*.
Source: Windows Help and Support, Wikipedia.	

4.10 Tips

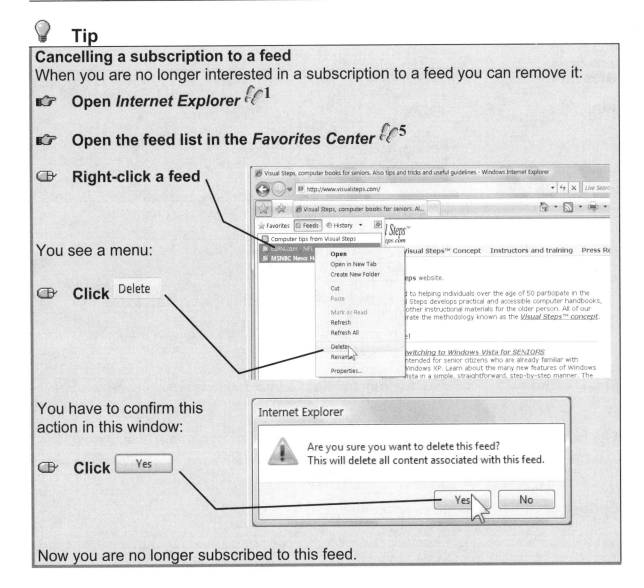

Tip

Cancelling a subscription to a feed
When you are no longer interested in a subscription to a feed you can remove it:

☞ **Open *Internet Explorer* ℰℓ¹**

☞ **Open the feed list in the *Favorites Center* ℰℓ⁵**

☞ **Right-click a feed**

You see a menu:

☞ **Click Delete**

You have to confirm this action in this window:

☞ **Click Yes**

Now you are no longer subscribed to this feed.

Tip

Saving a podcast
Instead of listening to it right away, you can also save a podcast:

☞   **Open the feed page MSNBC News Headlines** 🎧⁴

🖱   **Right-click a feed, for example**

   🎧   vh-01-28-2008-043013.m|

You see a menu:

🖱   **Click** Save Target As...

🖱   **Click** 🎵 Music

⌨   **Type** podcast MSNBC

🖱   **Click** Save

The download starts.

You see the message that the download is complete:

🖱   **Click** Open Folder

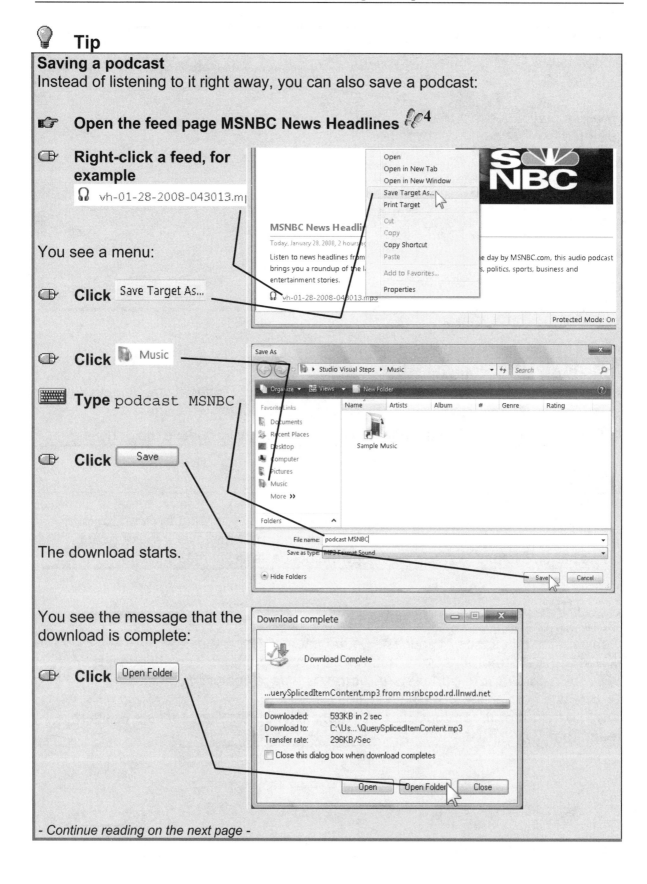

- Continue reading on the next page -

You see that the podcast is added to the Music folder:

You can play a podcast that is stored on your computer by double-clicking the file.

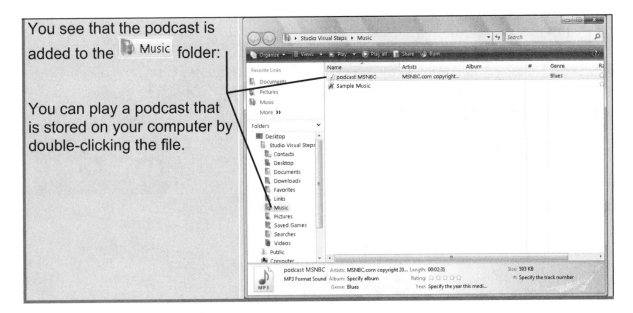

💡 **Tip**

Separate folders for podcasts

In the previous tip the podcast was saved to the Music folder. If you want to save more podcasts from one category, it is more convenient to create separate subfolders in the Music folder. In that way you can easily retrieve the podcasts.

💡 **Tip**

Listening to podcasts

You can play and listen to your podcasts on your PC. If you want to listen to your podcasts at another location, you can burn an audio CD and play it in your car or home stereo system. You can also copy the podcasts to your MP3 player.

💡 **Tip**

More podcasts

You can find thousands of podcasts on the Internet. For example:
www.podcastdirectory.com is a directory containing thousands of podcasts;
www.bbc.co.uk/radio/podcasts/directory is a page containing podcasts of broadcasts from all the BBC radio stations;
www.learnoutloud.com/podcast-directory is a directory for podcasts you can learn from.

5. Trading on eBay

Buying and selling goods on the Internet is fun and exciting. If you want to buy something, you can choose from thousands and thousands of items from all over the world. And if you want to sell something, you can reach a larger number of people by placing the information about it on the Internet.

EBay is the most widely known marketplace on the Internet. When you buy an item on *eBay*, you are buying from another *eBay* member, who is the seller. You are not buying from *eBay*. On *eBay* you trade the same way you do at an auction. The highest bidder is committed to buying the item, and the seller is obliged to sell the item to the highest bidder. In addition to the auctions, there are also items that are offered on *eBay* for a fixed price.

Before you can buy or sell an item on *eBay*, you need to register and sign in first. Selling items on *eBay* is not free; you have to pay *seller fees*.

In this chapter you can read how to buy or sell items on *eBay*.

In this chapter you learn how to:

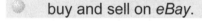   buy and sell on *eBay*.

⇨ **Please note:**

You cannot really practice using *eBay*; when you place a bid on an item you are really taking part in that auction. It is advisable to read through the information in this chapter first. Only when you really want to buy or sell an item, you can follow the steps described in this chapter.

⇨ **Please note:**

The creators of websites are constantly adding new information. The sreenshots used in this chapter may look different from what you see on your screen. This should not pose any problems; the basic features will not be removed. However, it is possible that certain features will be moved to a different location on the website.

5.1 Registering on eBay

The first step for buying and selling on *eBay* is to register as an *eBay* member. This means you have to enter your contact information. You also have to choose a user name and password.

☞ **Open *Internet Explorer*** $\ell\ell^1$

☞ **Surf to www.ebay.com** $\ell\ell^2$

You see the *ebay.com* start page:

On the left side of the window you see that items for sale can be found in many different categories:

☞ **Click** **Register**

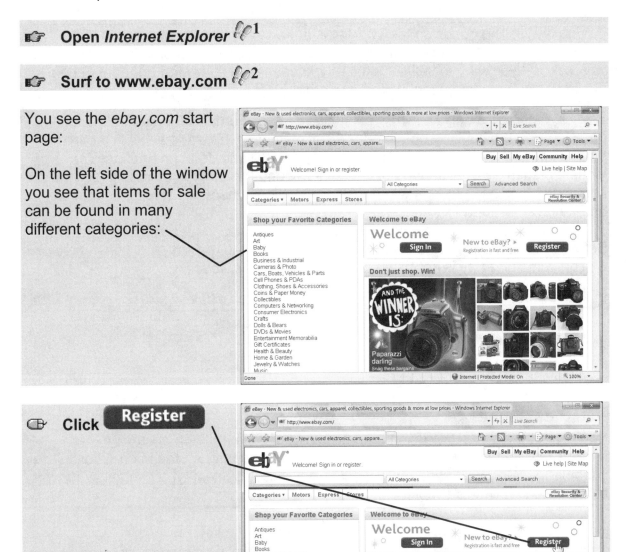

You see this window:

Type your information below

First name , Last name ,
Street address **and** City

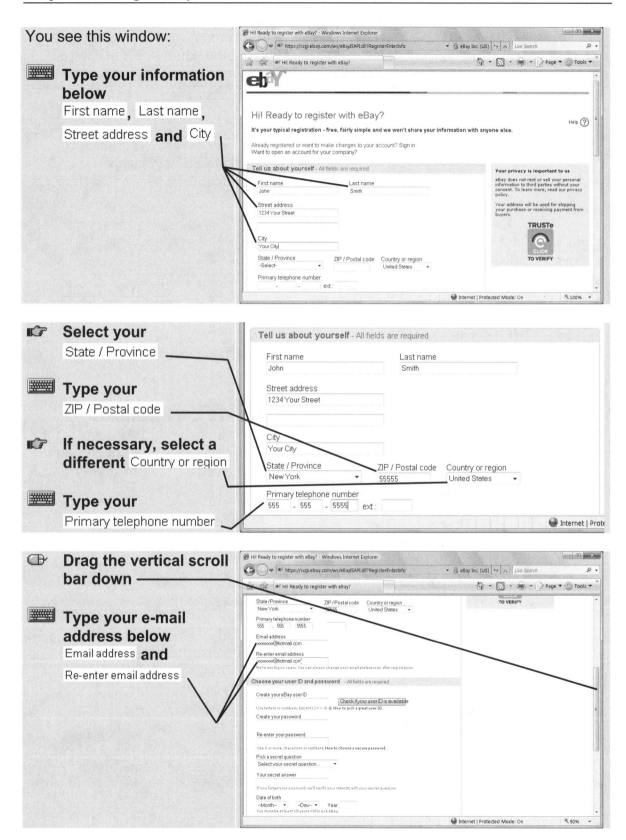

Select your State / Province

Type your ZIP / Postal code

If necessary, select a different Country or region

Type your Primary telephone number

Drag the vertical scroll bar down

Type your e-mail address below Email address **and** Re-enter email address

Now you need to create an *eBay* user ID. This is the name all *eBay* users will see. It does not have to be your real name. The name has to be unique for *eBay*. Do not use your e-mail address as your user ID, because that may lead to a lot of unwanted e-mails.

⌨ Type a user ID below

    Create your eBay user ID

🖱 Click

    Check if your user ID is available

When your user name is approved, you see the message

    ✔ This user ID is available .

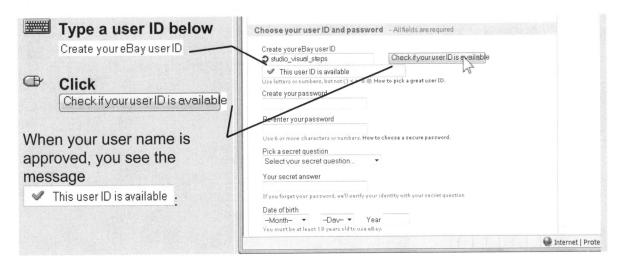

⊠ HELP! My user ID is rejected.

Your user ID can be rejected for several reasons. The user ID you entered may already be used by another *eBay* user. Or you included a character that is not allowed when you entered the user ID, for example, @ <> ( ) !, #, $, %, or &. Each user ID must contain at least six characters or more. If there is something wrong with the user ID you entered, you will need to enter a new one.

When you see a message in red print:

⌨ Type a new user ID below

    Create your eBay user ID

or:

🖱 Click one of the recommended user IDs below

    Recommended user IDs:

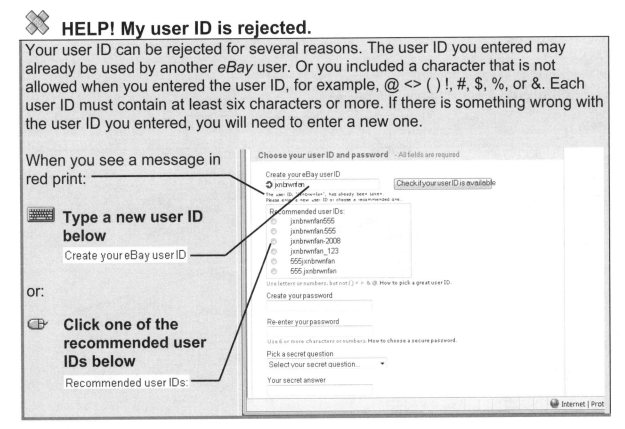

Now you need to create a password. Make sure not to choose a password that is too obvious.

Type a password below Create your password **and** Re-enter your password

☞ **Write your user ID, password and the e-mail address you entered down, and store it in a safe place**

If you ever forget or lose your password, *eBay* can verify your identity when you answer the secret question correctly. Then you can enter a new password for your account. You can select and answer the secret question now:

Click the box below Pick a secret question **and select a question**

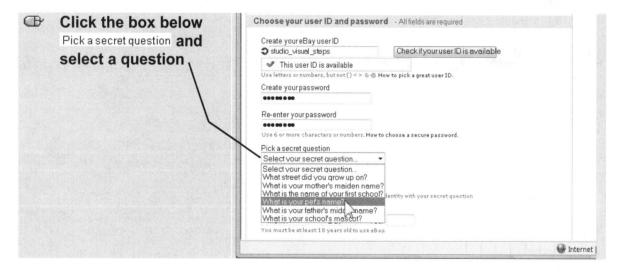

Type your answer below Your secret answer

Enter your date of birth below Date of birth

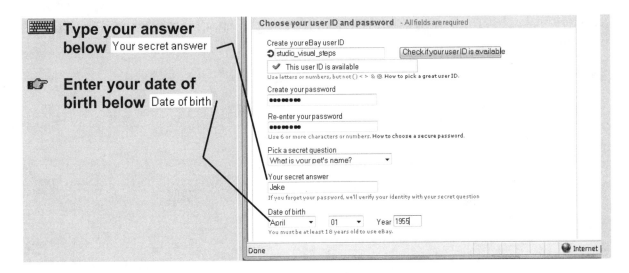

Please note:

To be able to continue, you need to agree to the *eBay* user agreement and privacy policy. You can read both documents by clicking User Agreement and Privacy Policy.

If necessary, drag the vertical scroll bar down

Click to check mark

☑ I agree that:

Click Register

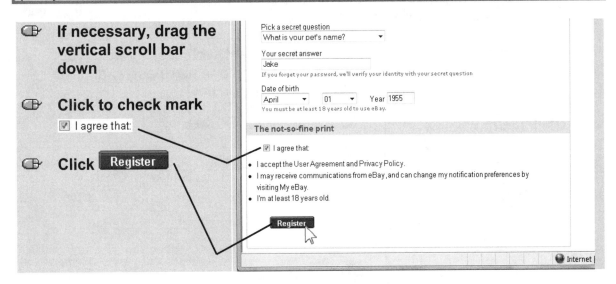

You see the message that you will need to confirm your registration by e-mail:

☞ **Click the link to your webmail account, for example**

Continue to Gmail Email

or:

☞ **Open your e-mail program and download your e-mail**

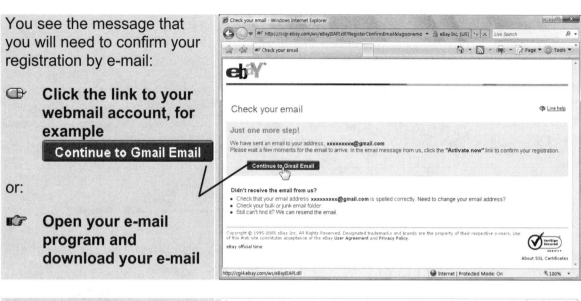

Here you see the e-mail message:

☞ **Click** **Activate Now**

The next window appears:

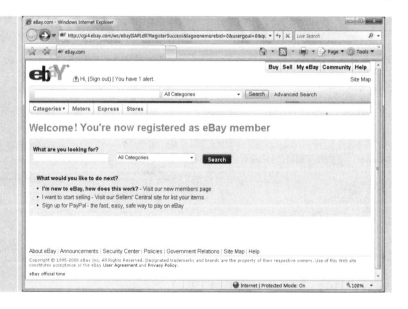

At this moment you are signed in to *eBay*. You are going to sign out and then sign in to *eBay* again. When you use a shared or public computer, it is advisable to always sign out after you finished your session.

To sign out:

$\mathbb{CP}$ **Click** Sign out

To sign in again:

$\mathbb{CP}$ **Click** Sign in

You see this window:

⌨ **Type your user ID next to** User ID

⌨ **Type your password next to** Password

$\mathbb{CP}$ **Click** Sign in

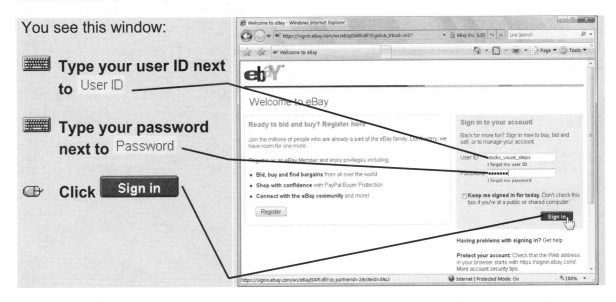

You may see this window now:

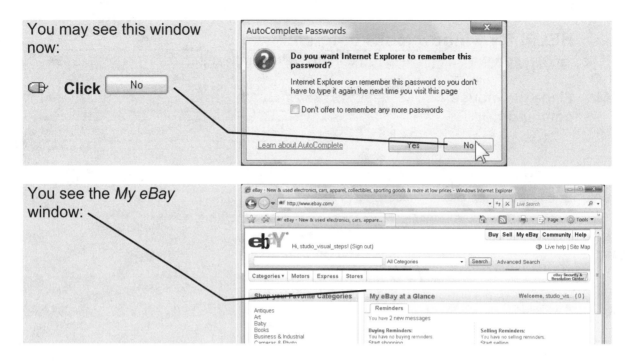

☞ **Click** No

You see the *My eBay* window:

You have registered for an *eBay* account and you have signed in. Now you can start buying or selling items on *eBay*!

5.2 Finding an Item

As soon as you have signed in, you can buy something on *eBay*. There are different ways to search for items. For example, you can search the *Categories* and *Subcategories*. In this example you will search for a computer mouse.

The categories are listed on the left hand side of the window:

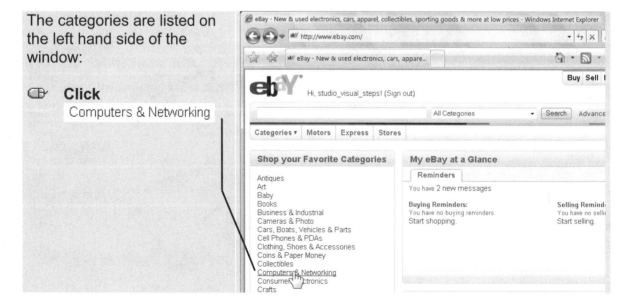

☞ **Click** Computers & Networking

HELP! My window looks different.

If you do not see the categories, you can display them like this:

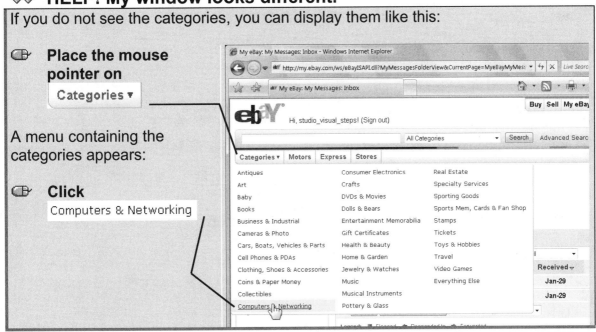

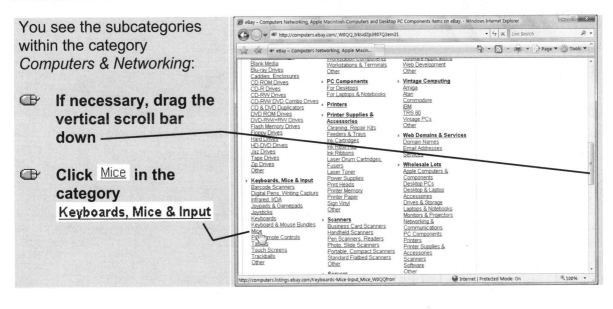

☞ **Place the mouse pointer on**

 Categories ▾

A menu containing the categories appears:

☞ **Click** Computers & Networking

You see the subcategories within the category *Computers & Networking*:

☞ **If necessary, drag the vertical scroll bar down**

☞ **Click** Mice **in the category** Keyboards, Mice & Input

You see how many items are currently being offered in the subcategory Mice:

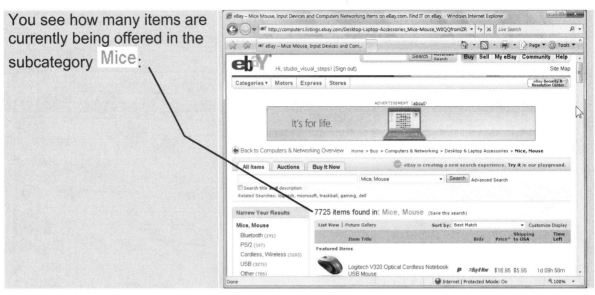

To see the rest of the items:

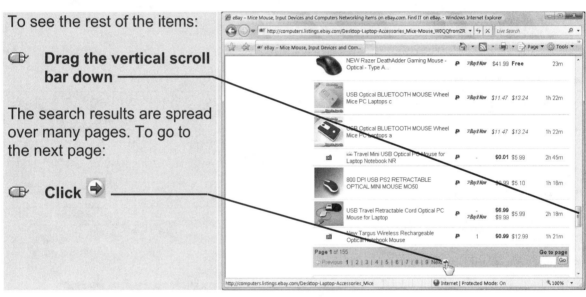

☞ **Drag the vertical scroll bar down** ─────

The search results are spread over many pages. To go to the next page:

☞ **Click**

You have searched by clicking a category within a category.
You can also search by keyword. You use the Search box for that.

☞ **Drag the vertical scroll bar up**

☞ **Click the Search box**

⌨ **Type:** mouse

☞ **Click** `Search`

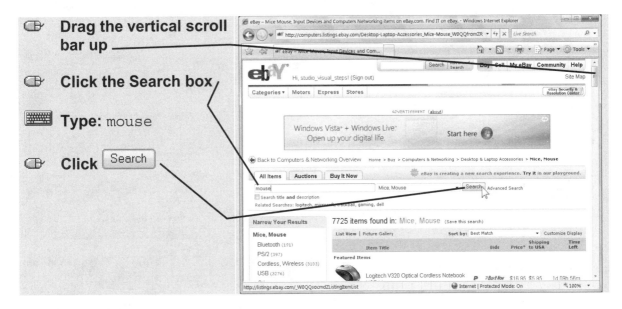

⇨ **Please note:**

The search is performed within the category *Mice, Mouse*. When you use the Search box `[____] Search Advanced Search` at the top of the window, all categories are searched.

Now you see the number of items containing the word 'mouse' that were found: —

For a more specific search:

☞ **Click** `Advanced Search`

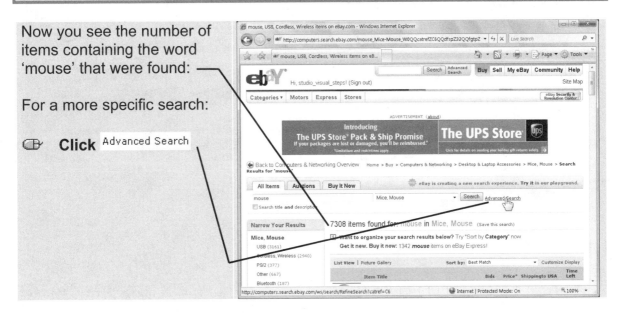

You can enter various search criteria when you perform an *Advanced search*. For example, you can choose to search both the title and descriptions of the items. You can also select the country you want to search in. On *eBay* you can buy items from all over the world. Take a look at the possible search criteria for yourself. In this example you will just add a maximum price.

🖱️ **If necessary, drag the vertical scroll bar down**

⌨️ **On the right side of** Max: US $ **, type:** 5

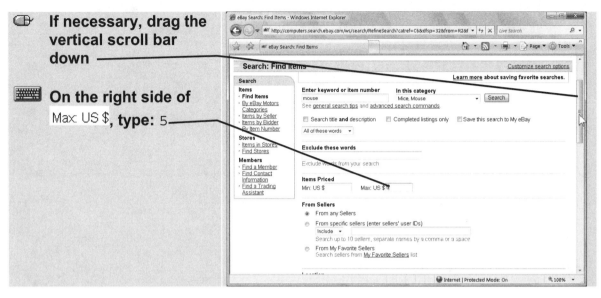

🖱️ **Drag the vertical scroll bar all the way down**

🖱️ **Click** Search

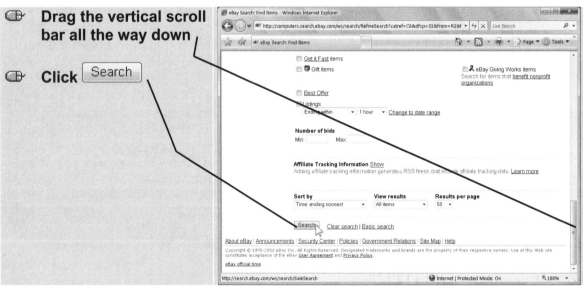

You see how many items remain after the *Advanced search*: ————

You see all items with the keyword 'mouse' with a price of $ 5.00 or less.

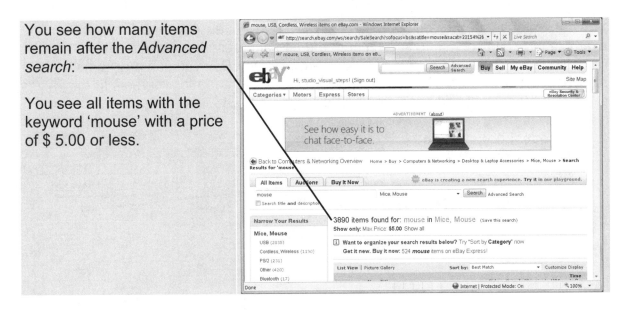

You have tried different search methods.

5.3 Finding Out More About an Item

Most listings on *eBay* contain a lot of information that is important for you as a buyer. There is information about the item as well as information about the seller. In this section you look at an item in detail and you ask the seller a question about the item.

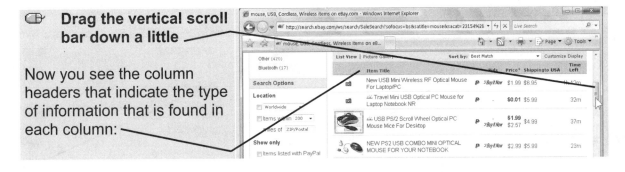

Drag the vertical scroll bar down a little ———

Now you see the column headers that indicate the type of information that is found in each column: ————

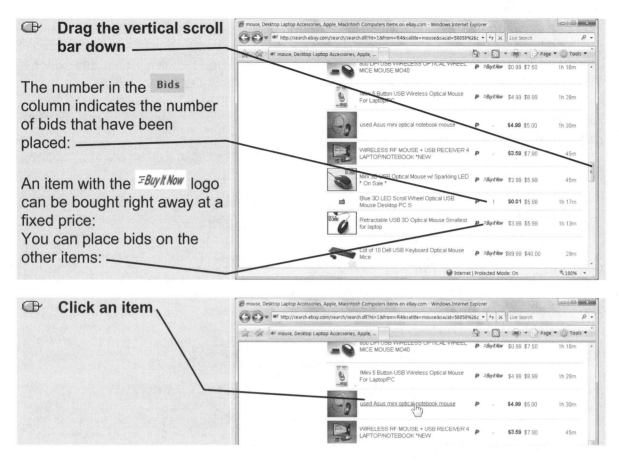

Drag the vertical scroll bar down ———

The number in the **Bids** column indicates the number of bids that have been placed: ———

An item with the *Buy It Now* logo can be bought right away at a fixed price:

You can place bids on the other items: ———

Click an item

If you use *Windows Vista*, you may now see the *Internet Explorer Security* window where you need to give your permission to continue:

Click **Allow**

You see a window containing more information about this item and about the seller. Each seller on *eBay* has a so called *feedback rating*. This rating is made up from the individual ratings given by people who have previously bought items from this seller. The score gives you an indication of the reliability of the seller.

Here you see the *feedback rating* of this seller:

For reasons of privacy, the name of the seller has been removed from this image.

You can ask the seller a question:

☞ **Click** Ask seller a question

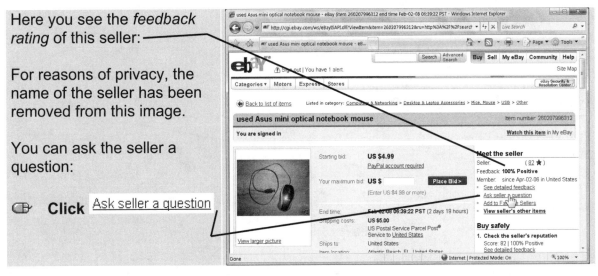

☞ **Click** Select a question about this item

☞ **Click the subject of your question**

⌨ **Type your question in the text box**

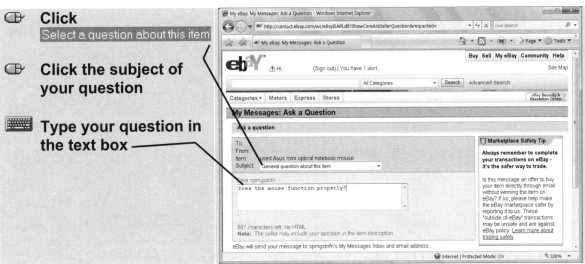

👆 **If necessary, drag the vertical scroll bar down**

👆 **Click to check mark**
☑ Send a copy to my email add|

👆 **Click** Send

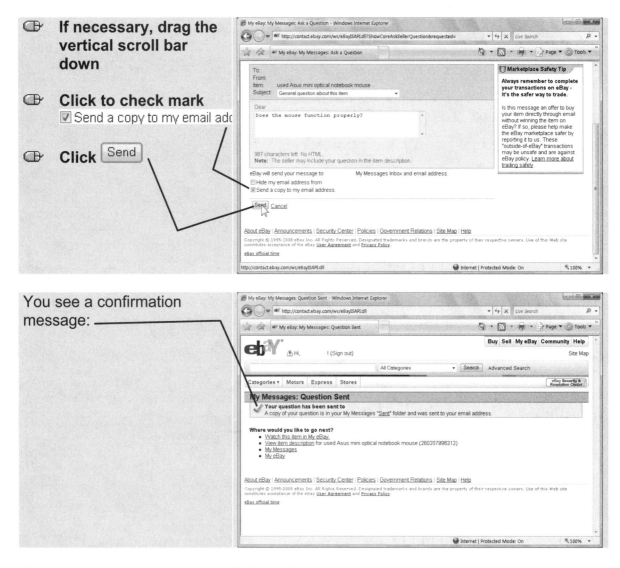

You see a confirmation message: ⎯⎯⎯⎯

Now you have to wait and see if the seller responds to your question. You can check *My eBay* to see if you have received a message from the seller.

👆 **Click** My eBay

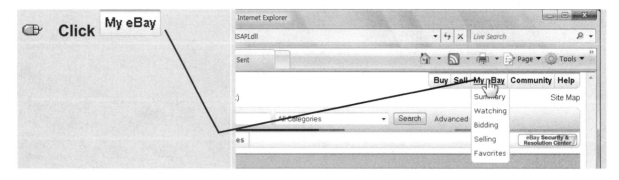

☞ **Click** Messages

In this example there is no response from the seller yet. You can take a look at the message you sent. From this message you can quickly return to the item.

You see there is no message
from the seller yet: ——

☞ **Click** Sent

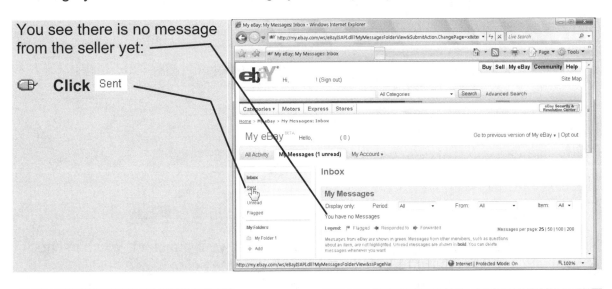

☞ **Click**
You've received a question ;
Asus mini optical notebook m

To return to the item:

👉 **Click the item number**
    260207996312

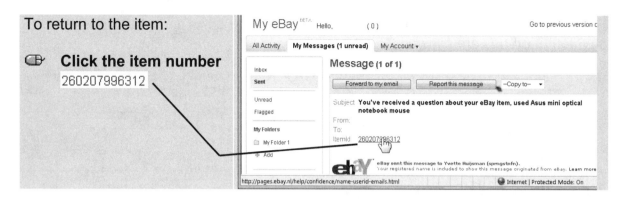

If you use *Windows Vista*, you may now see the *Internet Explorer Security* window where you need to give your permission to continue:

👉 **Click** [Allow]

You see the item you sent the question about. In the next section you can read how to bid on this item in the online auction. In the section after that you can read how to purchase an item at a fixed price.

5.4 Placing a Bid on an Item

Making the decision on how to buy an item will depend on how the item is offered. Are you going to pay a fixed price or are you going to place a bid? In the following example the item is offered in an online auction. You can read how to place a bid on an item.

➡️ **Please note:**

When you perform the actions described in this section, you are really participating in the auction for this item. This means you are obligated to buy the item if you are the highest bidder. Please make sure you only perform these actions for an object you really want to purchase.

If you do not want to place a bid on an item, you can just read through this section.

The bid you enter for the item is called a *maximum bid*. EBay will automatically bid on your behalf up to your maximum bid, not higher. Your maximum bid needs to be higher than the starting bid.

This way you may end up paying less than your maximum bid. However, it is also possible that you are outbid by someone whose maximum bid is higher than yours.

Before you place your bid, pay attention to the shipping costs and what kinds of payment methods are allowed.

You see the shipping costs and shipping method here: ———

The possible payment methods are listed here: ———

In this example only *PayPal* is accepted.

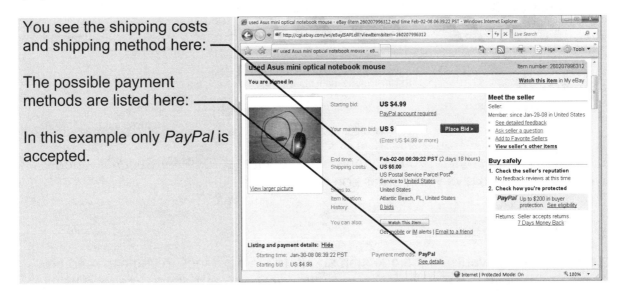

 Tip

Read the whole listing
Before you place a real bid in a real auction, make sure to scroll down and read all the information the seller has listed about the item. This may prevent unpleasant surprises.

You can enter your maximum bid like this:

Here you see the starting bid:

 Type your maximum bid next to

Your maximum bid: **US $**

☞ **Click** Place Bid >

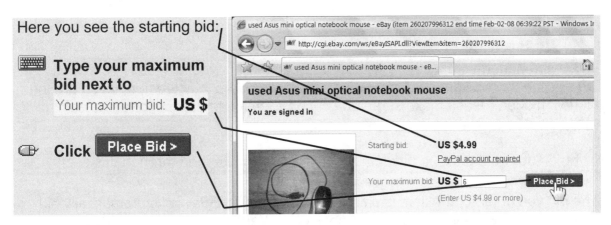

➡ **Please note:**

You are about to confirm your bid. If you choose to continue, you are obligated to buy the item if you are the highest bidder.

To confirm your bid:

☞ **Click** [Confirm Bid]

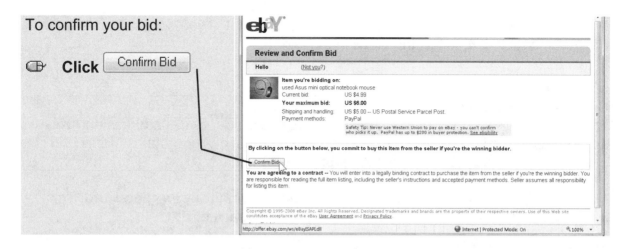

In the example the seller only accepts *PayPal* payments.

If there is a *PayPal* account linked to your *eBay* account, your bid is placed immediately.

You see this message:

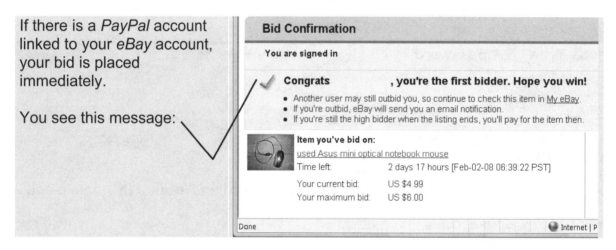

If there is no *PayPal* account linked to your *eBay* account yet, you see a message stating that you are unable to bid for this item.

If you want to open a *PayPal* account:

☞ **Click** Register with PayPal

If you already have a *PayPal* account:

☞ **Click**
Already have a PayPal accour

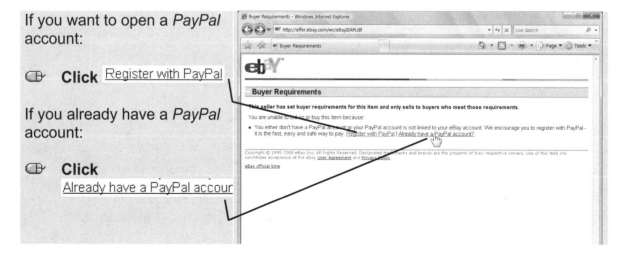

In this example the buyer already has a *PayPal* account. If you want to create a new *PayPal* account now, follow the steps in the next tip.

 Tip

Creating a PayPal account
The most important parts of your *PayPal* account are your e-mail address and your account password. Once your account is set up, you use your e-mail address and password to make or receive payments on the Internet.

Make sure you choose a password that is different from your *eBay* password. The password should have a minimum length of eight characters.

Type your e-mail address next to
*Email Address:

Type your password next to *Create a PayPal Password: **and** *Retype Password:

Drag the vertical scroll bar down

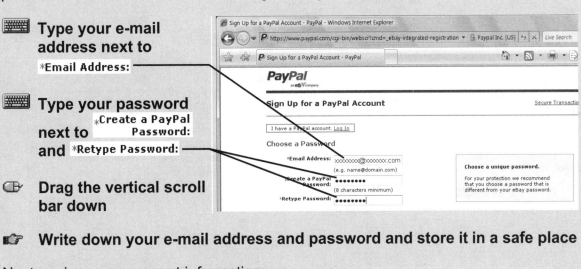

☞ **Write down your e-mail address and password and store it in a safe place**

Next, review your account information:

☞ **Check your address information**

If necessary, click Edit your address and phone number **to make changes**

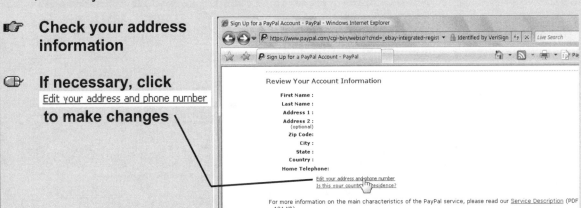

Next you will need to agree to the user agreement and privacy policy, and type the characters you see in the yellow box (for example [AV 63B]).
This is a security measure that helps *PayPal* prevent automated registrations.

- Continue reading on the next page -

☞ **Drag the vertical scroll bar down**

☞ **Click to check mark**

✓ **By checking the box,** I acknowled KB), and the terms incorporated the

⌨ **Type the characters displayed on your screen, for example**

☞ **Click** Sign Up

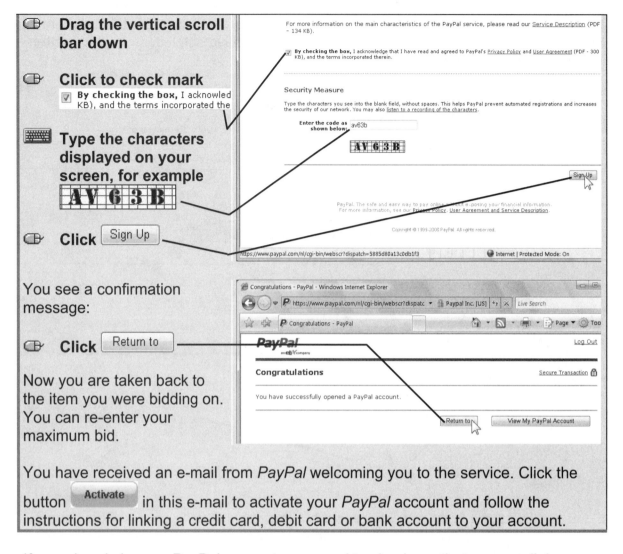

You see a confirmation message:

☞ **Click** Return to

Now you are taken back to the item you were bidding on. You can re-enter your maximum bid.

You have received an e-mail from *PayPal* welcoming you to the service. Click the button **Activate** in this e-mail to activate your *PayPal* account and follow the instructions for linking a credit card, debit card or bank account to your account.

If you already have a *PayPal* account, you need to sign in so that you can link your *PayPal* account to your *eBay* account.

⌨ **Type your e-mail address next to**

PayPal Email Address:

⌨ **Type your password next to** **PayPal Password:**

☞ **Click**

Link Your Account

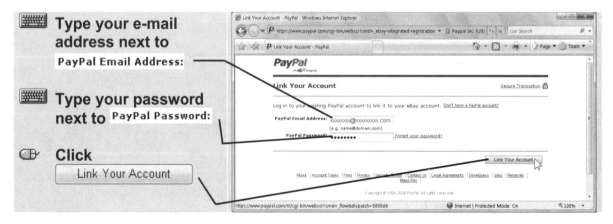

You may see this window where *Internet Explorer* offers to remember this password. Since you are using the *PayPal* password to make a payment, it is probably a better idea to decline this offer.

Click No

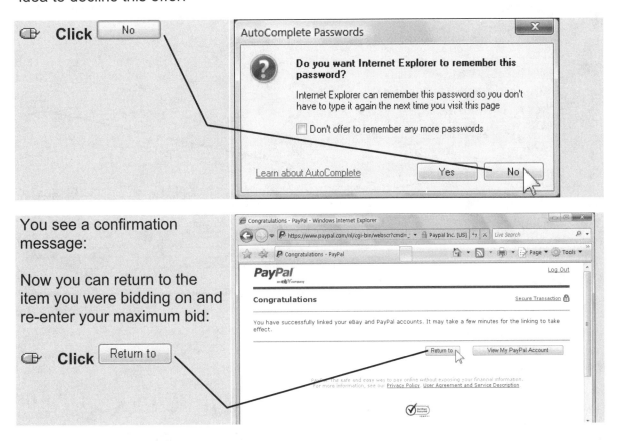

You see a confirmation message:

Now you can return to the item you were bidding on and re-enter your maximum bid:

Click Return to

If you use *Windows Vista*, you may see the *Internet Explorer Security* window again where you need to give your permission to continue:

Click Allow

Now you can place your bid again:

Type your maximum bid next to
Your maximum bid: **US $**

Click Place Bid >

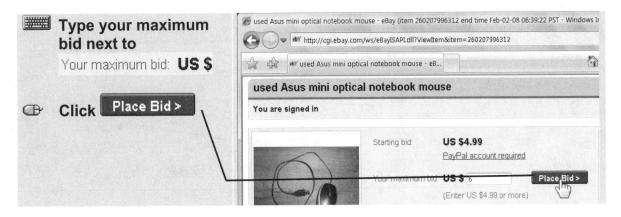

You are about to confirm your bid. When you do, you are obligated to buy the item if you are the winning bidder.

👆 **Click** [Confirm Bid]

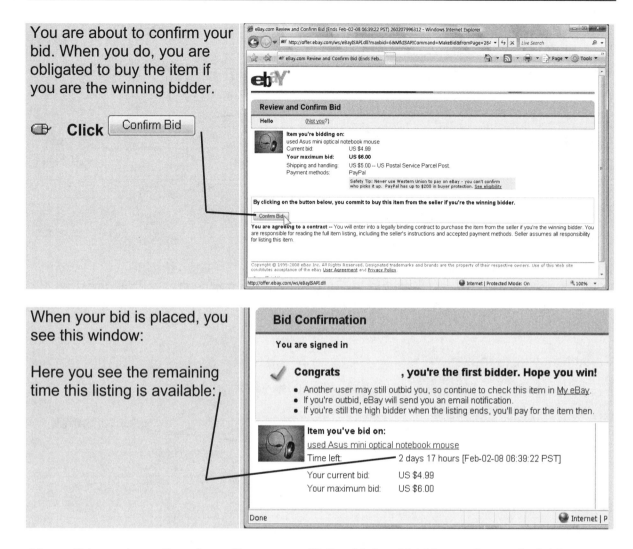

When your bid is placed, you see this window:

Here you see the remaining time this listing is available:

You will have to wait and see if you are still the highest bidder at the end of this period. You can follow what happens to the item on *My eBay*.

👆 **Click** [My eBay]

👆 **Click** [Bidding]

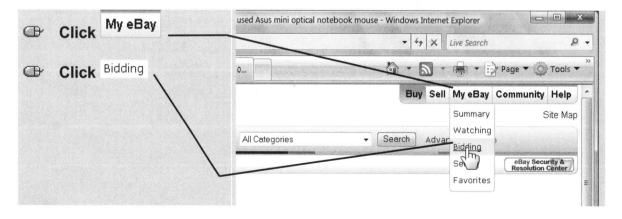

As long as you are the highest bidder, you see WINNING and the price is listed in green:

As soon as you are outbid, you see OUTBID and the price turns red.

If you are outbid and there is still time left on the listing, you can decide whether you want to increase your maximum bid. If you think the item is really worth it, you can place a higher bid. Remember, if you are the highest bidder you are obligated to buy the item from the seller.

To increase your maximum bid:

☞ **Click** `Increase max bid`

A small window appears:

⌨ **Type your new maximum bid next to** Increase your maximum bid:

☞ **Click** `Place Bid`

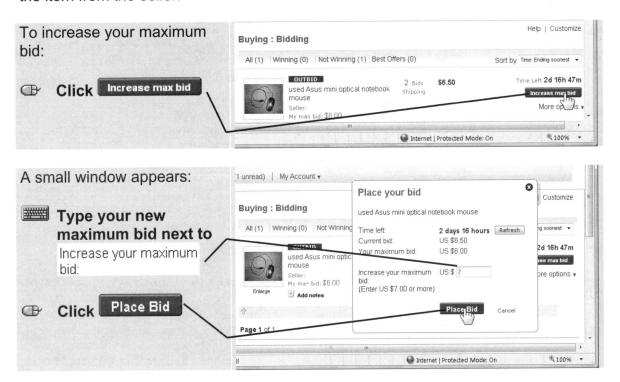

Each bid you place on *eBay* needs to be confirmed:

☞ **Click** Confirm Bid

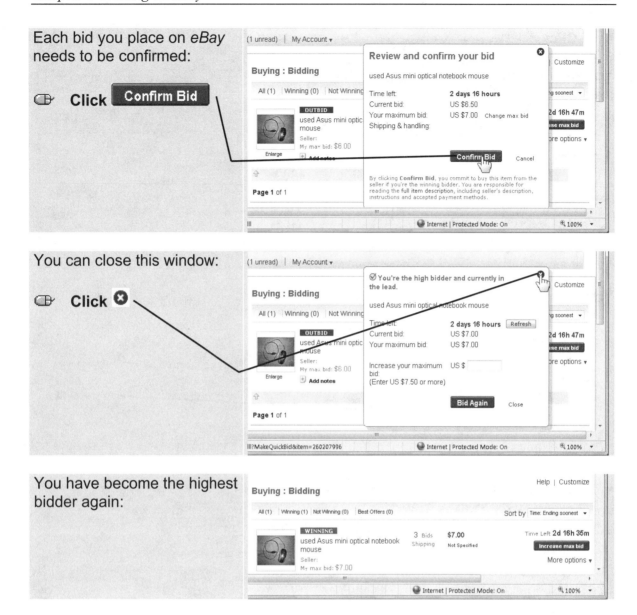

You can close this window:

☞ **Click** ✕

You have become the highest bidder again:

5.5 After Winning an Item

When the auction has ended and you are not the highest bidder, the item is listed in *My eBay* under Didn't Win . If you are the highest bidder, the item is listed under Won . You are also reminded by e-mail that you need to pay for the item. In this example the auction was won.

☞ **If necessary, open *My eBay*** 🖰[11]

🖰 **Click** Won (1)

You see the item you won is marked WON-NEED TO PAY:

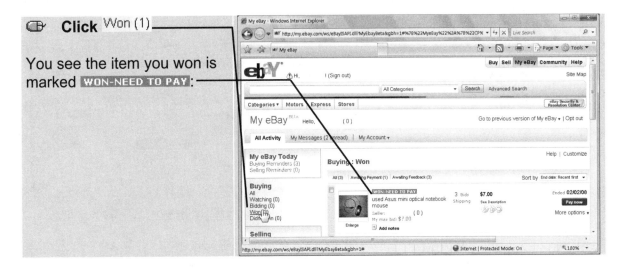

You can pay for the item like this:

🖰 **Click** Pay now

You see this window where you can check your shipping address and payment details:

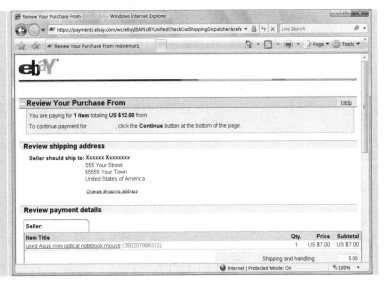

☞ **If necessary, drag the vertical scroll bar down** ——

Payment for this item can only be done by using *PayPal*: ——

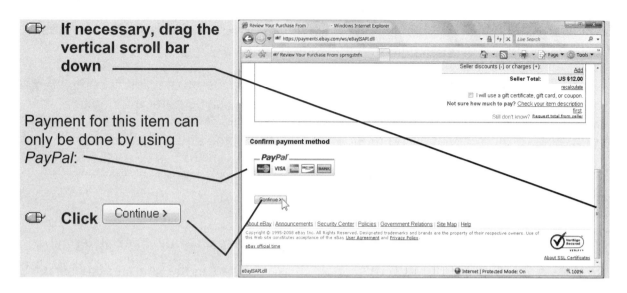

☞ **Click** [Continue >]

You are taken to the webpage where you can sign in to *PayPal* using your e-mail address and *PayPal* password to make the payment. Once you are signed in, you are taken to the page where you can complete your payment.

On this page you see your shipping address and the details of the item you ordered.

To complete your payment:

☞ **Click** [Pay]

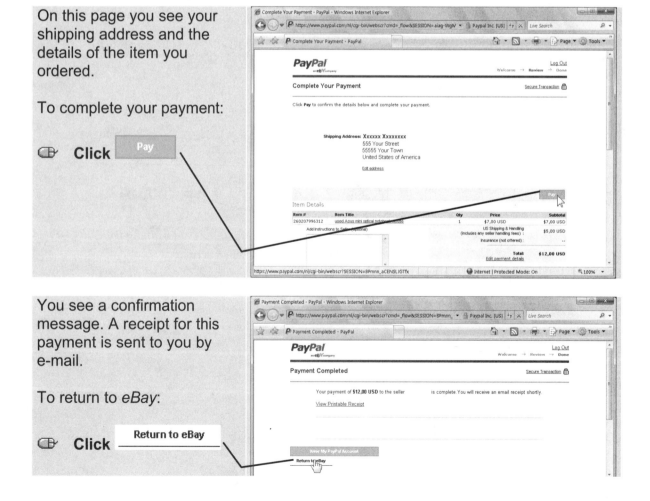

You see a confirmation message. A receipt for this payment is sent to you by e-mail.

To return to *eBay*:

☞ **Click** —— [Return to eBay]

You have read how to buy an item in an online auction. If you performed all actions described in this section, you have purchased an item on *eBay*.

As soon as you have received the item you bought and the transaction is completed, you can give feedback about the transaction. This means you enter a rating to express your opinion about how the transaction with this seller has transpired. You can read more about giving feedback in the tips at the end of this chapter.

5.6 Buying an Item at a Fixed Price

In this section you can read how to buy a *fixed price* item on *eBay*. In *eBay* terms: the item is listed as *Buy It Now*. This logo ⌐Buy It Now appears in the search results list.

⇨ **Please note:**

When you perform the actions described in this section, you risk having to buy the item for real. Please make sure you only perform these actions for an object you really want to purchase.

If you do not want to buy anything now, you can just read through this section.

In this example a CD is bought for the ⌐Buy It Now price.

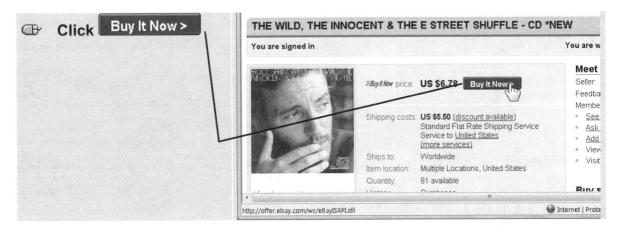

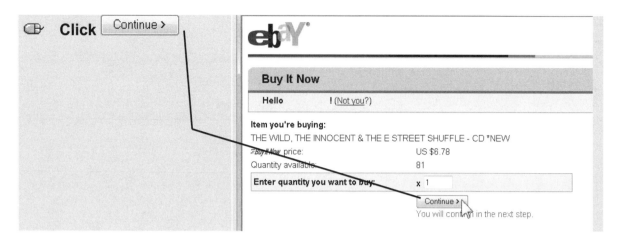

You are about to confirm that you are buying this item. If you do, you are obligated to buy the item. Pay attention to the shipping costs. Also, check which payment method suits you best. In this example you can decide between *Paypal*, Personal check or a Money order/Cashiers check.

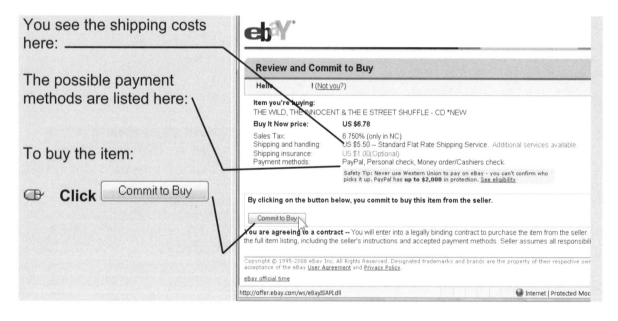

You see a message confirming your purchase:

☞ **Click** Pay Now >

You see this window where you can review your shipping address and payment information:

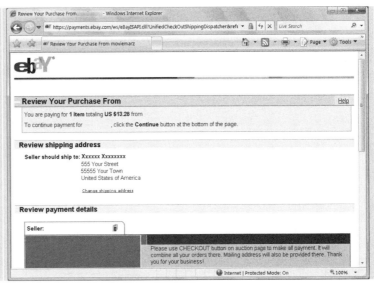

☞ **Drag the vertical scroll bar down**

☞ **Select ⊙ a payment method**

At the end of this section you can read a tip about the steps involved in using other payment methods like checks. In this example *PayPal* is selected.

☞ **Click** Continue >

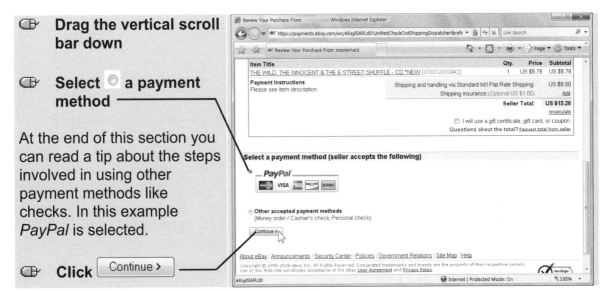

You are taken to the webpage where you can sign in to *PayPal* using your e-mail address and *PayPal* password to make the payment. Once you are signed in, you are taken to the page where you can complete your payment.

On this page you see your shipping address and the details of the item you ordered.

To complete your payment:

☞ **Click** [Pay]

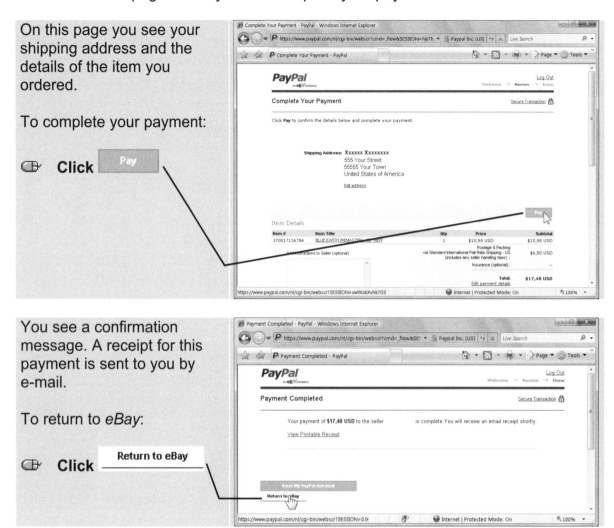

You see a confirmation message. A receipt for this payment is sent to you by e-mail.

To return to *eBay*:

☞ **Click** Return to eBay

You have read how to buy an item at a fixed price. If you performed all actions described in this section, you have purchased an item on *eBay*.

As soon as you have received the item you bought and the transaction is completed, you can give feedback about the transaction. This means you enter a rating to express your opinion about the way the transaction with this seller has transpired. You can read more about giving feedback in the tips at the end of this chapter.

You can safely assume the seller will send you the item. If that is not the case, or if the item is not the same as was described in the listing, communicate with the seller.

If the problem cannot be resolved, you can also report to *eBay* using the *Dispute Console* in *My eBay.* This is an online communication tool which helps you track, manage, and resolve your dispute as quickly as possible.

To open the *Dispute Console* in *My eBay*:

 Below Shortcuts **, click** Report an item not received

The *Dispute Console* is opened on a new tab or in a new browser window.

You can follow the instructions on this page to report your dispute:

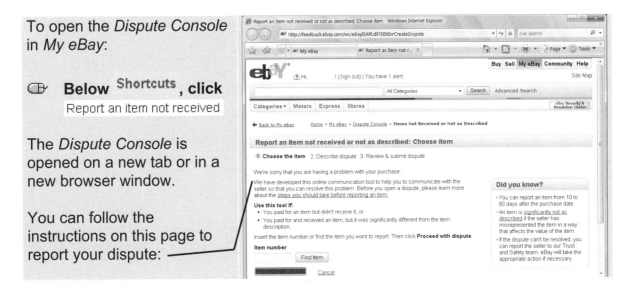

On the webpage http://pages.ebay.com/help/tp/using-dispute-console.html you can read more about the *Dispute Console.*

💡 Tip

Payment by check or money order

If you are paying by check or money order, you need to send the payment through the mail, based on the seller's instructions. Upon receipt of payment, the seller typically sends you a confirmation e-mail. You can always contact the seller for the shipping status.

If you are paying by personal check or money order, you see this window where you affirm that you are going to send your payment.

In the example the seller uses the *eBay* Checkout service to arrange his payments:

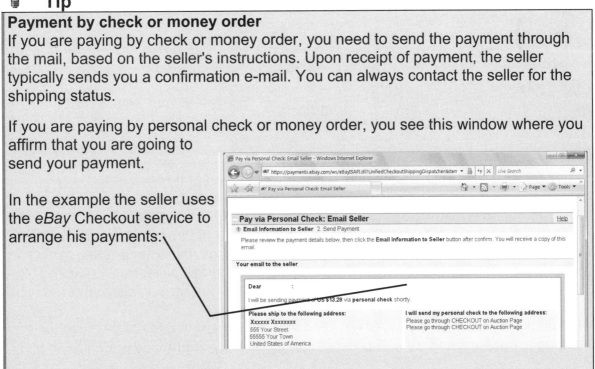

- Continue reading on the next page -

Drag the vertical scroll bar down

Here you see the total amount you have to pay, including shipping:

If necessary, you can type a note to the seller here

Click Email Information to Seller >

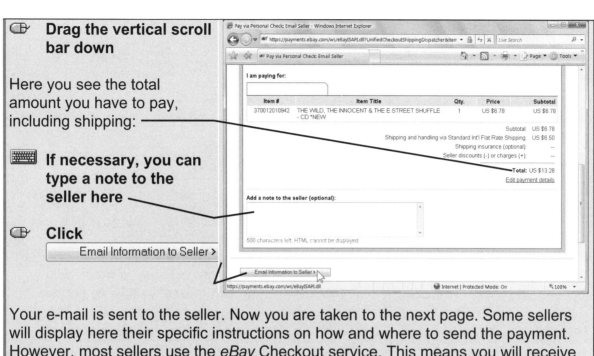

Your e-mail is sent to the seller. Now you are taken to the next page. Some sellers will display here their specific instructions on how and where to send the payment. However, most sellers use the *eBay* Checkout service. This means you will receive an e-mail containing the seller's address information and further instructions for sending the check. This could include whether or not you need to note the order number or confirmation number on the check or on the envelope.

As you see, there are no payment instructions on the page in the example. Instead they are mailed to your e-mail address.

You can go back to *My eBay* now:

Click ▶ My eBay **below** Where would you like to go n

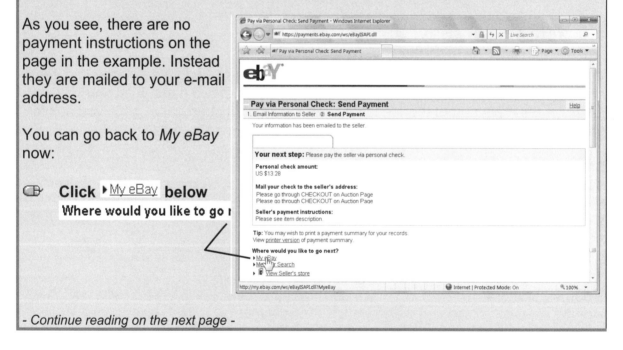

- Continue reading on the next page -

After you have sent the check, you need to mark the payment as sent in *My eBay*. There is a buying reminder for the item in *My eBay Today*:

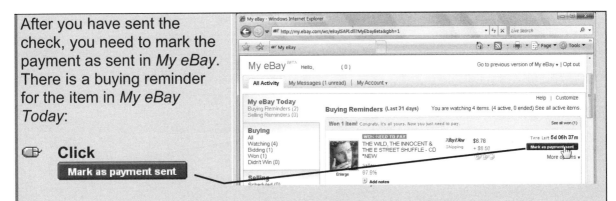

👉 **Click**

Mark as payment sent

The seller will send you the item as soon as he has received your payment.

As soon as you have received the item you bought and the transaction is completed, you can give feedback about the transaction. This means you enter a rating to express your opinion about the way the transaction with this seller has transpired.

You can read more about giving feedback in the tips at the end of this chapter.

You can read more about safe trading on the Internet in the *Background Information* at the end of this chapter.

5.7 Selling on eBay

When you have an *eBay* account, you can also put items up for sale. Listing an item on *eBay* will cost you a small fee. This fee is made up of two parts. First you pay an *insertion fee*. This part of the fee is based on the starting or reserve price you ask for an item. For auction style listings, the insertion fees are as follows:

Starting or reserve price:	Insertion fee:
$ 0.01 - $ 0.99	$ 0.15
$ 1.00 - $ 9.99	$ 0.35
$ 10.00 - $ 24.99	$ 0.55
$ 25.00 - $ 49.99	$ 1.00
$ 50.00 - $ 199.99	$ 2.00
$ 200.00 - $ 499.99	$ 3.00
$ 500.00 or more	$ 4.00

When you sell the item, you also pay a *final value fee*. When the item is not sold, the final value fee is not charged, and you can relist the item. If the item sells the second time, *eBay* will refund the insertion fee for the relisting.

Closing value:	Final value fee:
Item not sold	no fee
$ 0.01 - $ 25.00	8.75% of the closing value
$ 25.01 - $ 1,000.00	8.75% of the initial $ 25.00, plus 3.50% of the remaining closing value balance ($ 25.01 to $ 1,000.00)
Equal to or over $1000.01	8.75% of the initial $ 25.00, plus 3.50% of the initial $ 25.01 - $ 1,000.00, plus 1.50% of the remaining closing value balance ($1000.01 - closing value)

As an example, this section covers the process of selling a computer mouse. You have to decide for yourself which item you want to sell on *eBay*.
You can prepare yourself by answering a few questions. How will you describe the item? How much do you want to ask for the item? How much are you going to charge for shipping? How do you want the item to be paid? Also, make sure you have a digital photo of the item on your computer.

Before you can start, you need to sign in:

☞ **If necessary, sign in to *eBay*** 🦶¹²

☞ **Open *My eBay*** 🦶¹¹

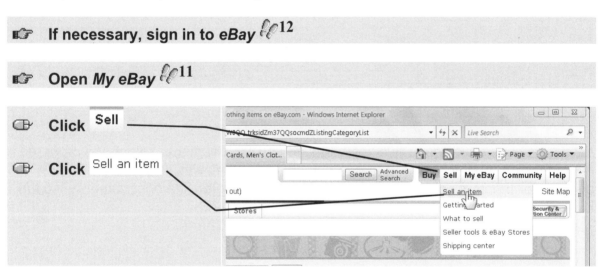

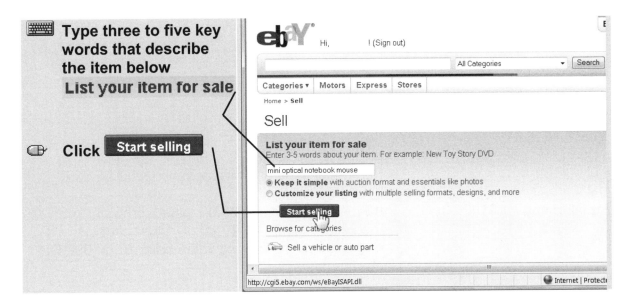

The first step in the selling process is creating a descriptive title for your item. *EBay* assumes you want to use the three to five keywords you just entered as the title. If you want to give more information in the title, you can change it.

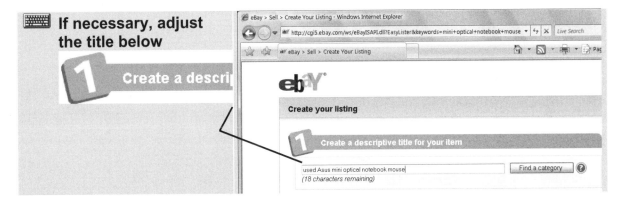

EBay has used the three to five keywords you entered earlier to select one or more categories or subcategories. You can decide for yourself which category is most suitable for the item you are selling. It is important to select the right category, so the item can easily be found by possible buyers.

Click the category of your choice

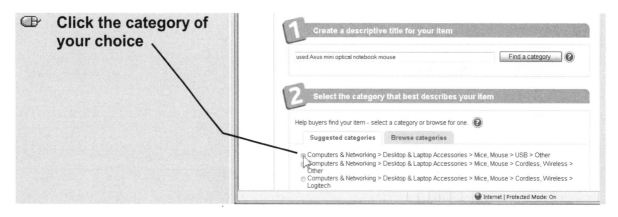

HELP! No category or the wrong category was found.

If no category is found based on the keywords you entered, or you think the categories that do show up are not suitable for the item you are selling, you can browse the categories yourself to make a choice:

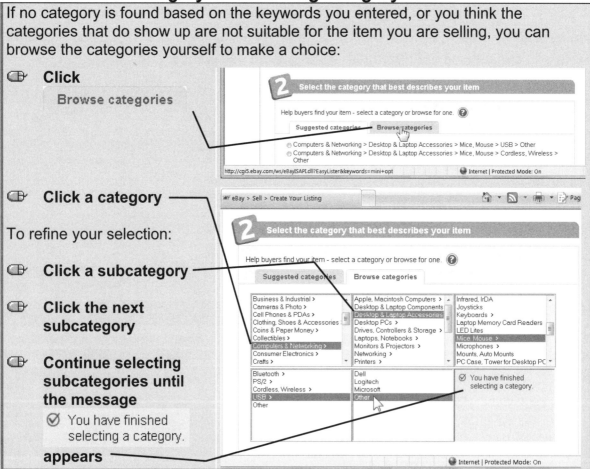

Click

    Browse categories

Click a category

To refine your selection:

Click a subcategory

Click the next subcategory

Continue selecting subcategories until the message

    ⊘ You have finished selecting a category.

appears

Now you can add a digital photo of the item you are selling. You can add one photo for free. To add additional photos, it will cost $ 0.15 each.

☞ **If necessary, drag the vertical scroll bar down** —————

☞ **Click** Add a photo

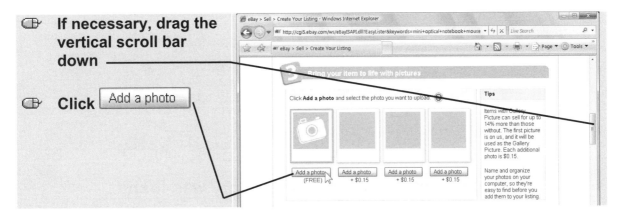

Depending on your *Internet Explorer* settings, a new window or a new tab is opened. Here you can browse your hard disk for the photo you want to add.

☞ **Click** Browse...

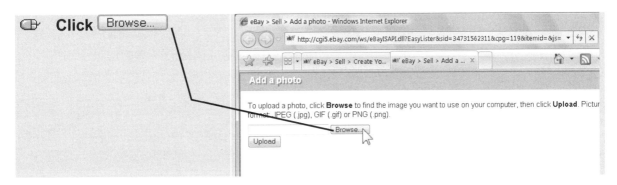

The *Choose File* window appears:

This window may look a bit different if you are working on a *Windows XP* PC. The actions you need to perform are the same.

☞ **If necessary, click** ▓ Pictures

☞ **Select a photo**

☞ **Click** Openen

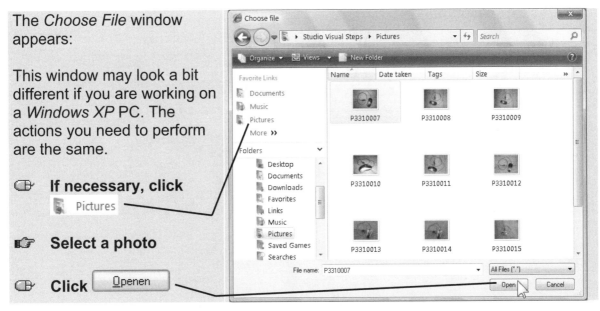

Now you can upload the photo.

Click [Upload]

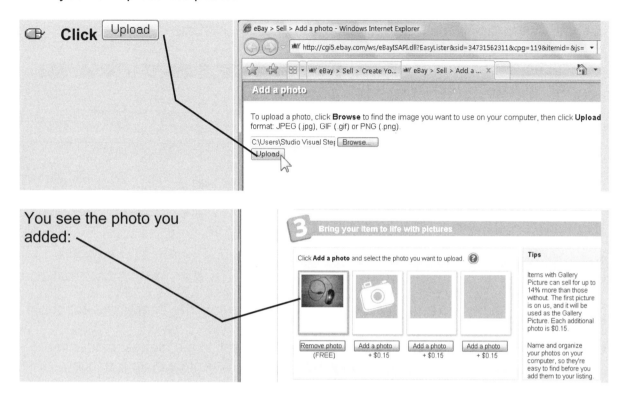

You see the photo you added:

The next step is to give your item a good description. First you need to indicate whether the item is new or used.

If necessary, drag the vertical scroll bar down

Click ▾ next to [Item condition]

Click [New] or [Used]

In this example the item is used.

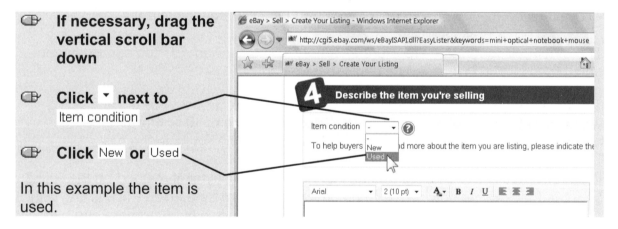

The next step is to add a description of the item. Make sure you have enough information and be honest about the state the item is in. If you make the item sound better than it really is, you may encounter disappointed buyers.

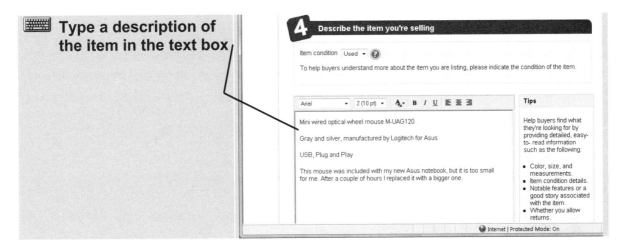

Now you have to decide how you are going to sell the item. The three most important selling formats are:

- *Online auction*: you receive bids on your item and sell to the highest bidder in a fixed length of time. You may also include a *Buy It Now* price in your auction, enabling buyers to buy the item immediately.
- *Fixed Price*: you list your items at a set *Buy It Now* price, so buyers can purchase immediately. There is no bidding. You may also include the *Best Offer* option in your *Fixed Price* listings.
- *Best Offer*: this means you consider 'Best Offers' from buyers (for example, '$ 250.00 or Best Offer').

The other selling formats are *Store Inventory* and *Classified Ad*. You can read more about these formats in *eBay's* extensive Help pages.

The Fixed Price selling format has some limitations: to create a Fixed Price listing with a quantity of one, you must have a feedback rating of 10 or more (or be ID Verified). Your feedback rating is created by buyers who evaluate the sale.

If you have a *PayPal* account and accept *PayPal* as a payment method on the listing, your feedback rating only needs to be 5 or more. To create a Fixed Price listing with quantities of two or more, you must have a feedback rating of 30 or more and be a registered user for at least fourteen days (or be ID Verified). If you have a *PayPal* account and accept *PayPal* as a payment method on the listing, your feedback rating only needs to be 15 or more.

To add a *Buy It Now* price to an auction, you must have either a minimum feedback rating of 10 or be ID Verified. If you are a *PayPal* account holder and accept *PayPal* as a payment method, you only need to have a minimum feedback score of 5.

Tip

ID Verify

ID Verify establishes an *eBay* member's proof of identity, helping both buyers and sellers trust each other. In the ID Verify process, a third-party company (Equifax in the US) works with *eBay* to confirm a member's identity by cross-checking contact information using consumer and business databases.

For ID Verify you must:

- Be a resident of the United States or US territories (Puerto Rico, US Virgin Islands, and Guam).
- Provide your home address, not your company's address.
- Pay a $ 5.00 application fee. When you have successfully passed the ID Verify process, the fee is charged to your *eBay* account. This is a **one-time** charge. If you do not complete the process or if you do not successfully pass the ID Verify process, you are **not** charged.
- Enter information such as your name and date of birth. You will also need to identify certain installment and credit accounts, and their associated monthly payments. The ID Verification process is not a credit check, the credit information is for identification purposes. Your personal information is cross-checked against consumer and business databases for consistency. When your information is successfully verified, you will receive an ID Verify icon in your member profile.

For more information, go to
pages.ebay.com/help/confidence/identity-idverify.html

Source: eBay Help

When you offer your first item on *eBay*, the selling format *Online Auction* is your only option. First you enter the price you want the auction bidding to start at.

Type the starting price next to

Start auction bidding at $

To select how long you want the listing to run:

👉 **Click ˅ next to**
lasting for

👉 **Click the number of days you want the listing to run**

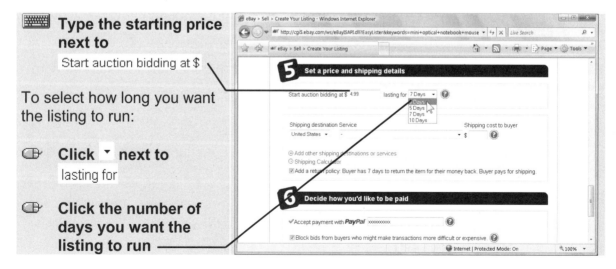

Now you can enter the shipping information: where will you ship your item and what is the cost? You can weigh the item (including the packaging) and look up the domestic and international shipping rate(s) using the hyperlink ⊙ Shipping Calculator .

When you know the shipping rates for the shipping service you want to use:

 **Type the shipping
rates below**
Shipping cost to buyer

☞ **Click the box below**
Service

☞ **Select the service**

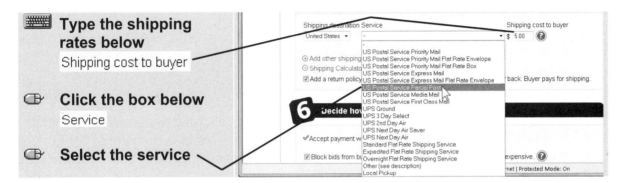

💡 **Tip**

Other shipping destinations or services

You can add more shipping destinations and/or services:

☞ **Click**
⊕ Add other shipping destinations or s

Now you can select the payment methods you want to accept. *PayPal* is a fast, easy and secure way to accept credit card or checking account payments. Since *PayPal* is regarded as the safest way to buy things on *eBay*, offering it as a payment option may help attract more buyers.

Every new seller is required to offer either *PayPal* or a merchant account credit card as an accepted payment method for his/her items.

Tip

PayPal

PayPal is a service you can use to pay and receive money online. After opening a *PayPal* account and registering your credit card, debit card, or bank account you can make secure purchases without revealing your credit card number or financial information to the seller. *PayPal* can be used on *eBay* and with thousands of other merchants worldwide.

As a seller on *eBay*, *PayPal* allows you to receive credit card payments for example, without monthly fees or the lengthy approval process necessary for setting up a merchant account credit card. You only pay a fee when you accept a payment.

For more information about *PayPal*, take a look at the official website at: www.paypal.com

Source: PayPal Help

In this example *PayPal* is offered as the only method of payment. If you do not have a *PayPal* account yet, you can wait until your item sells to create one. For now, just type your e-mail address in the box and sign up later.

PayPal is selected by default and cannot be turned off:

▤ **Type the e-mail address associated with your *PayPal* account**

☞ **Click**

Save and preview

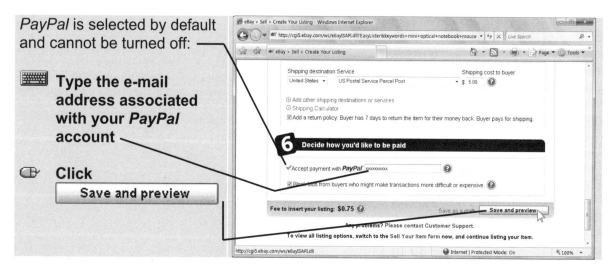

Windows Vista users may see the *Internet Explorer Security* window where you need to give your permission to continue:

☞ **Click** [Allow]

EBay requires an insertion fee for the placement of each listing, and a final value fee when the item is sold. In this example the insertion fee is $ 0.35. When the item is sold, an additional 8.75% final value fee must be paid to *eBay*.

You see this window, where you can review your listing:

Here you see a breakdown of the total insertion fee for this listing:

☞ **Drag the vertical scroll bar down**

You see what your listing will look like on *eBay*:

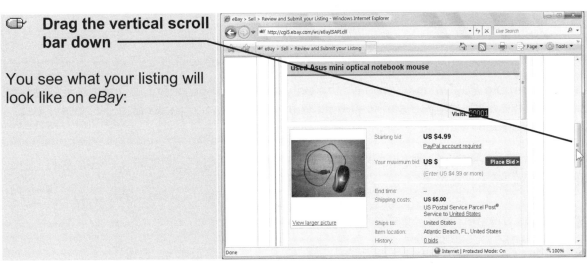

☞ **Drag the vertical scroll bar down**

You see how the listing will appear in the search results:

To change your listing:

☞ **Click** Edit listing

If you are satisfied:

☞ **Click** Continue >

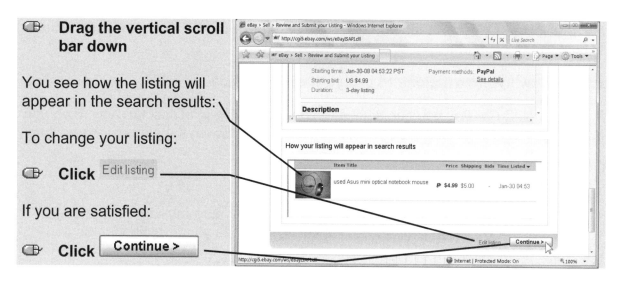

Now you have to create a *Seller Account* to be able to pay for your *eBay* seller fees. To do so, you need to sign in to your account again:

⌨ **Type your** User ID **and** Password **in the text boxes**

☞ **Click** Sign in

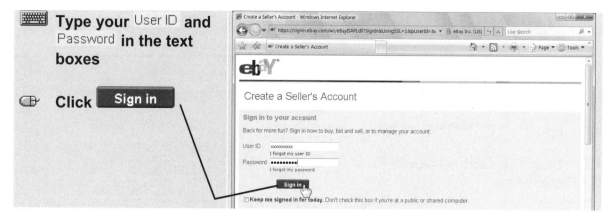

Now you have to select a payment method for your *eBay* seller fees. You can choose between *PayPal*, credit card, debit card or bank account. Proof of identity (with a credit card) is required to use a bank account to pay your fees.

☞ **Click the payment method you want to use**

In this example *PayPal* is used.

☞ **Click** Continue

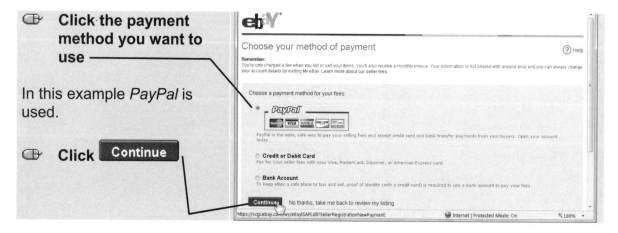

If you selected a payment method other than *PayPal*, you will see further instructions to finalize the payment.

☞ **Follow the instructions to pay your *eBay* invoice**

If you selected *PayPal*, you can sign in to your current *PayPal* account now. If you do not have a *PayPal* account yet, you can create one following the steps in the next tip.

 Tip

Creating a PayPal account
The most important parts of your *PayPal* account are your e-mail address and account password. Once your account is set up, you use your e-mail address and password to make or receive payments on the Internet.

Make sure you choose a password that is different from your *eBay* password. The password should have a minimum length of eight characters.

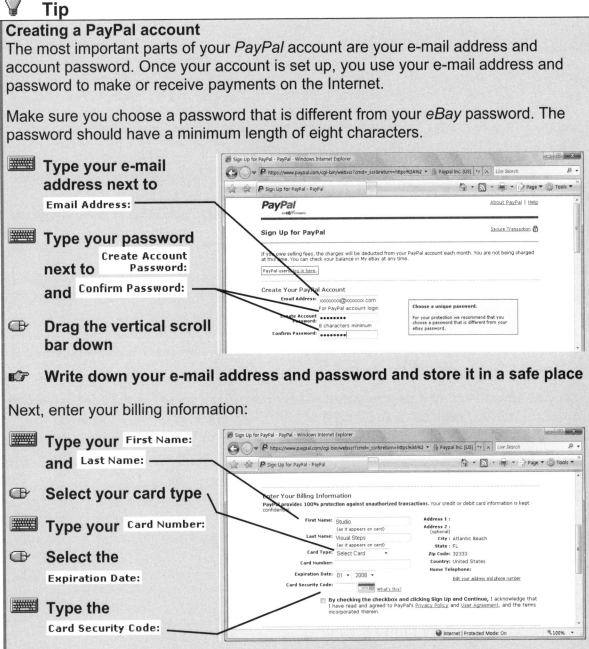

⌨ **Type your e-mail address next to**
Email Address:

⌨ **Type your password next to** **Create Account Password:**
and **Confirm Password:**

🖰 **Drag the vertical scroll bar down**

☞ **Write down your e-mail address and password and store it in a safe place**

Next, enter your billing information:

⌨ **Type your** **First Name:** **and** **Last Name:**

🖰 **Select your card type**

⌨ **Type your** **Card Number:**

🖰 **Select the** **Expiration Date:**

⌨ **Type the** **Card Security Code:**

- Continue reading on the next page -

☞ **Check your address information**

🖱 **If necessary, click** Edit your address and phone number **to make changes**

Now you only need to agree to the user agreement and privacy policy, and type the characters you see in the yellow box (for example 【A X 2 D G】). This is a security measure that helps *PayPal* prevent automated registrations.

🖱 **Click to check mark**
✓ **By checking the checkbox**

⌨ **Type the characters displayed on your screen, for example** 【A X 2 D G】 **in the box**

🖱 **Click**
Sign Up and Continue

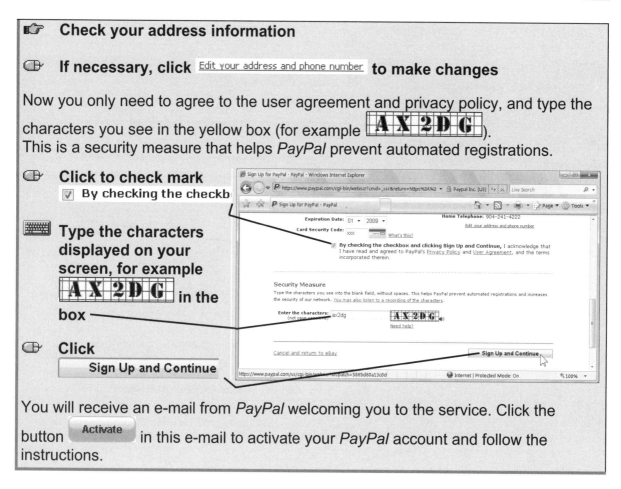

You will receive an e-mail from *PayPal* welcoming you to the service. Click the button **Activate** in this e-mail to activate your *PayPal* account and follow the instructions.

You can pay using your *PayPal* account like this:

🖱 **Click** log in here.

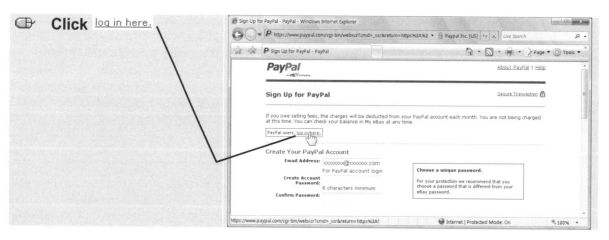

You see the *PayPal* login page:

Type your e-mail address next to
Email Address:

Type your password next to PayPal Password:

Click Log In

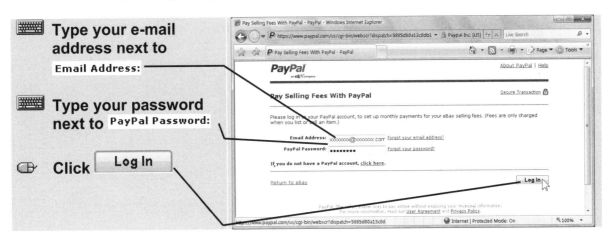

You may see this window where *Internet Explorer* offers to remember this password. Since you use the password to make a payment, this is not a good idea.

Click No

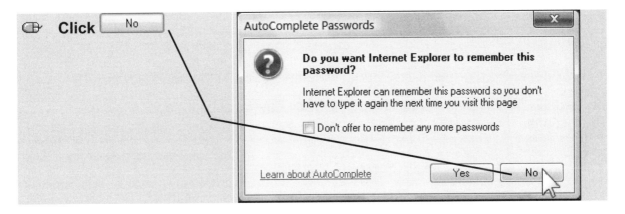

Now you can agree to the billing agreement and authorize *eBay* to debit payments from your funding source:

Click I Agree

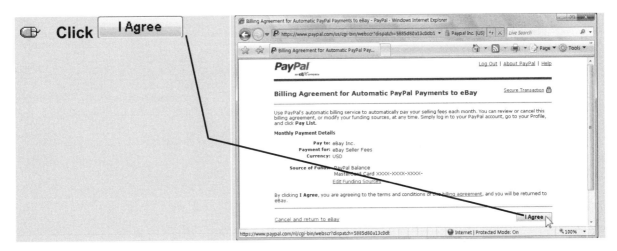

Windows Vista users may see the *Internet Explorer Security* window where you need to give your permission to continue:

☞ **Click** [Allow]

You are taken back to the page where you can review the listing for the item you are selling. Now you can place your item on *eBay*.

⇨ **Please note:**

You are about to offer the item on *eBay*. If you choose to continue, you are committed to selling the item to the highest bidder.

☞ **If necessary, drag the vertical scroll bar down**

☞ **Click**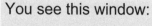

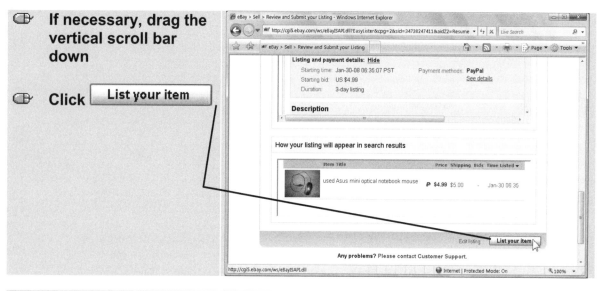

You see this window:

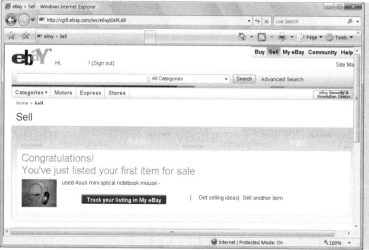

Your item is listed on *eBay*. Now you can sit back and wait for possible offers on the item. You may also receive messages from buyers that have a question about the item. You can follow the bidding and read the messages in *My eBay*.

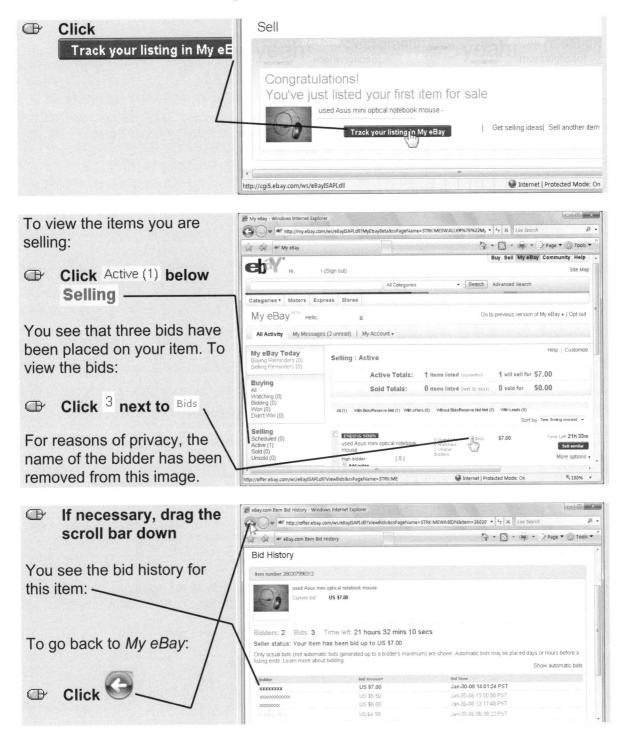

Click **Track your listing in My eB**

To view the items you are selling:

Click Active (1) **below** **Selling**

You see that three bids have been placed on your item. To view the bids:

Click 3 **next to** Bids

For reasons of privacy, the name of the bidder has been removed from this image.

If necessary, drag the scroll bar down

You see the bid history for this item:

To go back to *My eBay*:

Click

You can view your messages in *My eBay* like this:

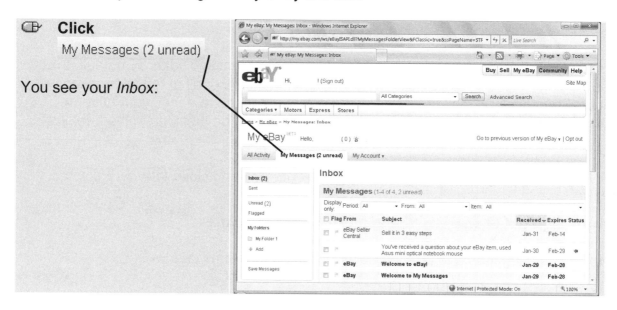

Click
My Messages (2 unread)

You see your *Inbox*:

You can also check the amount you owe to *eBay* in your Seller Account:

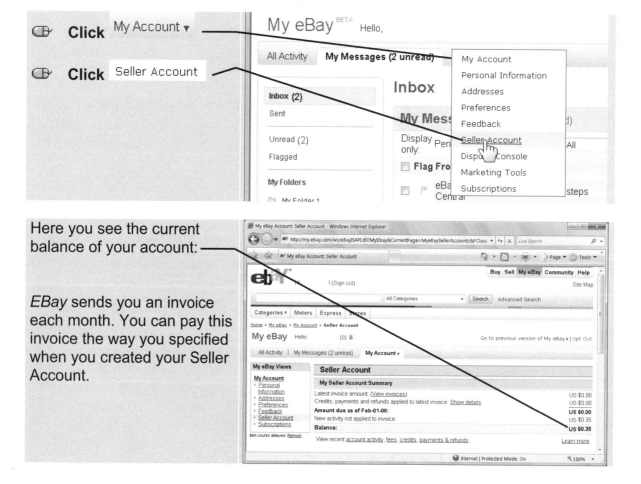

Click My Account ▼

Click Seller Account

Here you see the current balance of your account:

EBay sends you an invoice each month. You can pay this invoice the way you specified when you created your Seller Account.

When there is enough interest for the item you listed, you will eventually have a highest bid. Good communication with your customers and prompt shipping after the listing ends is crucial to your success as an *eBay* seller.

Once your listing is over, you need to contact your winning bidder. By default, the *eBay* Checkout service is active. This means that some or all of the information will be automatically e-mailed to your buyer. If not, you need to e-mail your buyer to exchange information. The buyer's e-mail address will be provided in the e-mail announcing the end of your listing.

When everything is settled, you can sign out of *eBay* and close *Internet Explorer*.

☞   **Sign out of *eBay*** 𝓁𝓁²³ **and close *Internet Explorer*** 𝓁𝓁³

In this chapter you have learned how to buy and sell items on *eBay*.

5.8 Background Information

Glossary

Buy it now	An item with the *Buy it now* label can be bought when you want it, at a set price.
Dispute Console	Online communication tool which helps you track, manage, and resolve your dispute with a seller as quickly as possible. Use this tool when you have not received an item you paid for, or when the item you received is not the same as the item that was described.
eBay	Online auction and shopping website in which people and businesses buy and sell goods and services worldwide.
Feedback rating	Feedback represents the permanent reputation of a buyer or seller as an *eBay* member. It is made up of comments and ratings left by other *eBay* members you have bought from and sold to.
Final value fee	Fee you are charged by *eBay* if your item is sold, ends with a winning bid, or is purchased. This fee applies whether or not you complete the sale with the buyer.
Insertion fee	Listing fee, the price *eBay* charges for listing your item for sale. This fee is charged to your seller's account at the time of listing. As with a newspaper ad, you need to pay this basic listing fee, even if your item is not sold.
Listing	The description of an item for sale on *eBay*. The listing usually contains photos and a description of the item, information about shipping costs and payment methods and the remaining time for the auction.
Maximum bid	The bid you place in an online auction. *EBay* will automatically bid on your behalf up to your maximum bid, not higher. Your maximum bid needs to be higher than the starting bid. This way you may end up paying less than your maximum bid.

- Continue reading on the next page -

My eBay	Your personal area on the *eBay* website. Here you can view your *My Messages* inbox, keep track of the items you are bidding on or selling, and edit your account information.
PayPal	Service you can use to pay and receive money online. After opening a *PayPal* account and registering your credit card, debit card, or bank account you can make secure purchases without revealing your credit card number or financial information to the seller. *PayPal* can be used on *eBay* and thousands of other online merchants worldwide.
Phishing	An attempt to criminally and fraudulently acquire sensitive information, such as usernames, passwords and credit card details, by masquerading as a trusted well-known company in an e-mail. Often links in phishing messages link to a spoofing website.
Seller account	To sell on *eBay* you need to register to become an *eBay* member and become a seller. Becoming a seller is free. During this one-time process you need to provide information to verify your identity and select how you will pay your seller fees.
Seller fees	Fees you pay to *eBay* for listing and selling an item on *eBay*. The seller fees consist of the *insertion fee* and the *final value fee*.
Spoofing	Fraudulent e-mail messages and websites. The sender address and other parts of the e-mail header are altered to appear as though the e-mail originated from a different source. The webpages mimic an actual, well-known website but are run by another party with fraudulent intentions.
Winning, Won	As soon as an auction ends and you are the highest bidder, you have won the item.

Source: eBay Help

Spoof and Phishing

Spoof or *phishing* messages are e-mail messages that are sent to trick computer users into revealing personal or financial information, like a password or credit card number. A common online phishing scam starts with a fake e-mail message that looks like an official notice from a well-known trusted source. This can be your bank, your credit card company, or an online shop or auction site you have dealt with before. The same message is sent randomly to thousands of e-mail addresses.

Often these e-mail messages contain a hyperlink to a webpage. Never click these links. It is possible that the web address mentioned in the e-mail is not the real address the hyperlink leads to. On the spoof website you are asked to provide personal or financial information.

These e-mails and the spoof websites they link to look so official that many think they are real. Unsuspecting people may comply and enter their credit card number or password. The information is sent directly to the criminal who sent the e-mails and made the fake website. Some of these fake webpages look the same as the *eBay* webpage. The real *eBay* web address always begins with http://www.ebay.com. When you sign in to *eBay*, the web address begins with https://signin.ebay.com.

Please note: *eBay* will **never** ask you to provide account numbers, passwords or other sensitive information through e-mail. If *eBay* does request information from you, a copy of that e-mail will be in your *My Messages* box in *My eBay*.
If you have any doubt that an e-mail really is from *eBay*, open a new browser window, type www.ebay.com, and sign in. Any e-mail that looks as if it is from *eBay*, mentions a problem with your account or requests personal information, and is not in *My Messages* in *My eBay*, is a spoof e-mail.

Spoof e-mails often include the *eBay* logo and an *eBay* address in the 'From' line (for example, 'From: support@ebay.com'). The e-mail may mimic common *eBay* e-mails, such as notifications of problems with your account or 'Ask seller a question' e-mails.

Spoof e-mails typically have the following characteristics:
- Requests sensitive information (example: Please update your credit card number);
- Starts with a generic greeting (example: Dear *eBay* member);
- Has an urgent tone for quick action (example: 'Ignoring this message will result in a suspension of your account within 24 hours'.);
- Contains links to webpages that resemble the *eBay* sign in page (example spoof web link: http://signin-ebay.com/).

Source: eBay Help

When you receive a suspicious e-mail

Do **not** click on any link in the e-mail. The purpose of spoof e-mail is to lead you to a website and attempt to collect personal information and commit identity theft or other crimes.

Report the e-mail by forwarding it to spoof@ebay.com. *EBay* will review the e-mail and let you know if it was legitimately sent by *eBay*.

Important: In order for *eBay* to investigate your report, you must forward the e-mail without adding attachments, adding text or altering text.

When you receive a suspicious e-mail that seems to originate from *PayPal*:

☞   **Go to www.paypal.com and sign in**

↪   **Click** Security Center **in the top right corner, then click** Report fake (phishing) email **or** Report fake (spoof) websites **below** ▶ **Take Action!**

Not every phishing message is caught by the phishing filter of your e-mail program or antivirus software. Never respond to messages from banks, credit card companies, online shops or auction sites that ask you for confidential financial information. Also, never click the hyperlinks in these messages.

If you think you might have provided information in response to a phishing message, take immediate action. For example, change your password. If you provided your credit card number or other financial information, contact your credit card company or bank.

Source: eBay Help, Paypal Help

Recognizing a secure website

When you buy something on the Internet or register with *PayPal,* you should always check if you are on a secure website before you enter your credit card details or bank details.

The most important difference between a secured and unsecured website is that on a secured website information is transferred using encryption technology. The user enters his or her data, such as a credit card number. This information is encrypted using special software and then transferred to the seller, who decrypts the information. Only specially authorized parties are capable of doing so. This way you can prevent hackers from stealing and using the information when it is sent over the internet.

The easiest and fastest way of recognizing a secure website is by means of the website address. Where this starts with 'https://' rather than simply 'http://', then you are on a secure website. The extra 's' stands for 'secure'.

Here you see an example:

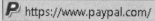 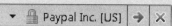

Another sign is the small padlock icon 🔒 which will be shown in the Address bar as soon as you enter the website. If this icon is missing, then the chances are good that the website is probably unsecured.

Please note: many websites have both secured and unsecured areas. Usually only the areas where you register or pay are secured.

Always make sure that you are on a secure website which ensures secure communication before you enter your personal or financial information.

5.9 Tips

 Tip

Giving feedback

As soon as you have received the item you bought and the transaction is completed, you can give feedback to the seller about the transaction. This means you enter a rating to express your opinion about the way the transaction with this seller has transpired. It is not mandatory to give feedback. Please note: for first time users, feedback is only possible after an initial five day waiting period following registration with *eBay*.

☞ **Open *My eBay* ℓ/℮11**

🖱 **If necessary, drag the scroll bar down**

🖱 **Click** `Leave feedback`

You see the window *Leave Feedback*:

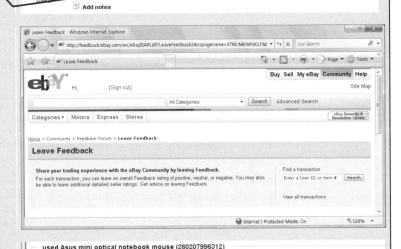

🖱 **If necessary, drag the scroll bar down**

To rate the overall transaction:

🖱 **Click your choice**
○ Positive   ○ Neutral   ○ Ne

⌨ **Type an explanation next to** Please explain:

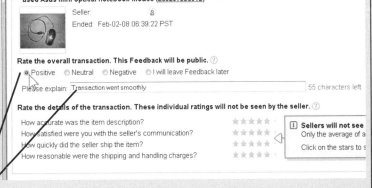

- Continue reading on the next page -

To rate the details of the transaction:

 In each row, click one of the ⭐⭐⭐⭐⭐

In case you are asked for an explanation, enter one.

 Click Leave Feedback

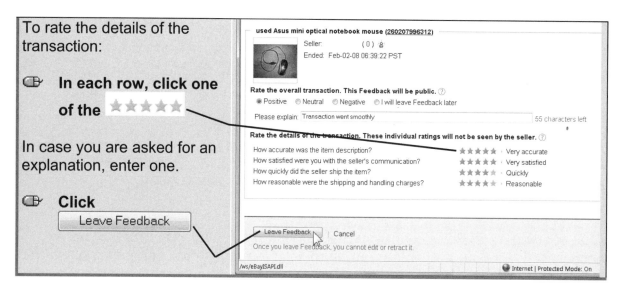

💡 **Tip**

Bidding and buying on eBay

Here is a summary of tips for buying and bidding on items with *eBay*:

- Before you buy an item or bid in an online auction, make sure to scroll down and read all the information the seller has listed about the item. This may prevent unpleasant surprises.
- Ask the seller one or more questions to learn all you can about the item.
- Check the seller's feedback to see what other buyers have had to say about doing business with the seller.
- Pay attention to the shipping costs listed by the seller. You may be able to save on shipping costs when you buy more items from one seller.
- Before you buy or bid, check if the seller allows a payment method that suits you.
- Do not bid on multiple similar items from different sellers if you only want one, because you may be the winning bidder in more than one auction.

Tip

Making safe payments on the Internet
Many people are afraid of buying items on the Internet using their credit card. You have probably heard stories about stolen credit card numbers, large charges that come out of nowhere and identity theft yourself.

As an alternative, *PayPal* is considered the safest way to make payments on the Internet. *PayPal* is a service that allows payments and money transfers to be made through the Internet. It serves as an electronic alternative to traditional paper methods such as checks and money orders.

After opening a *PayPal* account you register your credit card, debit card, or bank account with *PayPal*. You enter your financial information only once. When using *PayPal*, you have one account and one password that you can use to make payments on *eBay* and with thousands of other merchants worldwide. The main advantage of *PayPal* is that you can make secure purchases without exposing your credit card number or other financial information to the seller.

Please note: you should never let *Internet Explorer* remember your *PayPal* password on your computer. You use the combination of your e-mail address and password to make a payment. If you write down your password, make sure to keep it in a safe place.

 Tip

Is eBay safe?
Many people wonder if it is safe to buy on *eBay*. There is no easy answer to that question. As a buyer, you are dealing with an individual seller. These sellers come in many different shapes and sizes. There are good guys who want to make an honest trade, and promptly ship the item after receiving your payment. But everybody has heard the horror stories about the bad guys: sellers who sell defective items as new, or send a brick in the box of a digital camera, or send nothing at all. Of course there are scam artists who are trying to make a quick buck. But as a general rule: if an offer is too good to be true… it probably is!

The feedback rating of a seller tells you something about the way this person operates. But also take the time reading detailed feedback using the link See detailed feedback . And do not hesitate to ask the seller a question about the item. Good sellers will promptly respond to your question.

If problems arise, always make sure to report to both *eBay* and the seller using the *Dispute Console*. For more information:
http://pages.ebay.com/help/tp/using-dispute-console.html

6. Your Own Blog on the WWW

A *blog* is a website that is best described as a kind of online journal or diary on the Internet. A place where you can publish your thoughts, feelings, photos, special events, experiences and so on. The term blog is composed of the words website and log. A blog may also be called a *weblog* or *web log*. Someone who maintains a blog is called a *blogger*.

New entries are added to a blog on a regular basis. Some bloggers add new entries a couple of times a day. The most recent entries are always displayed on top of the page. Previous entries are listed below, in reverse chronological order. Older entries are usually kept in an archive. In addition to text, you can also add photos, videos and music to a blog.

You can read a blog, as well as comment on separate entries. The comments from readers are usually listed below each entry.

It is very easy to start and maintain your own blog. In this chapter you use the online application *Blogger* to do so. *Blogger* is a free service from *Google*, the company that makes the popular search engine, as well as *Google Earth* and *Google Maps.*

A blog on the World Wide Web can be viewed by everyone. The blogs owner can maintain the blog from any computer that has an Internet connection. This type of application is very interesting for people who travel frequently. Using their blog they can share their experiences with family and friends and read comments in return.

In this chapter you will learn how to:

- create a *Google* account;
- sign up to *Blogger.com*;
- set up your own blog;
- post a message with a photo to your blog;
- select a template for your blog;
- delete a post;
- moderate comments;
- read a comment;
- remove your blog.

6.1 Creating a Google Account

In this chapter you will learn how to create and use your own blog on the *Blogger* website. First you surf to this website:

☞ **Start *Internet Explorer*** ✌¹

☞ **Surf to the web address www.blogger.com** ✌²

After a while you see the *Blogger* home page:

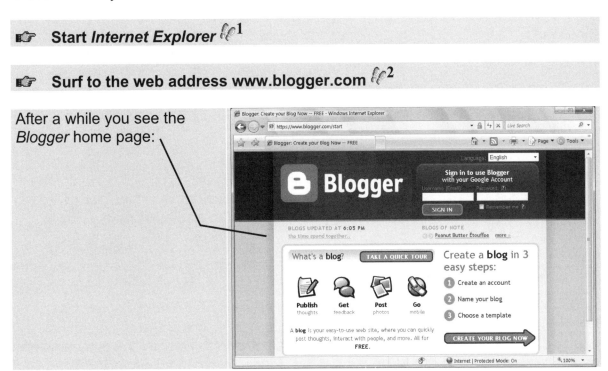

Blogger is one of the services provided by *Google*. *Google* will ask you to create an account to access these services. Using this account you will be able to use *Blogger* to start your own blog:

Click

CREATE YOUR BLOG NOW

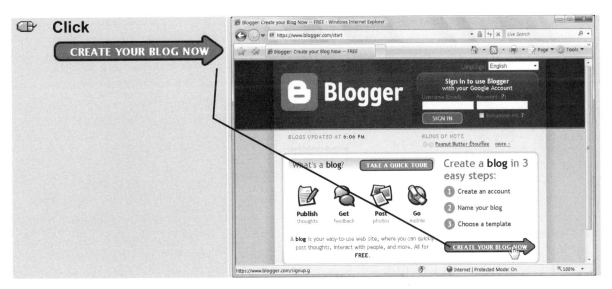

You see the webpage *Create a Google account*. Your account consists of an existing e-mail address and a password that you will now create. You need to enter each item twice at the top of the page.

Type your e-mail address next to Email address **and** Retype email address

Type your password next to Enter a password

You see if it is a strong password:

Type your password again next to Retype password

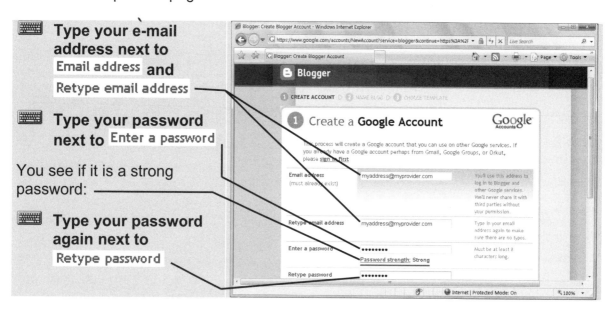

☞ **Write your e-mail address and password down and store them in a safe place.**

At the bottom of the webpage you enter your display name. This will be the name that is displayed on your blog:

Drag the scroll bar down

Type a name next to Display name

You see some funny-looking, colorful letters:

Type these letters in the text box

Click to check mark
☑ I accept the **Terms of Servi**

Click CONTINUE

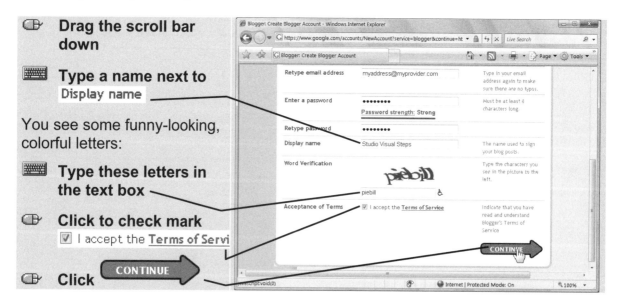

You have created a *Google* account. In the next section you are going to activate your *Google* account and set up your own blog.

6.2 Your Own Blog on Blogger

In the next step you enter a title for your blog and you create the blog address. Readers can open your blog directly using this blog address.

Type the title of your blog next to Blog title

In this example the name 'Studio Visual Steps' was chosen. Choose a title that suits you and enter it here.

Type a blog address next to Blog address

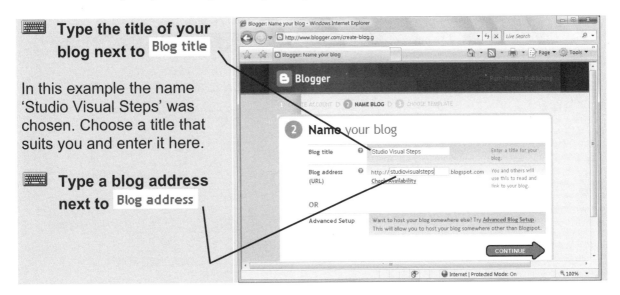

Now you are going to check if this blog address is available:

Click Check Availability

Do you see the message ⚠ Sorry, this blog address is not available ?

☞ **Change the blog address**

Click Check Availability **again**

If the address is available:

Click CONTINUE

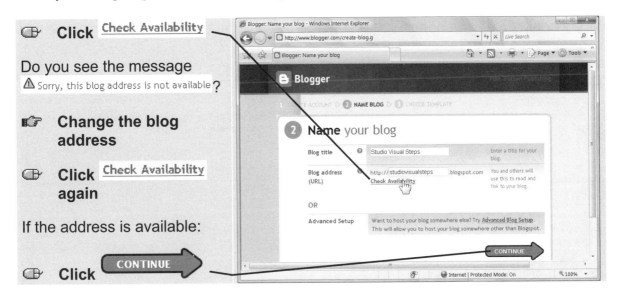

Now you see the window *Choose a template*. A *template* is a ready-made design for your blog. *Blogger* offers dozens of templates. A little further on in this chapter you will select your own template. For now you can just select the default template.

The first template is selected:

 Drag the scroll bar down

 Click CONTINUE

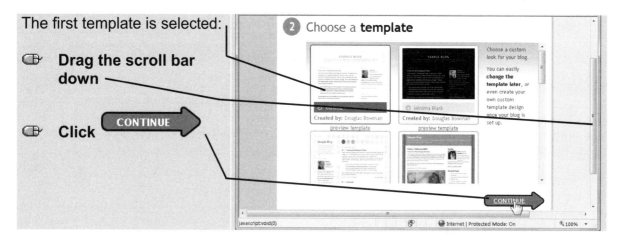

You have created your own blog.

 Click START BLOGGING

You see the page where you can write your first message. You sign out instead.

 Click Sign out

⊗ HELP! I see another window.

You may see this window.

 Click OK

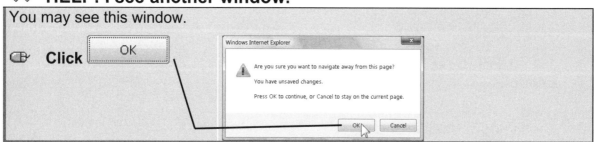

You see the *Blogger* home page:

An e-mail was sent to your e-mail address when you created your *Google* account. You can take a look at that e-mail now:

☞ **Open your e-mail program** $\ell\ell^6$

☞ **Press the button to receive your new messages** $\ell\ell^7$

☞ **Open the message titled 'Google E-mail Verification'** $\ell\ell^{13}$

This e-mail contains a hyperlink you can use to activate your *Google* account:

☞ **Click the first hyperlink**

Internet Explorer is opened automatically and you see a webpage:

You see the message that your account is now activated:

☞ **Click ☒ to close the new tab**

or:

☞ **Click ☒ to close the new browser window**

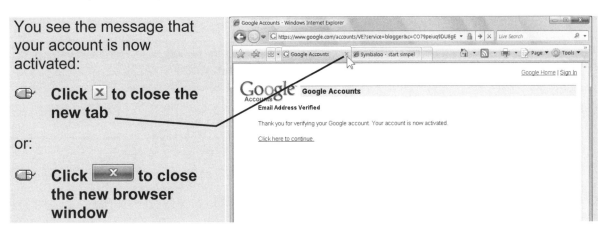

☞ **Close your e-mail program** $\ell\ell^3$

6.3 Posting the First Message

A blog is a digital journal. The blogger, the person who maintains the blog, posts new messages frequently. This might be on a daily, weekly or monthly basis. It is up to each individual blogger to decide how often postings are made. In this section you will see just how easy it is to make a new posting.

You see the *Blogger* home page. To be able to work on your blog, you need to sign in first:

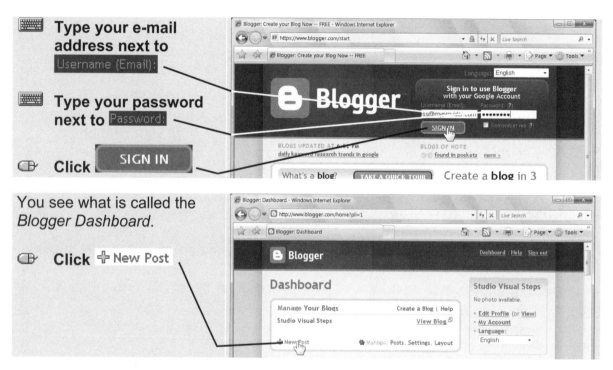

Type your e-mail address next to Username (Email):

Type your password next to Password:

☞ **Click** SIGN IN

You see what is called the *Blogger Dashboard*.

☞ **Click** ✚ New Post

You can type a message in this window:

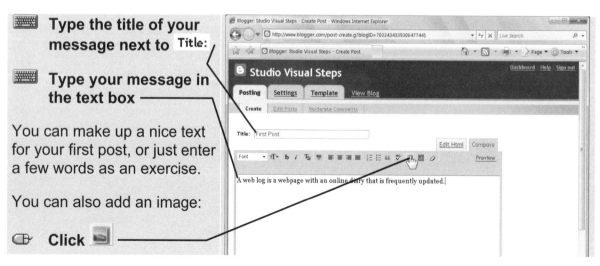

Type the title of your message next to Title:

Type your message in the text box

You can make up a nice text for your first post, or just enter a few words as an exercise.

You can also add an image:

☞ **Click**

Depending on the settings of your computer, a new webpage will be opened in a new tab or in a new browser window. You can add images from your computer or from the Internet. Here is how to add an image from your computer:

☞ **Click** Browse...

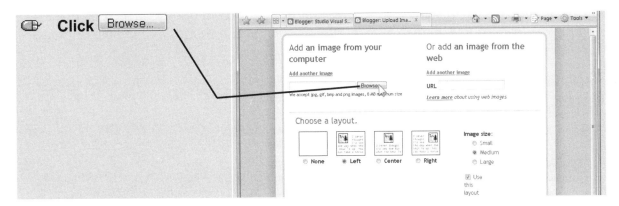

You see the window *Choose file*. It may look different on your computer than what you see in this example. You can choose a random image from your own photo collection. In this example one of the sample images that came with *Windows* is used.

☞ **Click** 📷 Pictures

You see the contents of the *Pictures* folder:

☞ **Double-click**

Sample Pictures

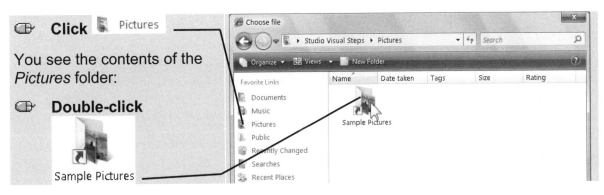

You see the sample images:

☞ **Click** Creek

The image is selected:

☞ **Click** Open

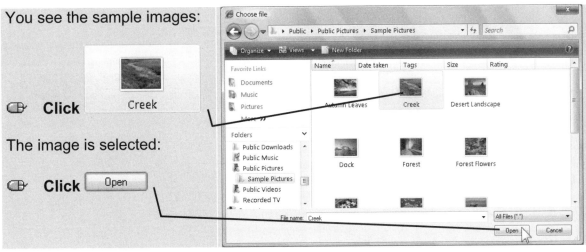

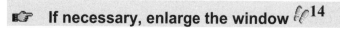
☞ **If necessary, enlarge the window** ✐¹⁴

Here you see which image will be added to your post:

Images can be displayed in different sizes:

🖱 **Click to select** ◉ Small

🖱 **Click to check mark**
☑ I accept the **Terms of Ser**

🖱 **Click**
UPLOAD IMAGE

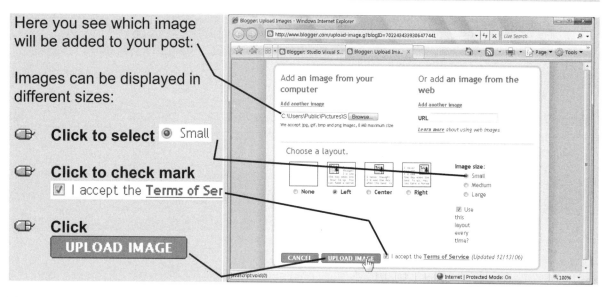

Now your image is copied to the *Blogger* website.

After a few moments your image is uploaded:

🖱 **Click** **DONE**

You see that the image is added to the text. Now you can check what it will look like on your blog:

🖱 **Click**
PUBLISH POST

☞ **Click**
View Blog

You see your first post with the image:

6.4 Editing Your Profile

Most bloggers will use a part of their blog for information about themselves. In this *profile* the blogger introduces himself. A profile is a simple way to create an 'about me' page as an addition to your blog. You can do that from the *Dashboard*:

☞ **In the top right corner, click** Customize **and then click** Dashboard

☞ **Click** Edit Profile

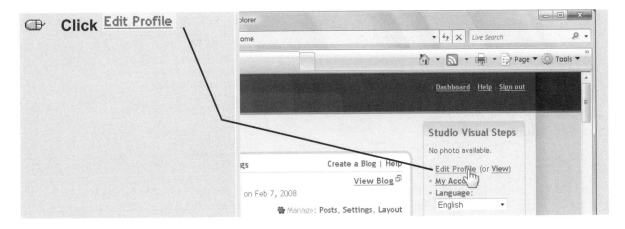

The user profile consists of several categories. The first category - *Privacy* - is at the top. Here you can select if you want to share your profile, and show your real name, your e-mail address and any other blogs.

In this example the information is displayed. You can decide for yourself whether you want to show your profile information.

☞ **Click to check mark** Show my real name

☞ **Drag the scroll bar down**

There are many categories on this page. You can add information to each category you want to use and skip the others. Remember, everything you enter here is visible for every reader of your blog.

⌨ **Type your first name next to** First Name

⌨ **Type your last name next to** Last Name

If you want to, you can add a photo to your profile here:

You can even add an audio clip:

☞ **Drag the scroll bar down**

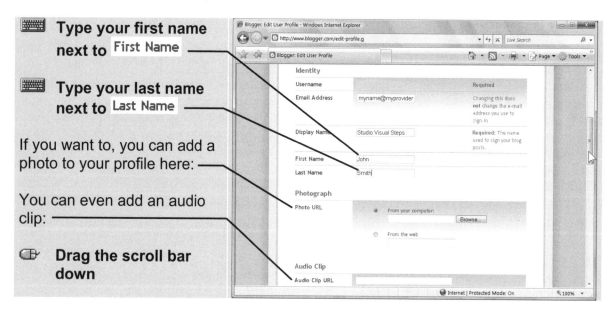

Click to select your gender here

You can also enter information about your home page, your location and your work. You can also skip these categories.

Type information in the categories you want to use

Drag the scroll bar down

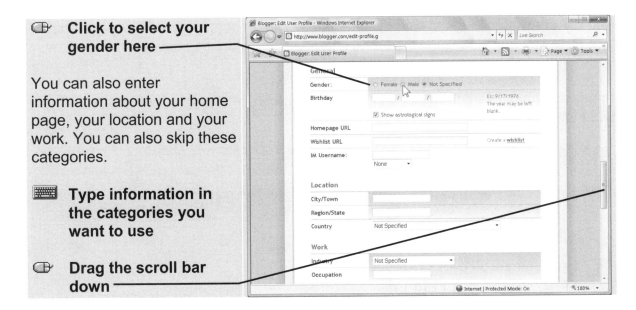

In the section **Extended Info** you can enter information about your hobbies and interests.

Type something about yourself in each category

Click

Save Profile

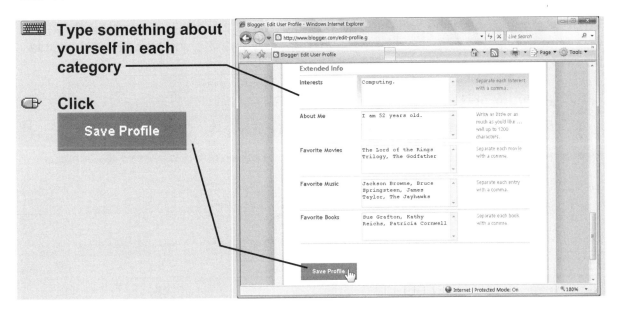

You automatically return to the top of the page. Here you see the link to your profile:

👆 **Click**
  View Updated Profile

You see the information you entered for your profile. You can return to your blog like this:

☞ **Drag the scroll bar down** ————

👆 **Click the title of your blog**

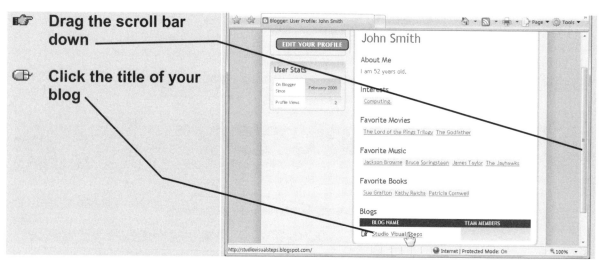

Your profile has been added to the right side of your web log: ————

Here you see the link VIEW MY COMPLETE PROFILE your readers can use to open your full profile:

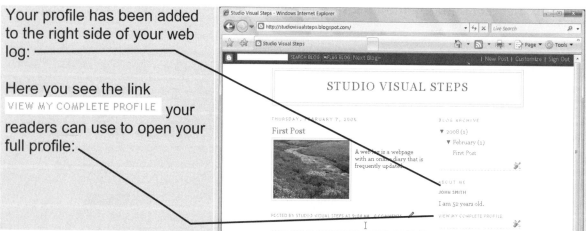

☞ **Open the *Dashboard*** 🖱️15

6.5 Selecting a Template for Your Blog

Blogger provides a number of ready-made templates. By using a template you can give your blog the look you like best. You can select a template on the *Dashboard* page:

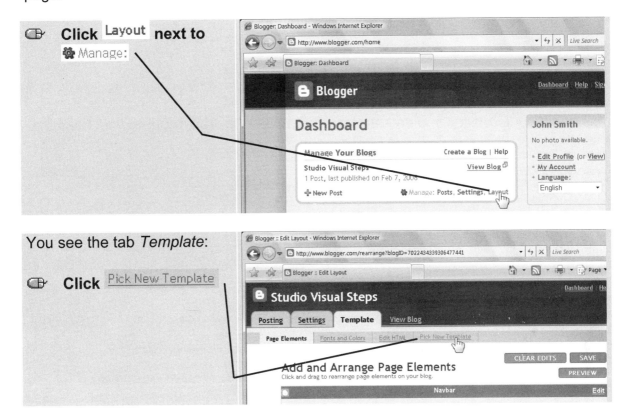

Click Layout **next to** 🔧 Manage:

You see the tab *Template*:

Click Pick New Template

You see a series of ready-made templates. In this example you select the template *Scribe*:

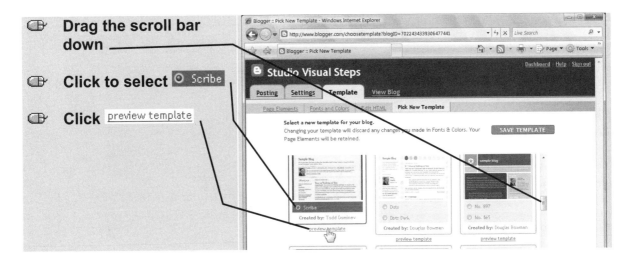

Drag the scroll bar down

Click to select ◉ Scribe

Click preview template

Your blog is opened in the *Scribe* template. Depending on the settings of your computer, you will see your blog in a new tab or in a new browser window:

☞ **Take a look at the new template**

⊂⊐ **Click X to close the new tab**

or:

⊂⊐ **Click X to close the new browser window**

You see the page with the templates again:

If you want to keep the current template:

⊂⊐ **Click**
SAVE TEMPLATE

You see the message
Your changes have been saved.

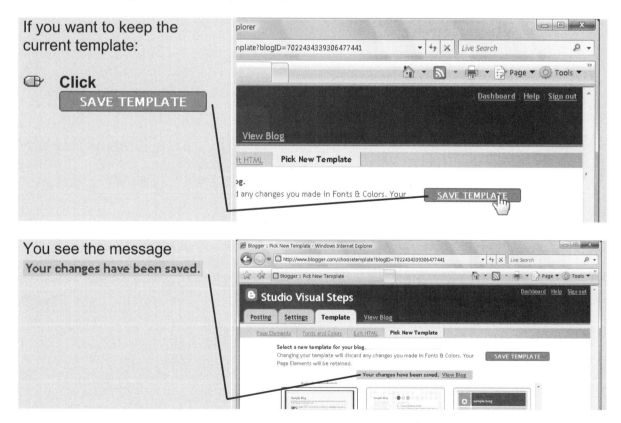

From now on, your blog will be displayed in the new layout.

6.6 Deleting a Post

You can always remove a post from your blog. You do that on the *Dashboard* page.

☞ **Open the *Blogger Dashboard* 📖¹⁵**

☞ **Add a new post 📖¹⁶**

☞ **Add an image to the new post 📖¹⁷**

⌨ **Click the tab**
Edit Posts

⌨ **Click Delete next to a post**

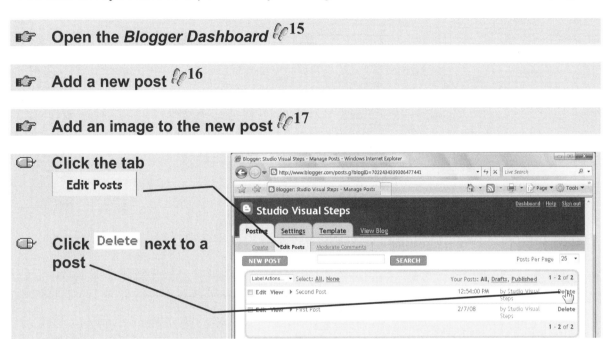

You see the post:

⌨ **Drag the scroll bar down**

⌨ **Click Delete It**

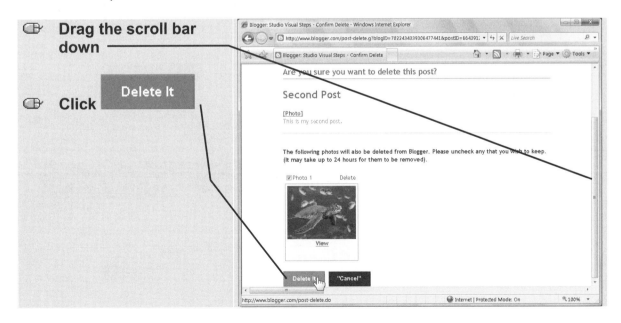

The post is deleted.

6.7 Adjusting Settings for Comments

A great thing about blogs is that it allows readers the ability to comment on your posts. You need to change a few settings for that. For example, you can select who is allowed to comment and how you can remove unwanted comments:

☞ **Open the *Dashboard*** ℓℓ¹⁵

You can adjust the settings for the comments using the link Settings:

Click Settings

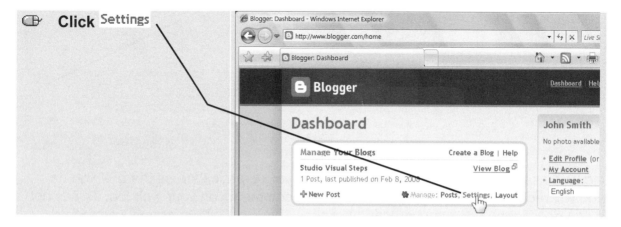

The creators of *Blogger* give you the ability to adjust a number of different settings. You see here various tabs and links. The tab *Settings* is already selected. You can adjust how the comments will be handled here:

Click Comments

You see the setting
Who Can Comment? :

Click to select
   ◉ Anyone

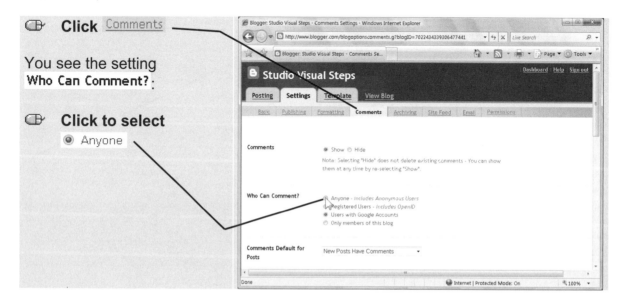

When you allow every visitor to comment, you may receive unwanted comments on your blog. It is therefore a good idea to enable comment moderation. Then you can decide which comments are placed on your blog and which comments are not.

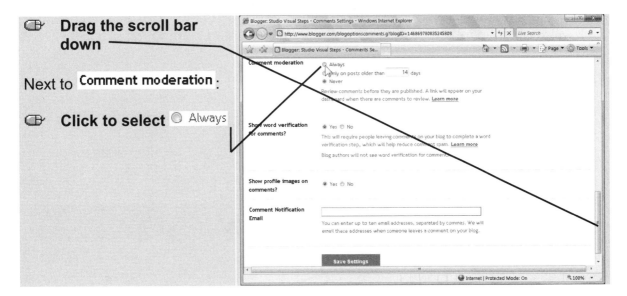

Drag the scroll bar down

Next to **Comment moderation**:

Click to select ○ Always

Now you see an extra text box. You can type your e-mail address there. If you do, you will receive an e-mail each time a reader comments on your web log. This is not really necessary, because you can also check the *Dashboard* for new comments.

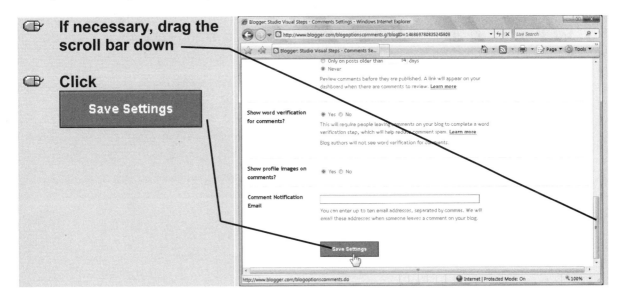

If necessary, drag the scroll bar down

Click

Save Settings

☞ **Sign out from *Blogger* now** ⸛18

6.8 Adding a Comment

You have signed out. Now you can visit your own blog and practice commenting on a post like a regular visitor.

☞ **Surf to your own blog** 🖱¹⁹

You see your blog the same way a visitor sees it:

Below each post you see the number of comments left by readers:

⌨ **Click** <u>0 comments</u>

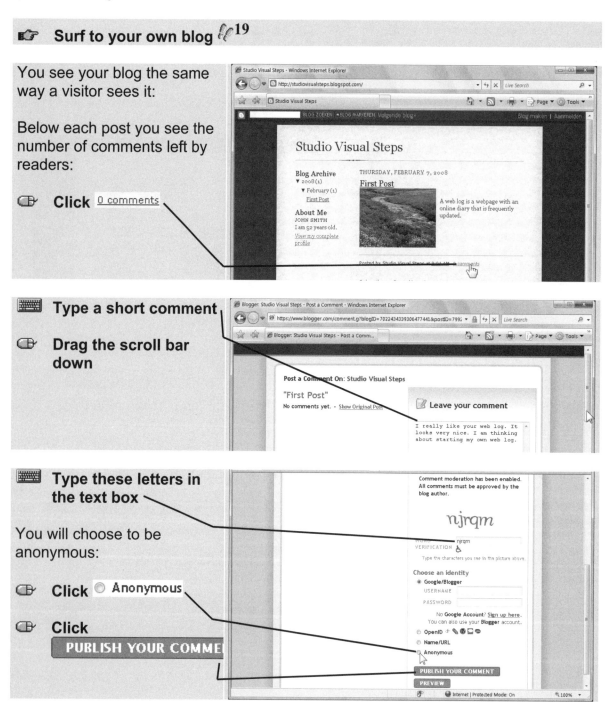

⌨ **Type a short comment**

⌨ **Drag the scroll bar down**

⌨ **Type these letters in the text box**

You will choose to be anonymous:

⌨ **Click** ○ Anonymous

⌨ **Click**
PUBLISH YOUR COMMEN[T]

Your comment is saved.

You see that visitors are notified that comments will only be added after blog owner approval:

⬚ **Click two times** ⬅

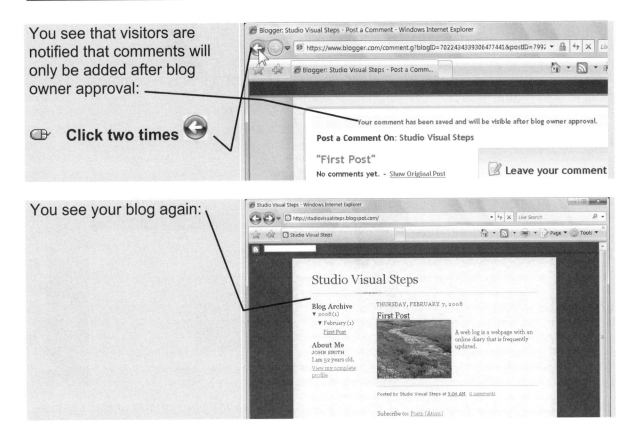

You see your blog again:

6.9 Publishing or Rejecting Comments

You decide whether or not to place this comment on your blog. To be able to do so, you will need to sign in again:

☞ **Sign in to *Blogger*** 🐾²⁰

You see the *Dashboard* page. In the box *Manage your blogs* you see there is one comment:

⬚ **Click** 1 comment

You can review your new comments by clicking the tab

Moderate Comments .

You see only a portion of the comment:

☞ **Click the comment**

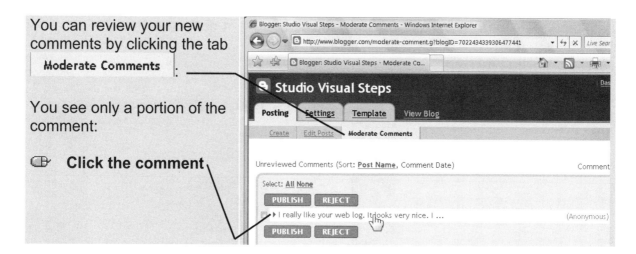

Now you see the full text. Below the comment you see two commands: Publish and Reject . If you select Reject the comment is deleted. You choose to publish this comment:

☞ **Click** Publish

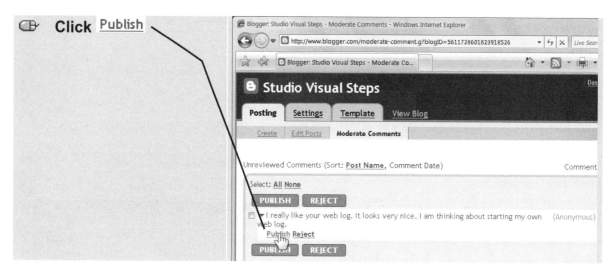

The comment is published.

☞ **Sign out from *Blogger*** ✍[18]

6.10 Reading Comments

People who visit your blog can also read the comments that other visitors have left. You can try that also:

☞ **Surf to your web log** ✍[19]

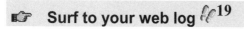

Last time there were 'comments'. Now you see there is '1 comments':

☞ **Go to the end of the first post**

🖱 **Click** 1 comments

The comment is displayed:

🖱 **Click** ⬅

You see the opening page of your blog again:

6.11 Removing Your Blog

You can remove a blog you no longer want to maintain by doing the following:

☞ **Sign in to *Blogger*** 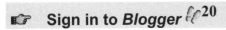20

You see the *Dashboard* of your blog:

☞ **Click** Settings

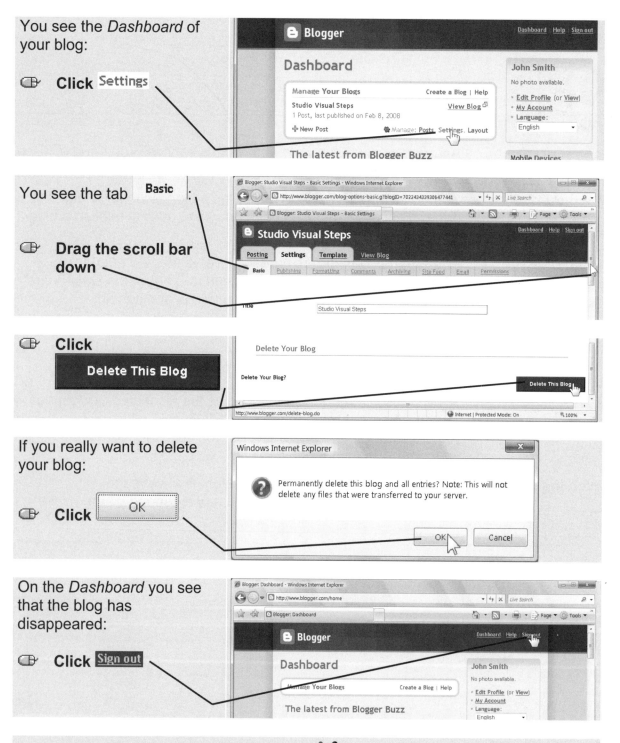

You see the tab **Basic** :

☞ **Drag the scroll bar down**

☞ **Click**

Delete This Blog

If you really want to delete your blog:

☞ **Click** OK

On the *Dashboard* you see that the blog has disappeared:

☞ **Click** Sign out

☞ **Close the *Internet Explorer* window** *ℓℓ³*

You have learned how to use *Blogger* to create your own blog. You can find a lot of information about using your blog in the *Blogger* Help feature. There you can also find a list with frequently asked questions and solutions to all kinds of problems.

6.12 Background Information

Glossary	
Account	An account gives the user access to a service. You need a *Google* account to be able to use *Blogger*.
Blogger	Someone who blogs, who maintains a blog. *Blogger* is also the name of the web program you can use to quickly publish a blog on the Internet.
Dashboard	The *Blogger Dashboard* contains everything you need to maintain your blog. When you sign in to *Blogger* the *Dashboard* is opened and you can access your blogs and settings.
Profile	Using the Profile feature in *Blogger* you can create a page containing personal information.
Template	The design that decides the layout of your blog.
URL	A URL, also called a web address, is the location of a webpage on the Internet. An example of a URL is http://www.blogger.com. The URL you select for your blog is the web address visitors use to access your blog.
Web log / Blog	A blog, also called web log or weblog, is a webpage with content that is frequently renewed and extended by the owner.

Source: Blogger Help

6.13 Tips

 Tip

Announce your blog
You maintain a blog expecting that it will be read. You can send an e-mail to family, friends and acquaintances to announce your blog and let them know the web address (URL) of your blog page.

 Tip

Adjusting the size of images
When you add an image you can choose between three sizes: small, medium and large. You can also adjust the image size manually:

☞ **Click the image**

The image is selected:

☞ **Place the mouse pointer on a corner handle**

☞ **Drag the corner handle down**

Tip

Deleting an image from a post
You can remove an image from a post like this:

On the tab *Edit Posts*:

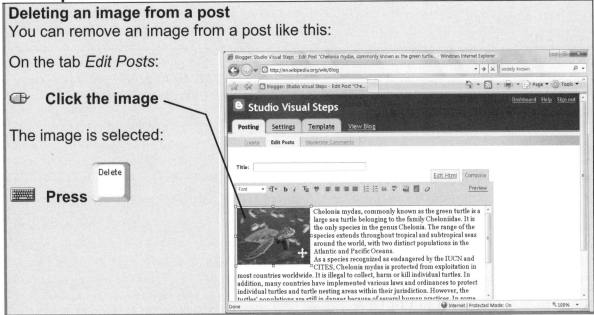

👉 **Click the image**

The image is selected:

⌨️ **Press** Delete

 Tip

Adding a hyperlink to a post
By selecting text, you can add a hyperlink to a website:

👉 **Select the word you
   want to add the
   hyperlink to**

👉 **Click** 🔗

⌨️ **Type the web address
   next to** URL:

👉 **Click** OK

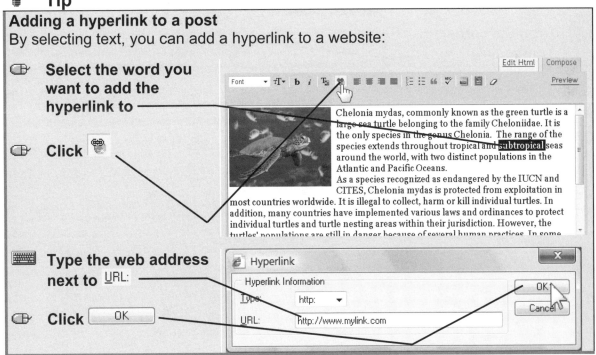

7. Making Friends in Facebook

Facebook is a free social networking website. The site is especially designed as an easy way to connect people with their friends and acquaintances, but it can also be used to get to know new people. You can use *Facebook* to meet people with similar interests, maintain a blog and share photos and videos with friends.

The name of the site refers to the paper face books depicting members of the campus community that some US colleges and preparatory schools give to incoming students, faculty, and staff as a way to get to know other people on campus. *Facebook* is not just one big site; it is made up of lots of separate networks based around things like schools, companies, and regions.

Facebook is a very inviting website. Anyone can look at the *Facebook* website and search for people who are in *Facebook.* But you need to sign up first in order to take full advantage of what *Facebook* offers and to be able to view the profiles of other people in your networks.

Facebook was created in 2004 and has about 65 million users worldwide. Signing up for *Facebook* is completely free! The costs of the application are covered by advertisements.

In this chapter you learn how to:

- sign up for *Facebook.com*;
- view and edit your profile;
- view and adjust your privacy settings;
- invite friends by e-mail;
- find, add and confirm friends;
- write notes;
- add a photo album;
- write on someone's Wall;
- deactivate your account.

➡ **Please note:**

The creators of *Facebook* are constantly adding new features. The screenshots used in this chapter may look different from what you see on your screen. This should not pose any problems; the basic features will not be removed. However, it is always possible that certain features will be moved to a different location on the website.

7.1 Surfing to Facebook

In this chapter you learn how to start and maintain your own group of friends on the *Facebook* website. First you surf to the *Facebook* website:

☞   **Open *Internet Explorer* ꝰ¹**

☞   **Surf to the website www.facebook.com ꝰ²**

You see the *Facebook* home page:

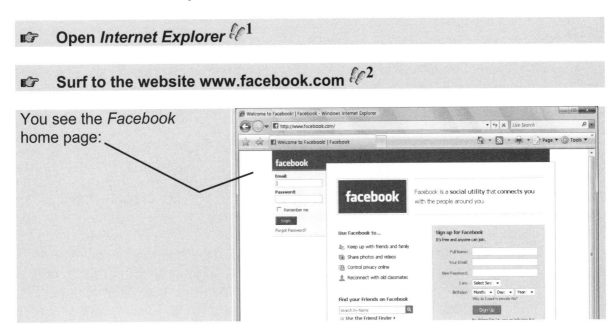

7.2 Setting Up a Facebook Account

To be able to use *Facebook*, you need to sign up for a free *Facebook* account. This account will give you access to *Facebook* so you can start your own group of friends:

⌨   **Type your full name next to** Full Name:

⌨   **Type your e-mail address next to** Your Email:

⌨   **Type a password next to** New Password:

🖰   **Select male/female**

⌨   **Fill in your birthday next to** Birthday:

🖰   **Click** Sign Up

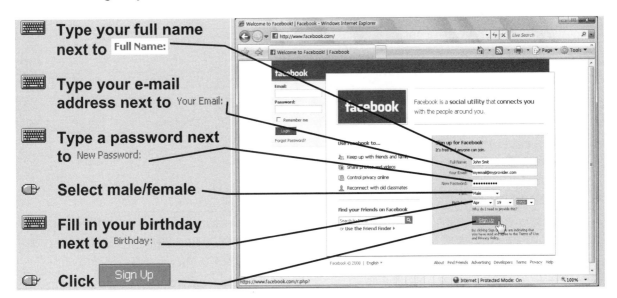

☞ **Be sure to write down your e-mail address and password and store them in a safe place.**

To prevent automated registrations, *Facebook* asks you to enter both words you see in the box by `Security Check`, for example **Cragin memory** :

⌨ **Type both words in the text box**

🖰 **Click** `Sign Up`

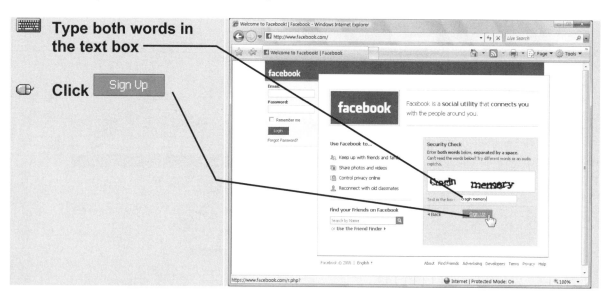

You see the message that you have received a confirmation e-mail:

You can close this window:

🖰 **Click** `X`

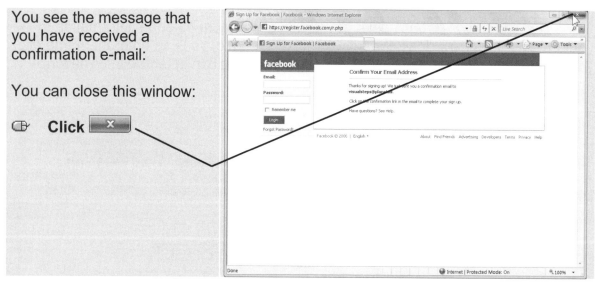

☞ **Open your e-mail program** ⌇⁶ **and receive your e-mail** ⌇⁷

☞ **Open the e-mail from *Facebook*** ⌇¹³

Here you see the e-mail message:

☞ **Click the link**

Hey John,

You recently registered for Facebook using this email address. To complete your registration, follow the link below:
http://www.facebook.com/c.php?code=4287152188&email=xxxxxxxxxxxx%40hotmail.com
(If clicking on the link doesn't work, try copying and pasting it into your browser.)

If you did not register for Facebook, please disregard this message.
Check out http://www.facebook.com/help.php?page=49 if you have any questions.

Thanks,
The Facebook Team

☞ **Close your e-mail program** ℓℓ³

The next window appears:

Facebook offers to help you find friends by using your e-mail address book. You do not need to do that now:

☞ **Click** Skip ▶

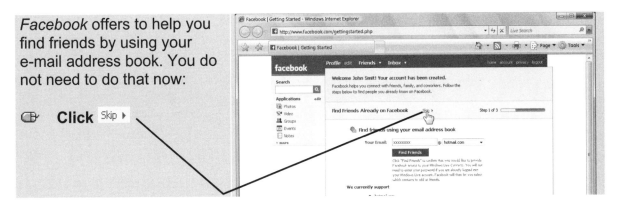

In the next window *Facebook* asks you to add some more personal information to your profile. To narrow down the network you belong to, you can enter the name of your high school. If you have additional education, you can enter the information about the college or university you went to.

⌨ **Type your high school next to** High School:

As soon as you start typing, a list appears with schools you can choose from.

☞ **Select your high school**

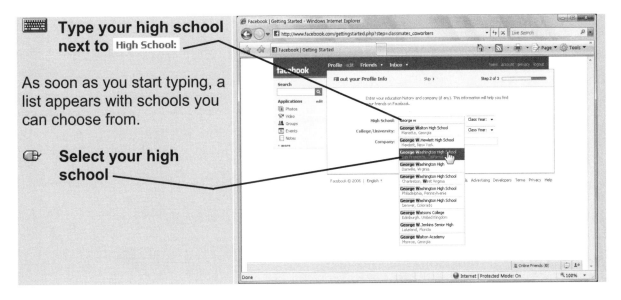

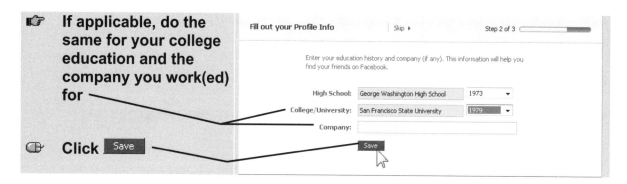

☞ **If applicable, do the same for your college education and the company you work(ed) for**

☞ **Click** Save

Now that you have added information to your personal profile, *Facebook* has selected a number of people you may know. The list includes people from the network San Francisco, CA:

☞ **Click** Skip ▸

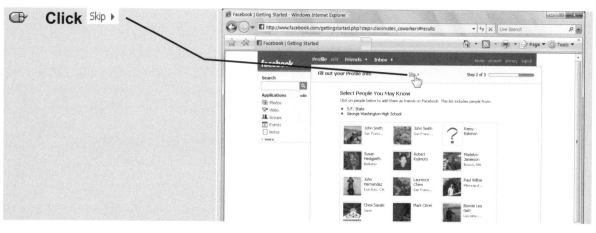

⌨ **Type your city next to** City/Town:

As soon as you start typing, a list appears with cities you can choose from.

☞ **Select your city**

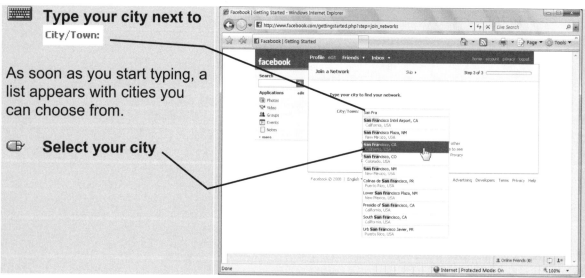

Facebook has selected a number of networks. You can choose the network you identify with most:

☞ **Click the network you want to join**

☞ **Click** Join

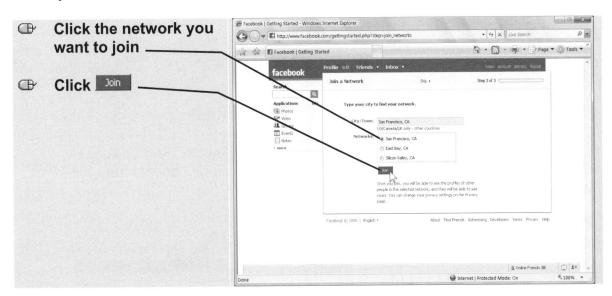

Your registration is complete and you are welcomed to *Facebook*.

You can sign out like this:

☞ **Click** logout

7.3 Viewing and Editing Your Profile

In the previous section you clicked logout. To be able to edit your profile in *Facebook*, you need to sign in again. You need your e-mail address and password for that:

Type your e-mail address below Email:

Type your password below Password:

Click Login

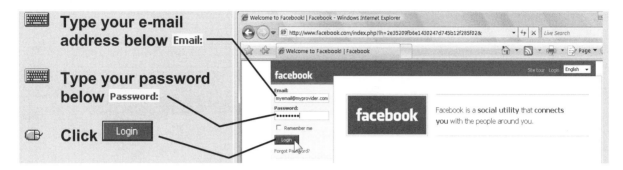

You see your home page on *Facebook*. Here you can surf to the page where you can edit your profile. Your profile contains personal information that will be visible for everyone in your network who finds you in *Facebook*.

Click edit next to Profile

You see your profile page with the categories Basic , Contact , Relationships , Personal , Education , Work and Picture .

In the category *Basic* you can enter your gender, hometown, and even your political or religious views.

☞ Enter the information you want to display in your profile

Click Save Changes

Now you can go to the next category ⎡ Contact ⎤. In this category you can enter your contact information. For example your address, your phone number, and the screen name you use in an instant messaging program. You see the icon 🔒 Only my friends. This means that by default the information in the *Contact* category can only be viewed by your friends. If you do not want to enter your address or phone number, you can skip this section.

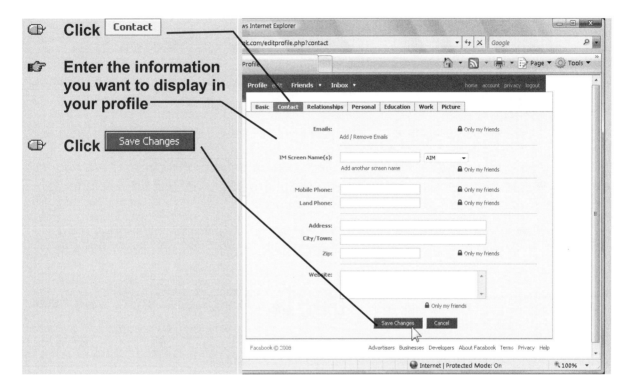

Click ⎡ Contact ⎤

☞ **Enter the information you want to display in your profile**

Click ⎡ Save Changes ⎤

In the category *Relationships* you can enter your current marital status, the name of your partner and (if applicable) your former name. If you want to use *Facebook* to meet new people, you can also select what you are looking for, for example friendship, or a date. You can also skip this category.

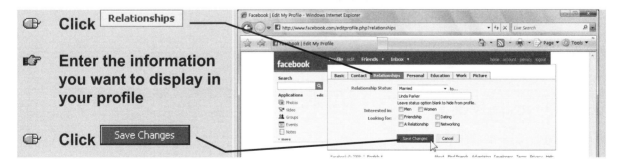

Click ⎡ Relationships ⎤

☞ **Enter the information you want to display in your profile**

Click ⎡ Save Changes ⎤

In the category `Personal` you can enter information about your hobbies and interests:

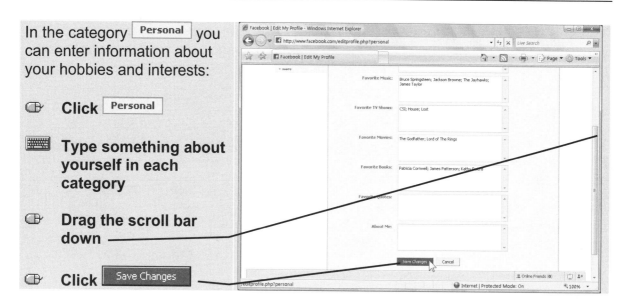

Click `Personal`

Type something about yourself in each category

Drag the scroll bar down ——

Click `Save Changes`

There are three more categories. In the category *Education* you can provide more information about the school(s) or college(s) you went to. In the category *Work* you can enter information about your current or previous job(s).

☞ **Add information to the category** `Education`

☞ **Add information to the category** `Work`

In the final category *Photo* you can add a picture to your profile. This will help your friends recognize you when they try to find you in *Facebook*.

Click `Picture`

Click `Browse...`

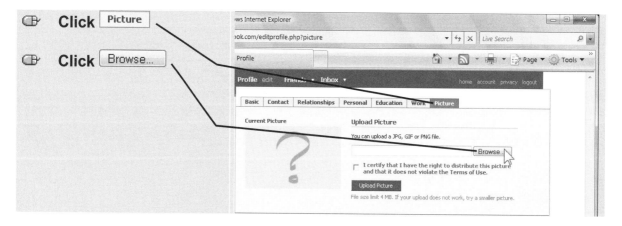

You see the window *Choose file*. It may look different on your computer than what you see in this example. You can choose a random image from your own photo collection. In this example a photo from the *Pictures* folder is used.

Click Pictures

You see the contents of the *Pictures* folder. You will see different photos on your screen:

Click a photo

Click Open

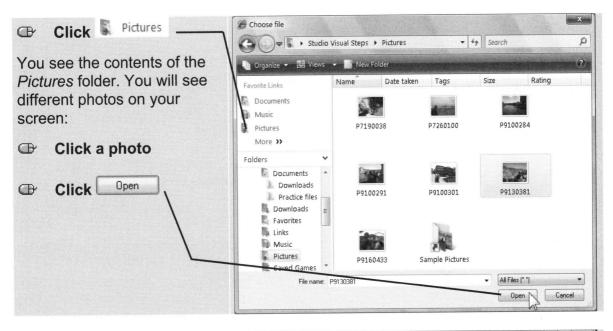

You see the location of the photo on the hard disk of your computer:

Click to check mark
☑ I certify that I have the right to and that it does not violate the T

Click Upload Picture

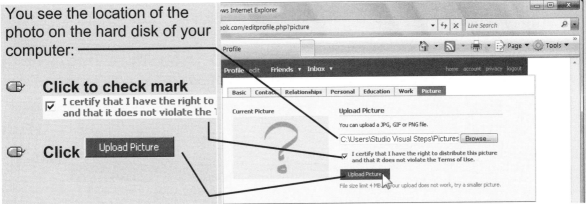

Now the photo is copied to the *Facebook* website:

In the bottom left corner you see the progress of the image upload:

You see the photo you just uploaded to the website. If necessary, you can adjust the thumbnail version of the photo that is used in the *Facebook* search results:

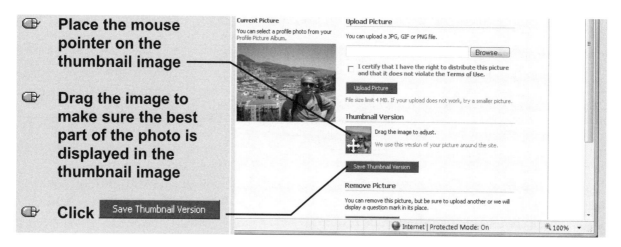

Place the mouse pointer on the thumbnail image

Drag the image to make sure the best part of the photo is displayed in the thumbnail image

Click Save Thumbnail Version

Now you can take a look at your profile page to see the results of the changes you made.

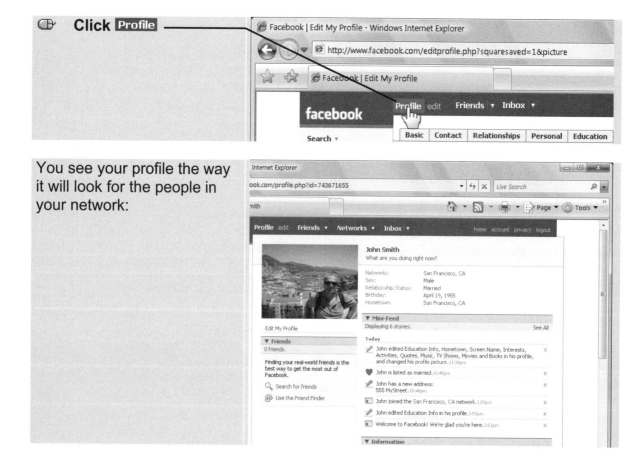

Click Profile

You see your profile the way it will look for the people in your network:

7.4 Viewing and Adjusting Privacy Settings

Take a look at your privacy settings. You can adjust these if necessary.

You see the *Privacy Overview*. This page contains four categories with settings you can adjust. For example, you can change the settings in the *Profile* category. You control who is allowed to view your profile.

You can choose who is allowed to see your profile in *Facebook*. By default, all your networks and all your friends can see your profile.

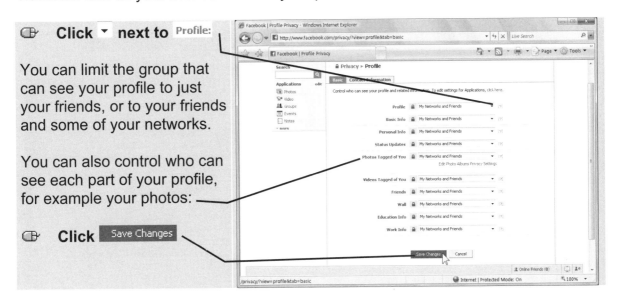

🖱 **Click** Contact Information

By default, your contact information is only visible to your friends:

☞ **If necessary, adjust these settings**

🖱 **Click** Save Changes

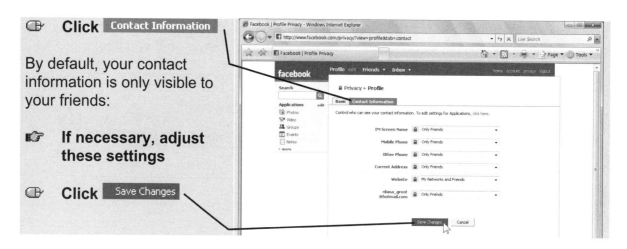

You see the page *Privacy Overview* again. You can go back now to your *Facebook* home page:

At the upper right side of the window:

🖱 **Click** home

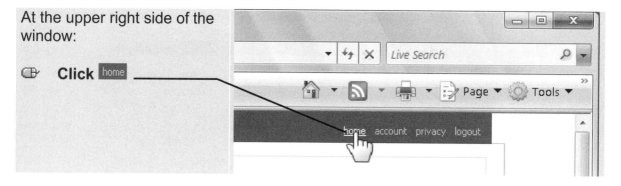

7.5 Inviting Friends

Facebook contains a special page where you can invite friends and acquaintances to take a look at your page in *Facebook*:

🖱 **Click** ▾ next to Friends

🖱 **Click** Invite Friends

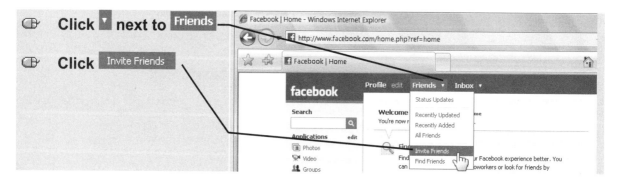

You see a page where you can send a standard invitation. You only need to add one or more e-mail addresses and you can type a personal message if you like:

Type one or more e-mail addresses next to To:

Type a personal message next to Message:

Click Invite

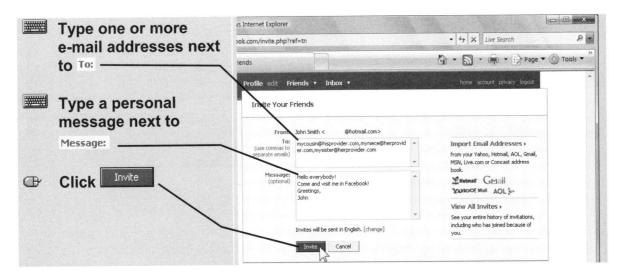

This is what the standard *Facebook* invitation e-mail combined with the personal message looks like:

After sending the invitation, you see the list of e-mail addresses it was sent to. You can return to your *Facebook* home page:

Click Go Home

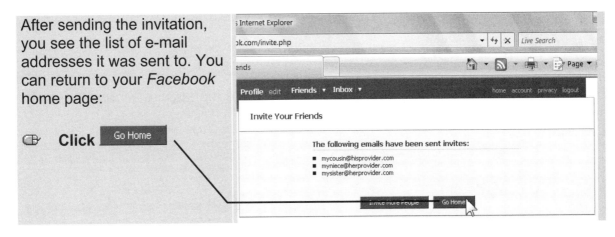

7.6 Finding and Adding Friends in Facebook

You can also look for friends that already have a *Facebook* account and invite them to your network of friends:

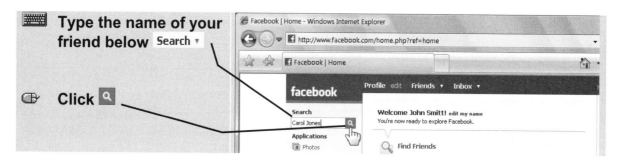

Type the name of your friend below Search ▼

Click 🔍

You see a list of *Facebook* members with a name similar to the name you have typed. If the person you are looking for is in this list, you can send him or her an invitation:

Click Add to Friends

You see the window *Add Carolina as a friend?*:

Click Add Friend

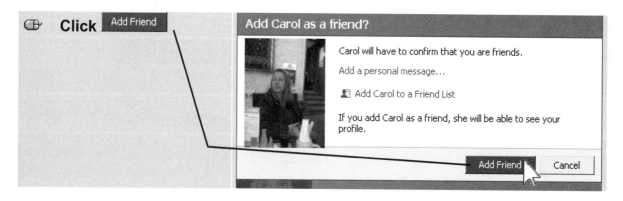

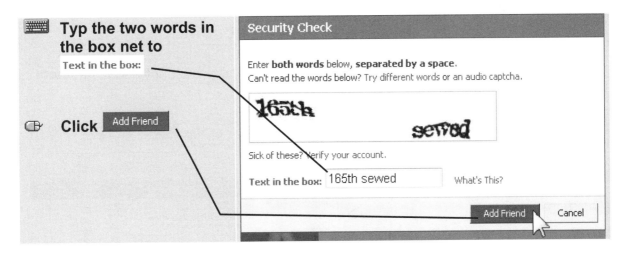

This way you can add more friends with a *Facebook* page. As soon as you have invited the friends you want to add, you can return to your *Facebook* home page.

☞ **Open your *Facebook* home page** ℓℓ²²

7.7 Confirming Friends in Facebook

The person you just added to your friends in *Facebook* needs to confirm that you two really are friends. He or she can also choose to ignore you.

You have to do the same thing when someone tries to add you as a friend. When that happens, you are notified by e-mail, and you see a 'friend request' on your *Facebook* home page. If you do not have any friend requests yet, you can just read through this section.

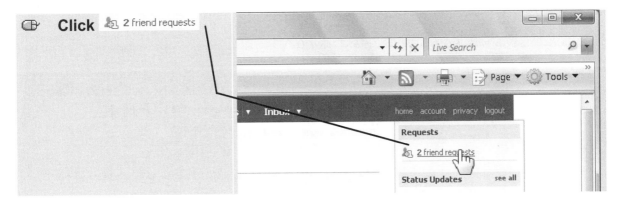

You see the names and the profile pictures of the people who want to add you as their friend. To add a friend:

Click Confirm

You see this window. Here you can select how you know this person. You can also skip this step:

Click Skip This Step

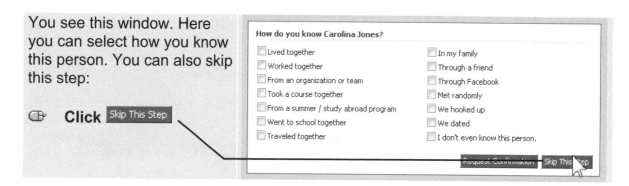

You see a confirmation message that now you are friends with this person.

☞ **Open your *Facebook* home page** 🐾²²

The people that belong to your group of friends are listed in a separate section on your *Facebook* home page:

Click Friends

You see your friends. In this example there is only one friend so far.

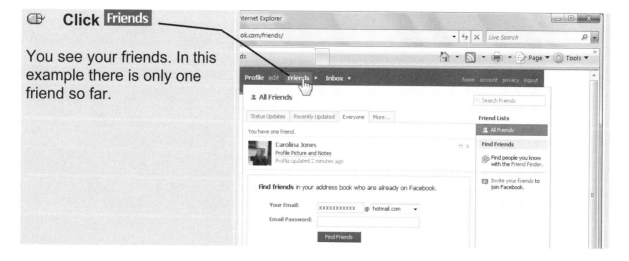

7.8 Writing Notes

In *Facebook* you can also maintain a blog, an online journal or diary on the Internet. This way you can keep your friends up-to-date on what is happening in your life. In *Facebook* each post on your blog is called a *note*. You can add a note like this:

Click ▢ Notes

Click + Write a New Note

Type a title for your note

Type a message

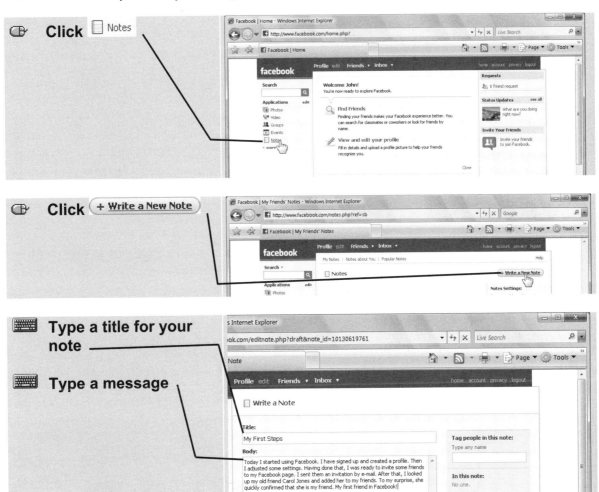

Another interesting thing about notes in *Facebook* is that you can *tag* your friends in your notes. A tag is a keyword that describes a file, or in this case, a note. Your friends can look up notes that are written about them, and you can look up the notes they have written about you. To be able to tag a friend, he or she must have confirmed that you are his or her friend. You can add a tag like this:

Type a name of a friend below

Tag people in this note:

Type any name

Facebook displays the names of the friends who are a match. In this example there is only one match:

Click the name of the friend you want to tag

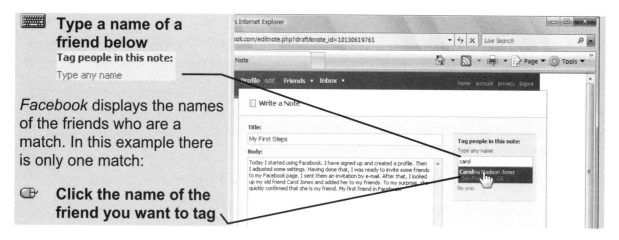

Now you can publish your note:

Drag the scroll bar down

Click Publish

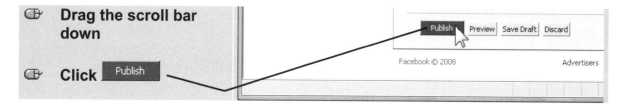

You can view your note on your profile page:

Click Profile

The note you just posted is listed as an action in your Mini-Feed:

Click the title of your note

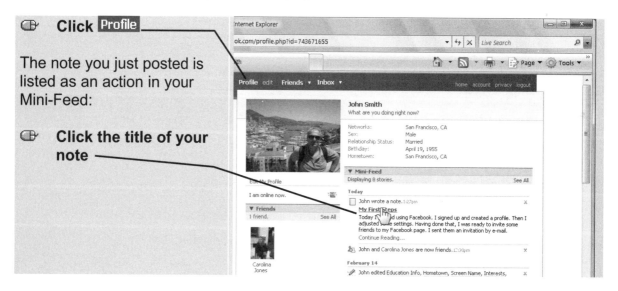

Tip

Mini-Feed and News Feed

The Mini-Feed is part of your profile. It shows the most recent actions you have taken in *Facebook*. The stories that are listed are all actions that people would have been able to see by clicking around the site. By default, the Mini-Feed is visible for everyone in your network who visits your profile.

Mini-Feed will **never** publish stories about whose profile or photos you view, whose notes you read, people you reject as friends or people you remove from your friends.

In addition to the Mini-Feed on your profile, there is a News Feed on your *Facebook* home page. This is a constantly updating list of new stories about your friends' activities on *Facebook*. For example, if a friend uploads a new photo album, you may receive a story about this in your News Feed.

There is a separate section for the News Feed and the Mini-Feed in the *Privacy* section of *Facebook*. You can use it to control what actions show up in your Mini-Feed. You can go there like this:

 Click privacy **in the top right corner, then click** News Feed and Mini-Feed

You see your note, and the friend you have tagged in this note:

 Tip

Notes about you

On the page where you view the note you have posted, you see the tab Notes about Me . As soon as one of your friends tags you in a note, you receive a notification and you can view that note there:

 Click Notes about Me

You see the note that was written about you. People who visit your profile, see John's Notes as well as Notes about John .

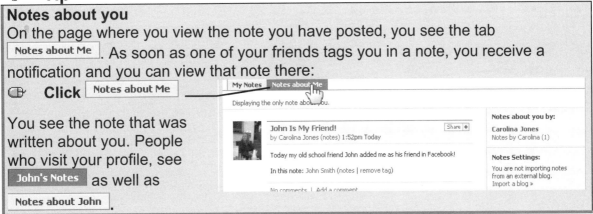

7.9 Adding a Photo Album

You can also add photos to your *Facebook* page. This is another way to keep your friends up-to-date with recent activities or events in your life:

☞ **Click** 🖼 Photos **below**
Applications

You see the page *Welcome to Facebook Photos.* Here you can create an album and upload your photos:

⌨ **Type a name for the photo album, for example** My cats

⌨ **Type a short description of the album**

You can also select who is allowed to view the photos. By default Everyone is selected:

☞ **Click** ▾ **next to** Privacy:

☞ **Click the group for which you want the photos to be visible**

☞ **Click** Create Album

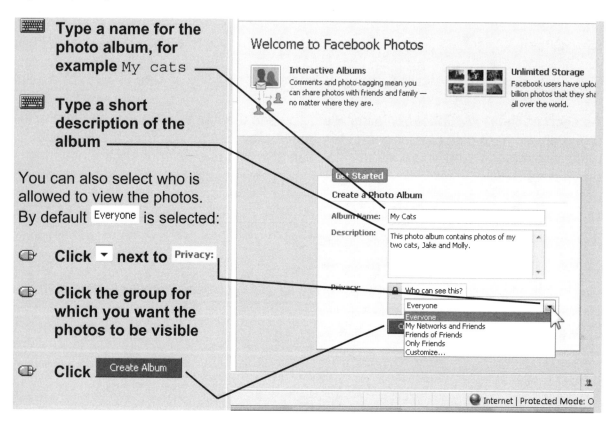

HELP! A security warning.

To be able to add photos, you need to install an add-on for *Internet Explorer*. If you have not done that yet, a window appears alerting you to a message in the information bar at the top of your browser window:

☞ **Click** | Close | **in the window**

☞ **Click the bar** 🛡 This website wants to install / to install it, click here... **below the *Internet Explorer* menu bar**

You see a menu:

☞ **Click** Install ActiveX Control...

If you use *Windows Vista*, your screen goes dark.
A window appears where you need to give your permission to continue.

☞ **Click** | Continue |
☞ **Click** | Install |

The *ActiveX control* is installed. Now you can start uploading photos.

As soon as the *ActiveX control* is installed, you see the names of the folders that are found on the hard disk of your computer. In this example, photos from the *Pictures* folder are added to the photo album. You can also add photos from another location on your hard disk.

☞ **Click** 📁 Pictures

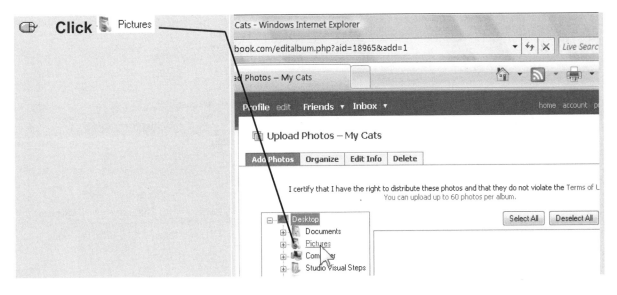

Click to check mark the photos you want to add ——

Click `Upload`

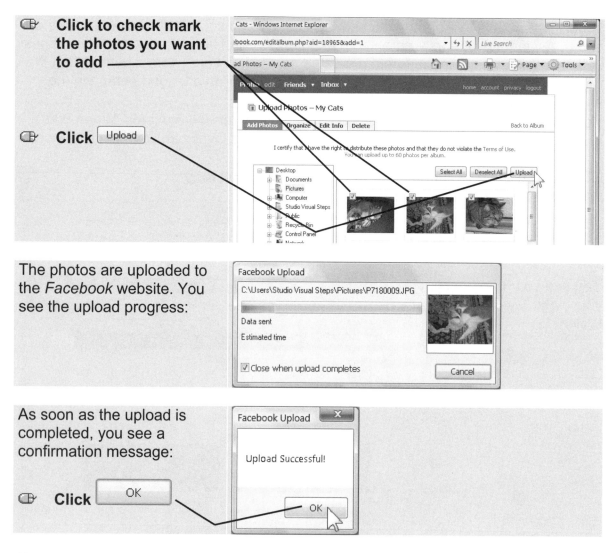

The photos are uploaded to the *Facebook* website. You see the upload progress:

As soon as the upload is completed, you see a confirmation message:

Click `OK`

Now you can edit your photo album:

Type a caption for each photo ——

Click ○ This is the album cover. **to select one photo as the photo album cover**

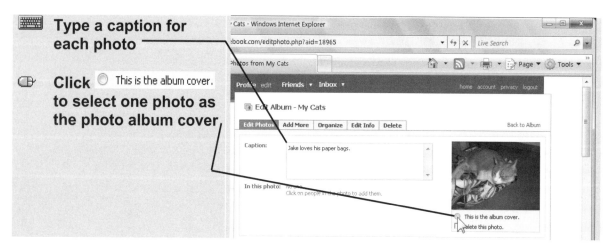

If there are people in a photo, you can tag them. To do so, you click a person in the photo. A window appears where you can enter or select his or her name. The names of the people that are in the photo are listed next to it in your photo album. When the people who look at the photos place the mouse pointer on a tagged person in the photo, his or her name will appear.

You can also go to the tab Organize to change the order of the photos. When you have finished making changes to your first photo album, you can save the changes:

Drag the scroll bar all the way down

Click Save Changes

You see your photo album on your page *My Photos*:

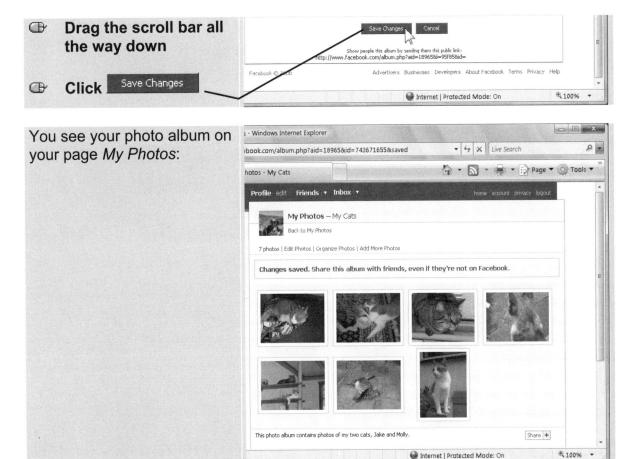

7.10 Viewing Your Profile

Now you can take a look at your profile to review what your friends will see when they visit you in *Facebook*:

☞ **Click** Profile

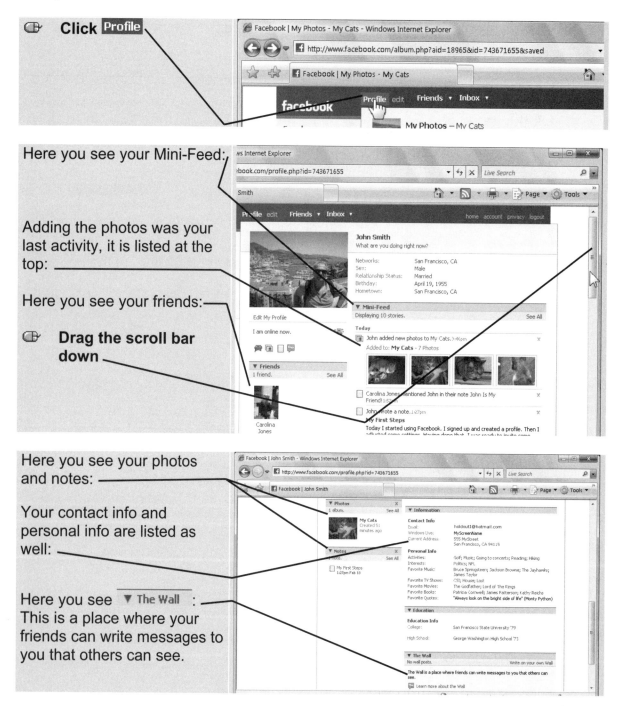

Here you see your Mini-Feed:

Adding the photos was your last activity, it is listed at the top: —————

Here you see your friends:—

☞ **Drag the scroll bar down** —————

Here you see your photos and notes: —————

Your contact info and personal info are listed as well: —————

Here you see ▼ The Wall : This is a place where your friends can write messages to you that others can see.

In the next section you can read more about the Wall.

7.11 Writing on the Wall

The Wall is a place where your friends can write messages to you or comments about you that others can see. By default, all your networks and all your friends can read the messages on your wall. It is very easy to leave a message on a wall.
You are going to leave a message for one of your friends. If you do not have any friends yet, you can just read through this section.

Click **Friends**

Click the name of a friend

You see the profile of your friend. You can find the Wall at the bottom of the page:

Drag the scroll bar down

Click the text box below ▼ The Wall

Type a message

Click Post

Now your message is listed on your friends' Wall:

You can delete a message you wrote on a wall using the link Delete :
Please note: your friend can also delete your message!

You can control the use of your wall from the *Privacy* page.

☞ **Click** privacy **at the top of the page, then click the** Profile **category**

☞ **Drag the scroll bar down** ⎯⎯⎯

☞ **Click** ▾ **next to** Wall:

If you want to limit the use of your wall to just your friends, then select Only my friends . If you do not want to use the wall at all, select No one .

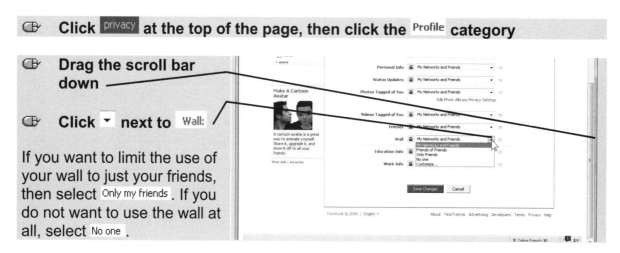

If you changed your wall setting:

☞ **Drag the scroll bar down and click** Save Changes

If you did not change a setting you can just continue reading.

7.12 Deactivating Your Account

If you ever want to stop using *Facebook*, you can deactivate your account. You can do that like this:

☞ **If necessary, drag the scroll bar up**

☞ **Click** account

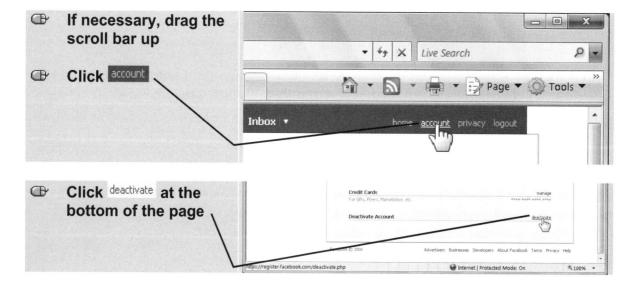

☞ **Click** deactivate **at the bottom of the page**

As a part of their customer service, *Facebook* will ask you why you are deactivating your account. You can select a reason from the list.

Click to select a reason for deactivation

A yellow box appears with suggestions from *Facebook* to solve any issues you have with the website.

Click to select
☑ Opt out of receiving emails from Facel

Click Deactivate

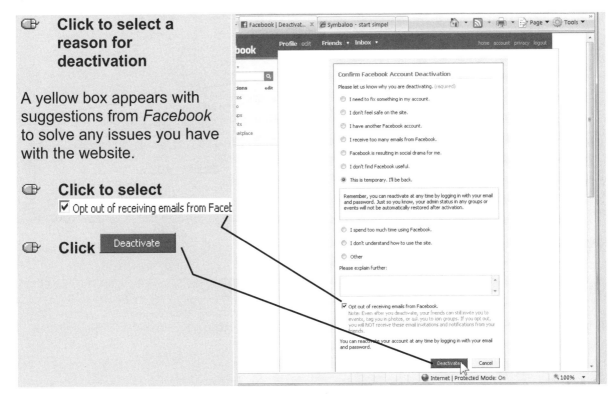

Your account is deactivated and you will no longer receive any e-mails from *Facebook*. Your profile and all information associated with your account are no longer accessible for other *Facebook* users. If you ever want to reactivate your account, you can just log in with your e-mail address and password.

☞ **Close *Internet Explorer*** 🐾³

In this chapter you have been introduced to the most important features of *Facebook*. You know how to edit your profile and to invite and find friends.

💡 **Tip**

Help
If you want to learn more about *Facebook,* you can refer to the extensive Help section of the website. Keep in mind that the creators of *Facebook* frequently add new features to the service. You can also find information about these new features in the Help section. You can access the Help section like this:

Click Help **at the bottom of the page**

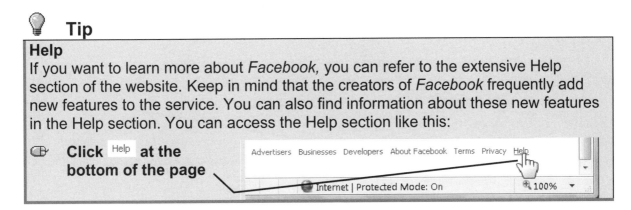

7.13 Background Information

Glossary	
Account	An account gives the user access to a service. You need an e-mail address and a password to access *Facebook*.
ActiveX control	Technology used to create active web content. These controls need to be installed in *Internet Explorer* separately.
Applications	Applications are tools that allow you to interact with your friends and networks. Examples of applications that *Facebook* has built are Photos, Notes, and Groups.
Deactivate	If you deactivate your account, your profile and all information associated with it, are immediately made inaccessible to other *Facebook* users. What this means is that you effectively disappear from the *Facebook* service, but you always have the option to reactivate your account at a later date.
Facebook	*Facebook* is a free social networking website. The site is designed as an easy way to connect people with their friends and acquaintances, but it can also be used to get to know new people.
Friend	Person who has confirmed your 'Add Friend' request.
Mini-Feed	When looking at a profile, Mini-Feed will show you the most recent *Facebook* actions by that user.
News Feed	A constantly updating list of news stories about your friends' activities on your *Facebook* home page. For example, if a friend uploads a new photo album, you may receive a story about this in your News Feed.
Note	The Notes page is the center for sharing your life through your writing. You can tag friends in the notes you write.
Poke	You can poke someone to get his or her attention.
Profile	Your profile contains all the information about you that your friends and people in your networks can see. You can easily restrict what parts of your profile people can see from the *Privacy* page.
Tag	Keyword or name you can add to a note, photo or video.
Wall	Message board that is embedded in your profile. It is a place where your friends can write messages to you or comments about you that others can see.

Source: Facebook Help

7.14 Tips

 Tip

What are you doing right now?

In *Facebook* you can enter a status message to let the people that visit your profile know what you are doing:

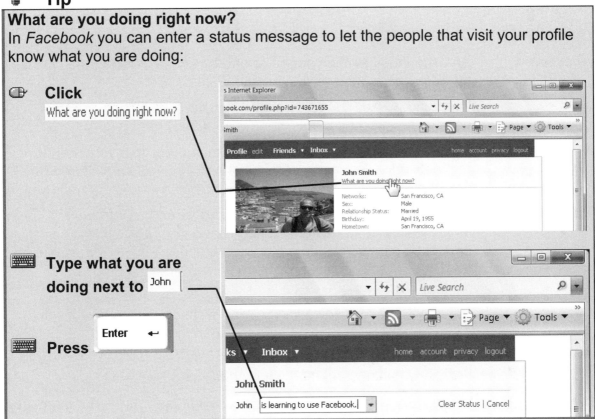

 Tip

Quickly navigate inside your profile

At the top of your profile there are a couple of buttons you can use to quickly jump to a certain section of your profile.

Tip

Joining another network

In *Facebook* you are limited to one regional network. But in addition to a regional network, you can also join up to four school, college or company networks.

☞ **Click** account

☞ **Click** Networks

For example, to join a college network:

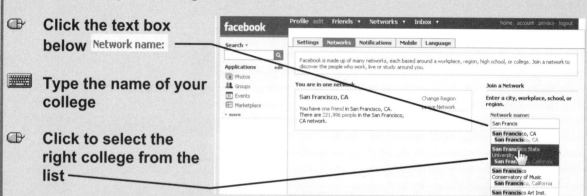

☞ **Click the text box below** Network name:

⌨ **Type the name of your college**

☞ **Click to select the right college from the list**

To be able to join their network, most colleges and companies require you to prove your affiliation by entering a working e-mail address you received from them. You must be able to access this e-mail address to confirm your affiliation.

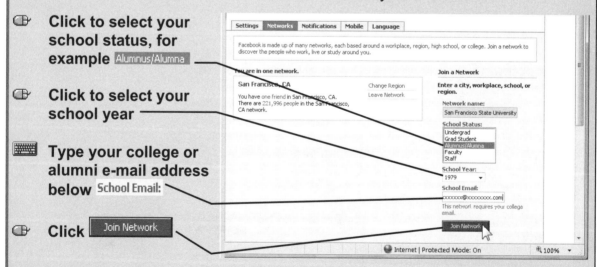

☞ **Click to select your school status, for example** Alumnus/Alumna

☞ **Click to select your school year**

⌨ **Type your college or alumni e-mail address below** School Email:

☞ **Click** Join Network

An e-mail will be sent to the e-mail address you specified above. This e-mail contains a confirmation link that you need to click in order to join this network.

Tip

Joining a group

In *Facebook* you can also join *groups*. A group consists of *Facebook* members with a similar interest. For example, people that like the same band or type of car, or people that have the same hobby. You can join up to 200 groups. You can search for a group like this:

☞ **Click** 👥 Groups **below**

Applications

For example, you can search for a group of fans of the singer/songwriter Jackson Browne:

☞ **Click the text box**

⌨ **Type** Jackson Browne

⌨ **Press** Enter ↵

You see a list of groups that have something to do with Jackson Browne. You can view a group like this:

☞ **Click the name of the group you are interested in**

If you like this group, you can join it:

☞ **Click** Join this Group

A window appears:

☞ **Click** Join

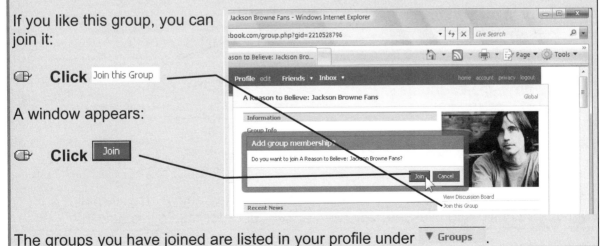

The groups you have joined are listed in your profile under ▼ Groups .

Tip

Poking someone

In *Facebook* you can *poke* your friends and other people in your network. A poke is a way to interact with your friends in *Facebook*. A poke does not have a specific purpose. You can use it for example to get the attention of a person, without sending a message.

☞ **Click** Friends

☞ **Click** Poke Carolina!

You see this message:

⌨ **Type both words in the text box** ———

☞ **Click** Poke

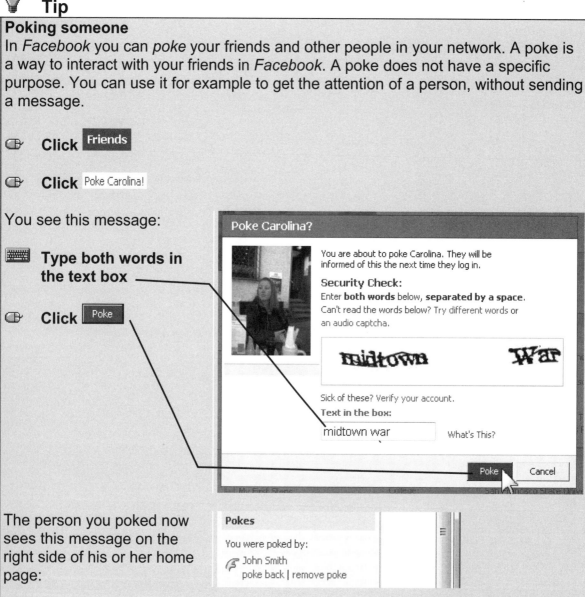

The person you poked now sees this message on the right side of his or her home page:

The person you poked can either poke back , or remove poke . He or she can also click your name to go to your profile.

Notes

Write your notes down here.

8. Global e-mailing with Windows Live Hotmail

Webmail is a convenient way to send and receive your e-mail, no matter where you are in the world. Webmail requires just two things: a webmail address and a computer that is connected to the Internet.

Webmail is very simple: you surf to the website of the webmail provider. There you enter your password to open your personal webmail page. On this page you can read the e-mails you have received and write and send new e-mails.

Most Internet Service Providers (ISPs) offer a free webmail service to their subscribers. In that case you can keep using your regular e-mail address. You can find more information about this on the website of your Internet Service Provider.

You can also use a free webmail service such as *Windows Live Hotmail*. It is easy to sign up for a free e-mail address. This address will give you access to your personal webmail page in *Windows Live*.

Having this type of e-mail address is very convenient when you are on vacation and still want to be able to send or receive e-mail.

In the following sections you will learn how to:

- create a *Windows Live Hotmail* address;
- open your personal webmail page;
- send and receive a webmail message;
- create a new folder;
- move a message to another folder;
- delete a message;
- change the theme;
- display the reading pane.

⇨ **Please note:**

Windows Live Hotmail is a website that is frequently updated. The screenshots you see in this chapter may differ slightly from what you see on your screen.

8.1 Creating a Windows Live Hotmail address

Windows Live is a collection of several free *Microsoft* services. One of these services is *Windows Live Hotmail.* To be able to use this service you need a *Windows Live ID.* This is a free e-mail address that ends with *@hotmail.com* or *@live.com*.

 Please note:

Do you already have an e-mail address that ends with @live.com or @hotmail.com?
Then you can skip this section.

You are going to create a *Live Hotmail* address:

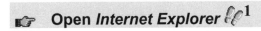

☞ **Open *Internet Explorer*** 🖐¹

☞ **Surf to the web address www.live.com** 🖐²

 Please note:

The sign up webpage for *Windows Live Hotmail* is frequently renewed. The screenshots you see in the following examples may look a bit different from what you see on your screen. For example, a certain button or link you need to click may have been moved or have a slightly different name. In that case, take a good look at the window to find the correct link.
If necessary, follow the instructions in the windows. Using these instructions you should not encounter any difficulty creating a new *Live Hotmail* account.

You see the *Internet Explorer* window with the *Windows Live* webpage:

In this example you see the link to open the sign in page in the upper right corner:

☞ **Click** Sign in

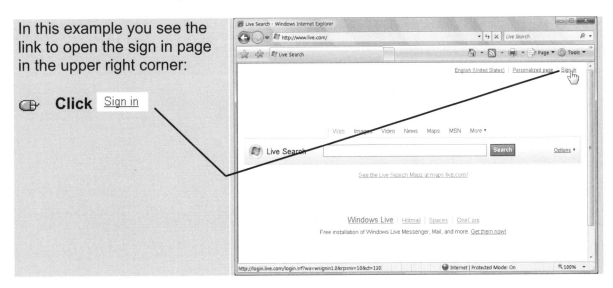

In this window you can either sign in to your *Windows Live Hotmail* account or sign up for a new one.

You do not yet have a *Live Hotmail* address yet, so you choose to sign up for one:

☞ **Click** Sign up

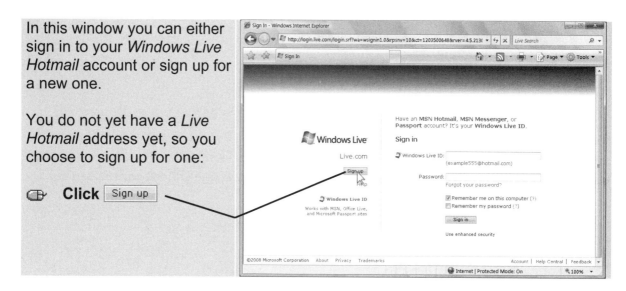

You are going to make a new *Windows Live ID*. This ID consists of an **e-mail address** that you create for yourself plus a corresponding **password**. The e-mail address may contain letters, numbers, a period (.), a dash (-) or an underscore (_). Spaces are not allowed in an e-mail address.
An e-mail address may look like this: **my_name@hotmail.com**
In this example an e-mail address that ends with **@hotmail.com** is created. You can decide for yourself if you want a **@hotmail.com** address or a **@live.com** address.

☞ **Click** ▾ **next to** live.com

☞ **Click** hotmail.com

☞ **Click next to**
   *Windows Live ID

⌨ **Type the e-mail address you have in mind**

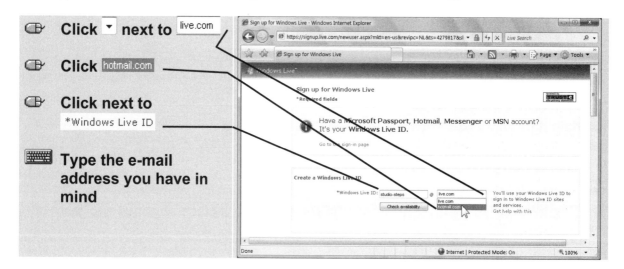

Next, you need to check if this e-mail address is available:

☞ **Click** Check availability

If the address is already in use, you see a notification in red:

In that case you can choose one of the possibilities from the list, or type a different e-mail address and check the availability again.

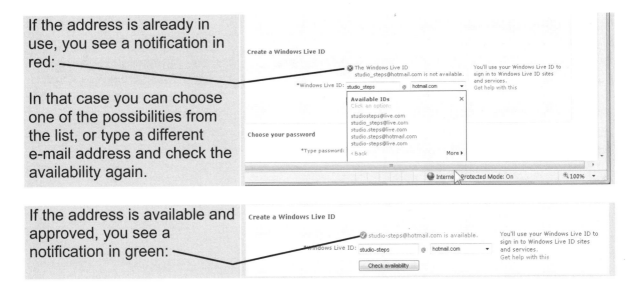

If the address is available and approved, you see a notification in green:

Now you can continue with the sign up procedure. Think of a good password. The password should contain at least six letters or numbers. The password is case sensitive, so if you use a capital now, you will need to use a capital when you login.

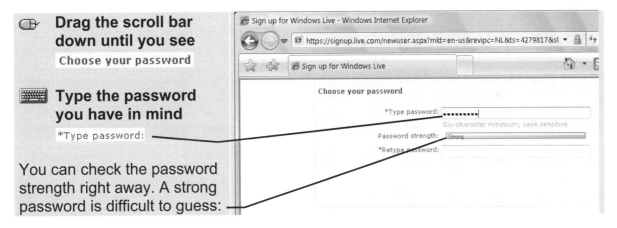

Drag the scroll bar down until you see Choose your password

Type the password you have in mind *Type password:

You can check the password strength right away. A strong password is difficult to guess:

 Tip

Write down your new e-mail address and password on a piece of paper and store it in a safe place.

You have to retype the password to confirm it and prevent mistakes:

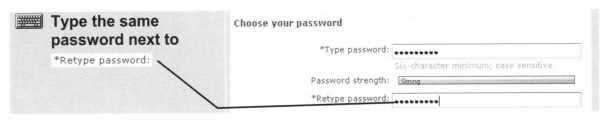

Type the same password next to *Retype password:

➡️ **Please note:**

If necessary, use the scroll bar to see the next question.

Now you can choose a security question and enter an answer. Make sure to choose a question only you know the answer to. If you ever forget your password, your answer to this question gives you temporary access to your account.
You can also enter another e-mail address that *Live Hotmail* may use to send you your forgotten password.

 If available, type an e-mail address next to Alternate e-mail:

To select a question:

👆 **Click ▾ next to** *Question: **and select a question**

 Type your answer next to *Secret answer:

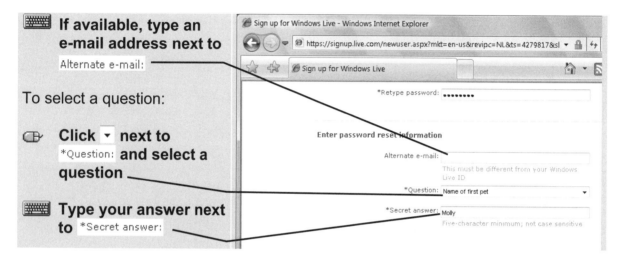

Now you are asked to provide your account information. Your first and last name will be sent with all of your outgoing messages.

 Type the requested information below Your information

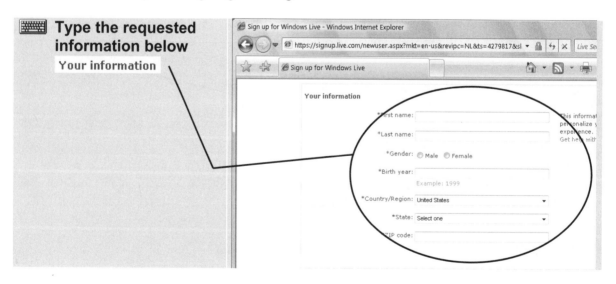

The next step is the registration check. To perform this check, you have to type the letters and numbers you see on the image. This is a way to make sure a real person is signing up for the account and not automated software.

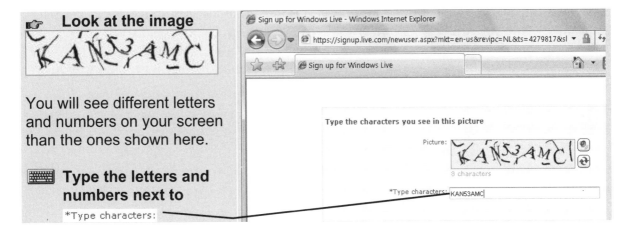

☞ **Look at the image**

You will see different letters and numbers on your screen than the ones shown here.

⌨ **Type the letters and numbers next to**

*Type characters:

💡 **Tip**

Are you having difficulty reading the characters?
Then you can click to get a new image. If you still have a problem reading the characters after that, you can click 🔊. Now the letters and numbers are read aloud to you. Make sure the speakers of your computer are turned on.

Now you see two hyperlinks to the *Microsoft* service agreement and privacy statement:

To read these agreements:

🖱 **Click**
Windows Live Service Agreeme
and Privacy Statement

Depending on the settings of your computer, the agreements are opened in a new tab or a new browser window. You can close these windows or tabs after reading the agreements. Now you need to accept the service agreement and privacy statement:

🖱 **Click** I accept

HELP! Error.

If you failed to enter part of the requested information, or you did not enter it correctly, you see an error message. You are requested to enter the missing information, or change the incorrect information.

☞ **Read the instructions and enter the requested information**

Now you have a webmail address. This webmail address is also called a *Windows Live ID*, because it also gives access to other *Windows Live* services. You can start using the webmail service. To see how you can sign in next time, close *Internet Explorer*:

☞ **Close *Internet Explorer*** $\ell\ell^3$

8.2 Opening Your Webmail Page

Now you can use any computer connected to the Internet to open your webmail:

☞ **Open *Internet Explorer*** $\ell\ell^1$

☞ **Go to the web address www.live.com** $\ell\ell^2$

➡ **Please note:**

This website is frequently updated. The screenshots used in the following examples may appear different from what you see on your screen.

You see the *Windows Live* webpage:

Click Sign in

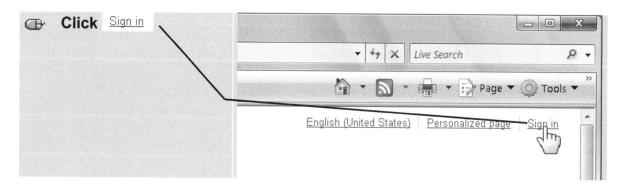

You see the webpage for signing in. If you are working on a different computer than the one you used to sign up for your *Windows Live ID*, you see this window:

Type your new e-mail address and password

You can decide whether to allow this computer to remember your e-mail address and password:

Click Sign in

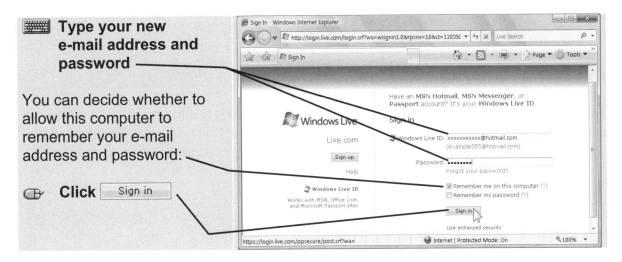

If you are working on your own computer, the one you just used to sign up for your *Windows Live ID*, you see this window:

Place the mouse pointer on your webmail address

xxxxxxxxxx@hotmail.c

The button Sign in appears next to it.

Click Sign in

Type your password

If necessary, click to check mark
☐ Save my password (?)

Click Sign in

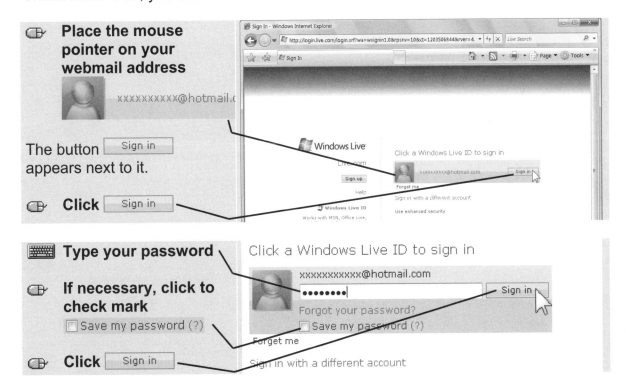

Please note:

If you decide to save your password, your e-mail address and password are entered automatically on this computer from now on.

You see the *Windows Live* webpage again:

☞ **Click** `Hotmail` **at the bottom of the page**

You may see another window where you can choose between the classic version and the full version of *Windows Live Hotmail*. The classic version is suitable for slower Internet connections; the full version requires a broadband connection.

☞ **Read the information on your screen and decide what is best for your situation**

In this chapter the full version is used.

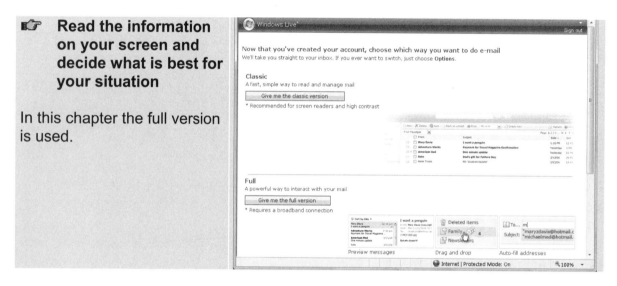

Now you see your personal webmail page. If you cannot see everything, you can enlarge the window:

☞ **If necessary, enlarge the window** 𝓵𝓵^14

Here you see your name and e-mail address: ——

The toolbar and the folders in the window are similar to those in *Windows Mail* and *Outlook Express*: ——

You have received a welcome message from *Windows Live Hotmail*: ——

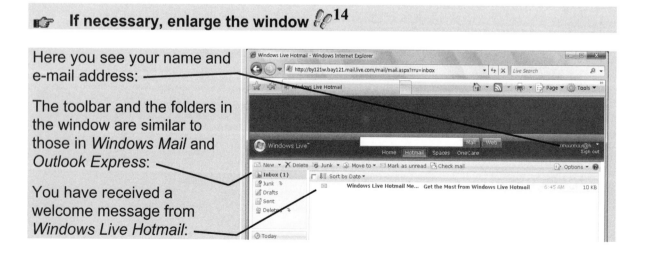

8.3 Sending and Receiving a Webmail Message

You are going to create a new message and send it to yourself:

Click ☐ New ▼

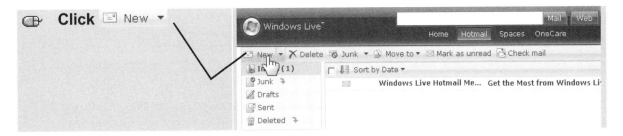

Now you see an empty e-mail message:

Type your own webmail address next to ☐ To...

Type next to Subject: :
test message

Type a text in the main message window

You can click Show Cc & Bcc to send a CC or BCC to others:

Click ☐ Send

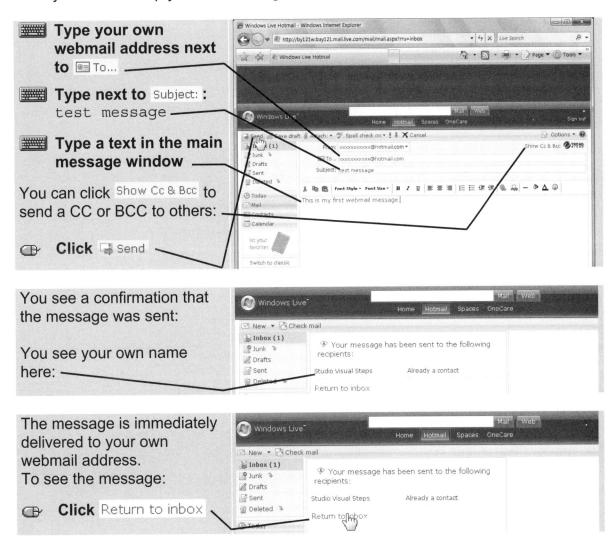

You see a confirmation that the message was sent:

You see your own name here:

The message is immediately delivered to your own webmail address.
To see the message:

Click Return to inbox

If the message has not yet been delivered to your *Inbox*, you can renew the webpage:

If necessary, click
🖳 Check mail

Click the new message

You see the message: ─────

Advertisements will often be included at the end of the message. These ads make it possible for *Microsoft* to offer this service for free.

8.4 Creating and Using a New Folder

The basic structure of the webmail program is similar to *Windows Mail*, the e-mail program packaged with *Windows Vista* or *Outlook Express,* available in *Windows XP*.

On the *Windows Live Mail* webpage there are similar folders where messages are stored:

You can easily add new folders to organize your e-mail messages. Here is how to do that:

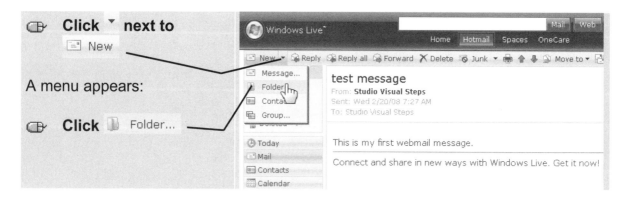

Click ▾ **next to**
📧 New

A menu appears:

Click 📁 Folder...

The new folder is added to the folder list. Type a name for the new folder:

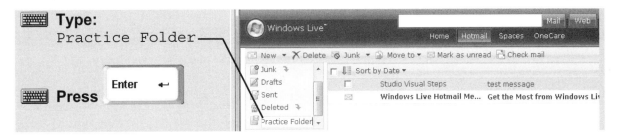

The new folder *Practice Folder* is now included in your list of folders. You can move your test message to this folder. First you select the message:

Now you can select the folder you want to move this message to:

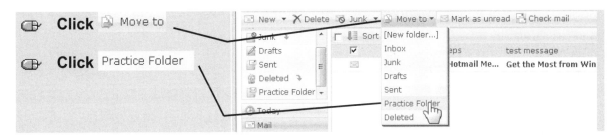

The message has disappeared from your *Inbox*. You can check to make sure it really is stored in the new folder:

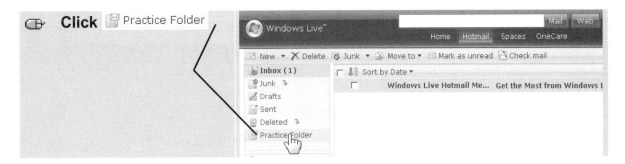

You see that the message is found in the new folder:

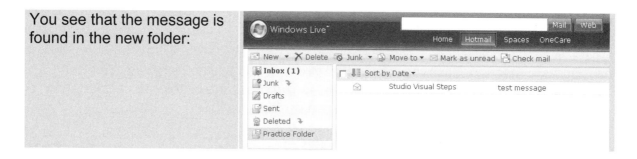

8.5 Deleting a Message

You can delete messages you no longer want to save. You are going to try that with the message you just moved. First you select the message:

☞ **Point to** ✉

The check box ☐ appears.

☞ **Click to check mark** ☑
the test message

Now you can delete the message:

☞ **Click** ✕ Delete

The message is moved to the folder 🗑 Deleted .

8.6 Emptying the Deleted Folder

As long as a message is in the 🗑 Deleted folder, it can still be retrieved. You can open it, or move it to one of the other folders. The message is deleted permanently when you empty the *Deleted* folder. You can do that like this:

Right-click 🗑 Deleted

A menu appears:

Click ✦ Empty folder

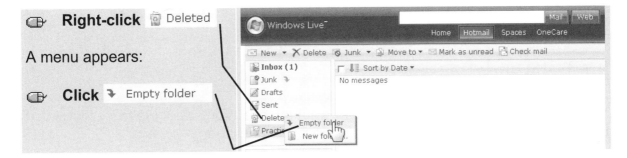

You have to confirm that you really want to empty the folder:

Click OK

The *Deleted* folder is now empty. You return to your *Inbox*:

Click 📧 Inbox (1)

8.7 Changing the Theme

You can adapt the *Windows Live Hotmail* window to your own preferences. For example, you can change the colors of the window by selecting another theme:

Click 📄 Options ▾ **in the top right corner**

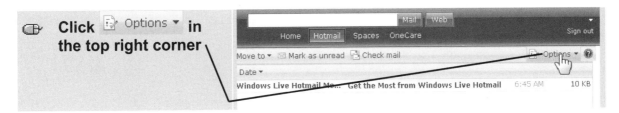

You see a menu. You can select a different color below **Themes** :

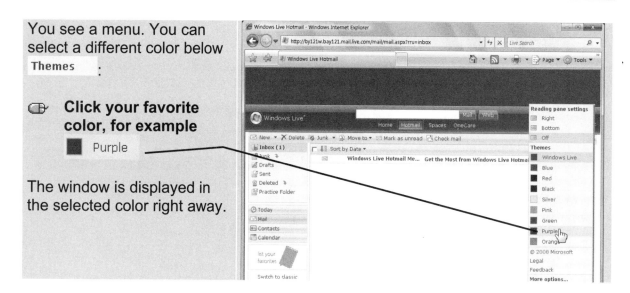

☞ **Click your favorite color, for example** ■ Purple

The window is displayed in the selected color right away.

To return to the default window colors:

☞ **Click** 🖹 Options ▾ , ■ Windows Live

8.8 Displaying the Reading Pane

When you use *Windows Mail* and *Outlook Express*, you probably display the contents of your messages in a reading pane. This way you can quickly read your messages in your *Inbox* very easily without having to open each one individually. This is also possible in *Windows Live Hotmail*.

☞ **Click** 🖹 Options ▾

Below **Reading pane settings** you can choose where you want to display the reading pane. You select 📑 Bottom :

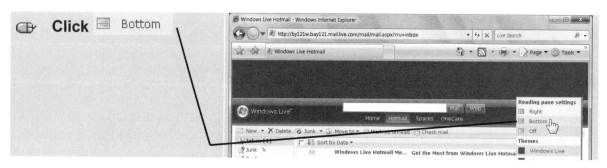

☞ **Click** 📑 Bottom

The reading pane is now displayed below the message list.

👉 **Click the *Windows Live Hotmail* welcome message**

The message is displayed in the reading pane:

You can use the scroll bar ▣ to see the rest of the message:

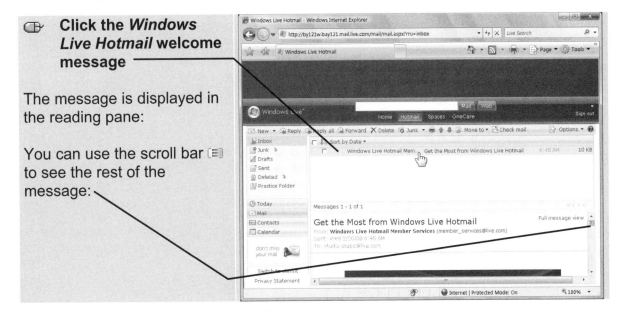

8.9 Signing Out

When you are done reading your messages, you can sign out:

👉 **Click** `Sign out`

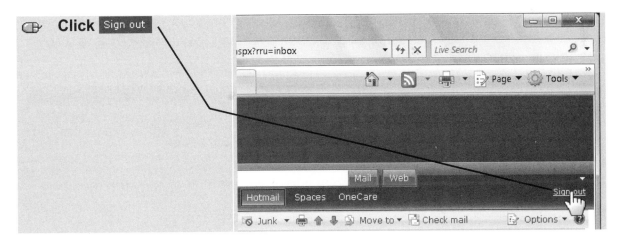

You have signed out. Now you see an MSN webpage.

👉 **Close the *Internet Explorer* window** ✌️³

You now have your very own *Windows Live Hotmail* address at your disposal. You can use this convenient webmail service on any computer in the world that is connected to the Internet.

8.10 Background Information

Glossary	
Deleted	Deleted webmail messages are moved to the *Deleted* folder. To permanently remove a deleted item: delete the message in the *Deleted* folder.
Inbox	The folder where all of the webmail messages you receive are placed.
Outlook Express	E-mail program that comes with *Windows XP*.
Reading pane	Here you can view the message's contents without opening the message in a separate window.
Theme	Color scheme used for the *Windows Live Hotmail* window.
Webmail	E-mail service that is offered through a website. If you have a webmail address, you can read your e-mail on your webmail page on any computer in the world that is connected to the Internet.
Webmail address	E-mail address you can use with a webmail service. For example the addresses which end with @hotmail.com or @live.com.
Webmail message	E-mail message sent or received using a webmail service.
Webmail page	Webpage where you can read, write and send your webmail messages.
Windows Live Hotmail	Free webmail service from *Microsoft*.
Windows Mail	E-mail program that comes with *Windows Vista*.

8.11 Tips

💡 Tip

Sending and receiving attachments

You can send and receive attachments in *Windows Live Hotmail* the same way you do in your regular e-mail program. To add an attachment to a new message:

☞ **Click** ☐ New ▾ **to open a new message**

☞ **Click** 📎 Attach: ▾

☞ **Click** File

Now you can select the file you want to add in the window *Choose file*. For example a document or an image. Use the button ⌈ Open ⌉ to attach the file. Now you can send the message like a normal webmail message.

Please note: if you choose Photo instead of File , you will need to install the 'Microsoft MSN Photo Upload Control' add-on first. *Microsoft Photo Upload* allows basic image editing of your photos before you attach them to your message. For example, you can rotate the photo or change its size. You can also add multiple photos to a message. Follow the instructions in each window that appears to install this add-on. You only need to do this once.

After installing the add-on the window looks like this. The contents of the *Pictures* folder are displayed in the window. This enables you to quickly select, edit and add the photos to your message.

If you receive an e-mail message with an attachment, you follow these steps:

☞ **Click the attachment, for example** 📎 P7180011.JPG (42.9 KB)

In the window *File Download* you can choose between ⌈ Open ⌉ and ⌈ Save ⌉.

If you choose ⌈ Save ⌉, you can choose a location in the *Save as* window.

If you choose ⌈ Open ⌉, you see a security warning first:

☞ **Click** ⌈ Allow ⌉ **in this window**

The photo is opened in *Windows Photo Gallery*.

Tip

Adjusting additional options

You can adapt *Windows Live Hotmail* further to suit your particular needs. To open the window containing extensive options:

Click

You can adjust many different things in the *Options* window, for example:

`Manage your account`: here you can edit your personal information, send automated vacation replies and forward mail to another e-mail account.

`Junk e-mail`: here you can enter safe and blocked senders and select a setting for the junk e-mail filter.

`Customize your mail`: here you can adjust the reading pane, select a different language, create a personal e-mail signature and save sent messages.

`Customize your contacts`: here you can clean up your duplicate contacts, import contacts and export contacts.

 Tip

More information?

If you would like more information about working with *Windows Live Hotmail*, you can also refer to the Help section. You can open the *Help* window like this:

Click in the top right corner of the window

Depending on the settings of your computer, the Help section is opened in a new window or a new tab:

By default, the `FAQ` (Frequently Asked Questions) is displayed in this window:

If you want to take a look at the table of contents:

Click `Table of contents`

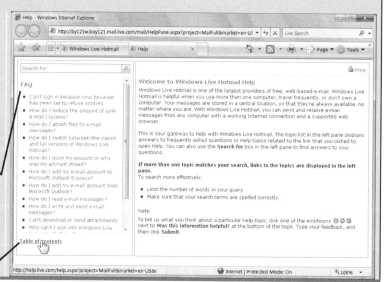

Tip

Other windows
In addition to the reading pane, you can display several other panes in the *Windows Live Hotmail* window.

You can open the corresponding panes by clicking these buttons:

| Today |
| Mail |
| Contacts |
| Calendar |

Today : this button shows you a webpage with MSN headlines.

Mail : use this button to return to the e-mail pane.

Contacts : this button takes you to the pane where you can view and edit your online address book.

Calendar : here you can write down your appointments in your online calendar. This calendar works the same way as the program *Windows Calendar* that comes packaged with *Windows Vista.*

9. Chatting with Windows Live Messenger

Windows Live Messenger lets you easily communicate with friends or family. Anyone can participate if they belong to your list of *contacts* and are *online* at the same time. You can instantly type messages back and forth with any of the *contacts* you have previously created. This is what is called *chatting*.

In addition to this, *Windows Live Messenger* allows you the opportunity to make a video call using a webcam and a microphone. This is a way to communicate face to face with your friends, family or co-workers.

Windows Live Messenger is available around the world. It does not matter where your contacts are located. The only requirement is that each party has the program *Windows Live Messenger* installed on their computer. A fast Internet connection is also highly recommended.

You can sign in to *Windows Live Messenger* with the webmail address you created in the previous chapter. This webmail address is also called your *Windows Live ID*.

In this chapter you learn how to:

- download and install *Windows Live Messenger*;
- open *Windows Live Messenger*;
- sign in to *Windows Live Messenger*;
- add a contact;
- send and receive *instant messages*;
- make a video call using a webcam;
- change your status;
- sign out.

➡ Please note:

Windows Live Messenger and the *Windows Live* websites are frequently updated. The screenshots you see in this chapter may differ slightly from what you see on your screen.

9.1 Downloading and Installing Windows Live Messenger

In this section you are going to download the latest version of *Windows Live Messenger*. You can download *Windows Live Messenger* from the *Windows Live* website.

⇨ **Please note:**

Do you already have the latest version of *Windows Live Messenger*?
Then you can skip this section plus the following section. Continue reading on page 270.

☞ **Open** *Internet Explorer* 𝒪𝒪¹

☞ **Surf to the website www.home.live.com** 𝒪𝒪²

⇨ **Please note:**

The *Windows Live* windows are often changed and renewed.
The screenshots you see in this chapter may look a bit different from what you see on your screen. For example, a certain button or link you need to click may have been moved or have a slightly different name. In that case, take a good look at the window to find the correct link.

⊕ **Click** Messenger

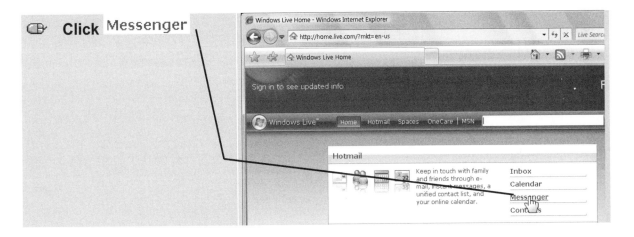

You see a webpage with information about *Windows Live Messenger.* Here you can download the latest version of the program for free:

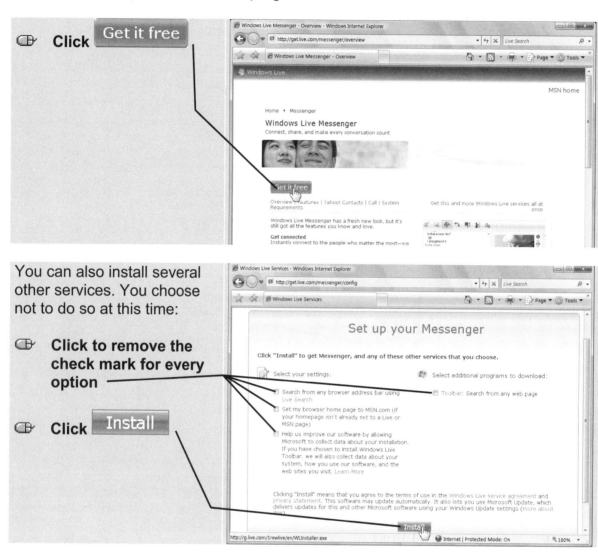

Click [Get it free]

You can also install several other services. You choose not to do so at this time:

Click to remove the check mark for every option

Click [Install]

You choose to install the program right away.

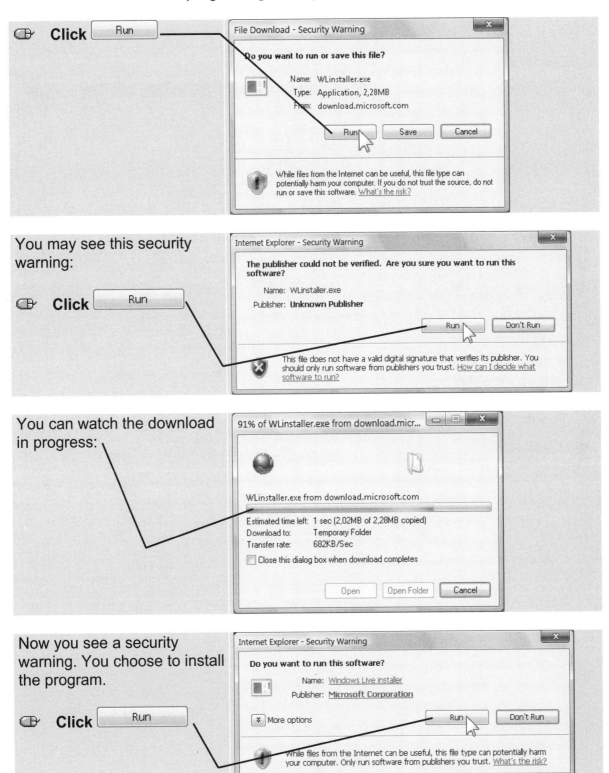

If you work on a *Windows Vista* computer your screen goes dark and you see a window where you need to give your permission to continue:

Click Continue

Windows Live checks for *Windows Live* programs that are already installed on your computer. This may take a few minutes.

Now *Windows Live Messenger* is installed:

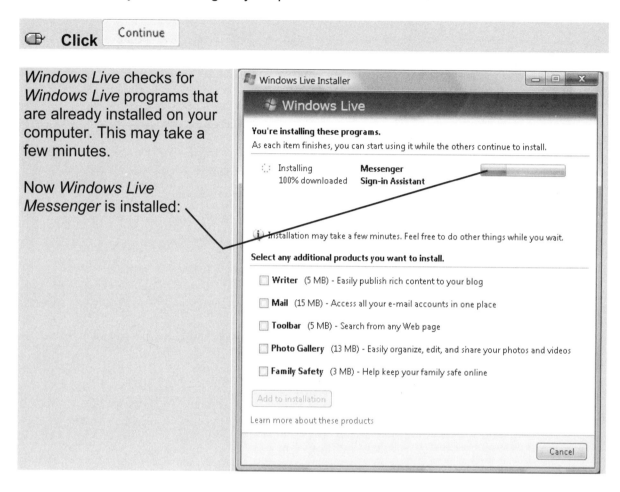

As soon as the program installation has completed, you can close this window:

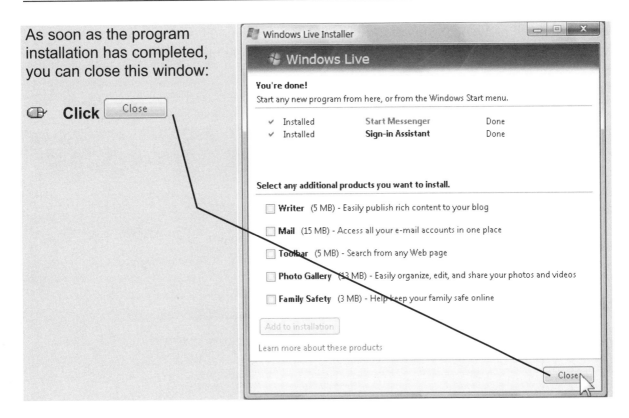

 Click [Close]

The *Windows Live Messenger* sign in window opens.

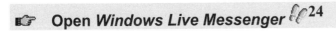 **Close** *Internet Explorer* $\ell\ell^3$

9.2 Signing In to Windows Live Messenger

In the previous chapter you created a *Windows Live ID*. This is a free webmail address that ends with **hotmail.com** or **live.com**. This webmail address gives you access to *Windows Live Messenger* and other *Windows Live* services.

❖ HELP! I did not create a Windows Live ID yet.

You can do that now, using the instructions in chapter 8.
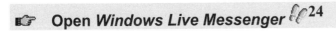 **Work through** *section 8.1 Creating a Windows Live Hotmail address*

The *Windows Live Messenger* window is opened. If that is not the case on your computer:

 Open *Windows Live Messenger* $\ell\ell^{24}$

Type your e-mail address and password

You can choose to have the computer remember your e-mail address and password:

If you want to sign in automatically as soon as you open *Windows Live Messenger*, click to check mark ☐ Sign me in automatically:

☞ **Click** Sign in

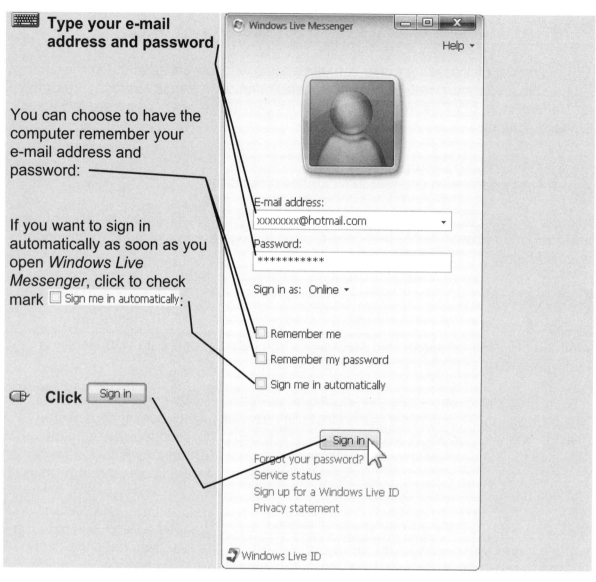

Now you see the *Windows Live Messenger* window and the *Welcome* window.

You can close the *Welcome* window:

☞ **Click** X

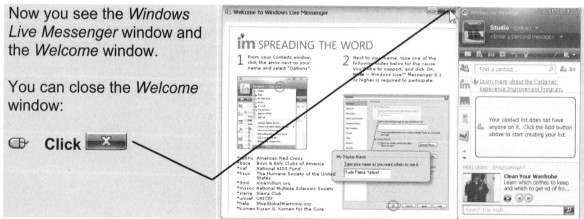

9.3 How Does Windows Live Messenger Work?

The main goal of *Messenger* is to connect people who are online at the same time. To be able to communicate, both parties need to have an e-mail address (preferably a *Live Mail* or *Hotmail* address), and *Windows Live Messenger*. There are two ways to make contact:

- you add a contact to your list;
- a contact wants to add you to his or her contact list.

In order to understand how all this is possible, it is good to know how *Windows Live Messenger* functions. Take some time to read through the *Background Information* you find below.

With the program *Windows Live Messenger* you can communicate with friends or family members that are *online* at the same time.

It works like this. Somewhere there is a central *Windows Live* computer that monitors which *Messenger* users have signed in. Every user has his or her list of contacts (friends and acquaintances). The *Windows Live* computer continuously updates the status of these contacts. You see their names in your *Messenger* window, and you see if they are online or not. If you want to communicate with a contact that is online, you can start a 'conversation'.

Messenger becomes active as soon as you connect to the Internet and sign in to the service. *Messenger* works best when it is kept active. This way you have the best chance to get in touch with a contact that is also online.

For people who use a dial-up connection, this may be very expensive. But if you use a broadband Internet connection, for example cable or DSL, you can keep *Messenger* active.

9.4 Adding a Contact Yourself

You can start communicating with a contact by entering his or her *Live Mail* or *Hotmail* address in *Messenger.*

In this example there are no contacts yet:

☞ **Click**

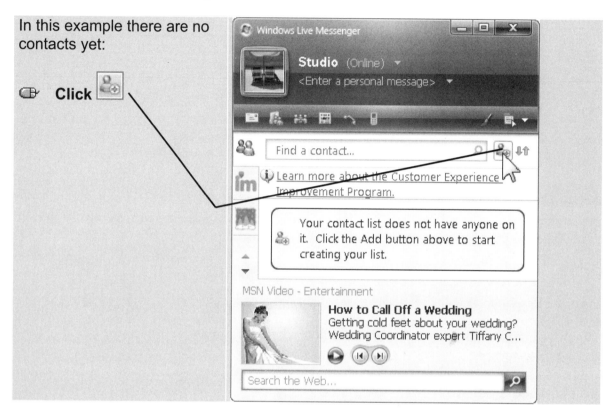

HELP! I already see contacts in my list.

Windows Live Messenger automatically displays the contacts you created in *Windows Live Hotmail*. These non-*Messenger* contacts can be recognized by the little address book 📖 in front of their name.

If you double-click the name, a new webmail message addressed to this contact is opened.

If you have the *Live Mail* or *Hotmail* address of your contact, you can quickly add him or her to your contacts list.

Here you can enter the full e-mail address of your contact:

⌨ **Type the e-mail address of your contact** —

When you add a contact, this person is automatically notified when he or she signs in to *Live Messenger*.

You can add a personal invitation to the default message if you want to.

👆 **Click the box below**
Personal invitation: ———

⌨ **Type a personal message**

You can also send the invitation by e-mail:

👆 **Click to check mark**
☑ Also send an e-mail invitation to

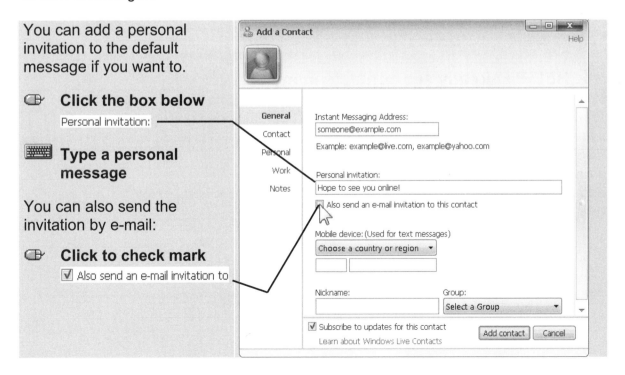

Below Nickname: you can enter a name for this person that you want to see in your contacts list. If you do not enter a name here, you will see his or her e-mail address in your contacts list instead.

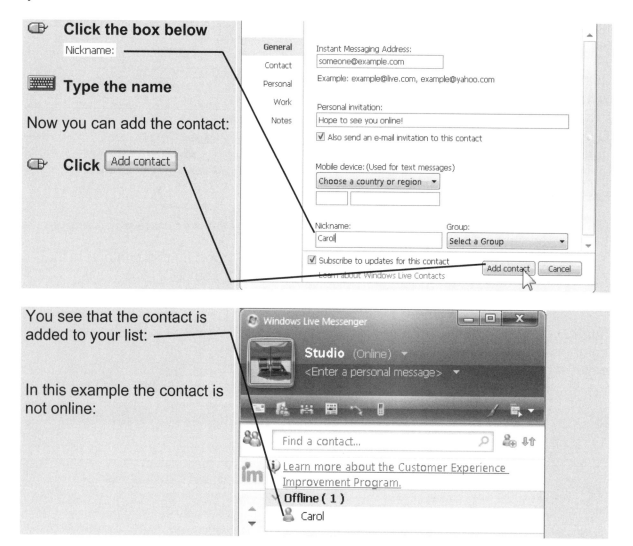

 Click the box below

Nickname:

⌨ **Type the name**

Now you can add the contact:

Click Add contact

You see that the contact is added to your list:

In this example the contact is not online:

You have added your first contact. You see that adding a contact is very easy if you know the e-mail address of your family member, friend or co-worker.

💡 **Tip**

Adding Yahoo Messenger users
Windows Live Messenger is compatible with *Yahoo Messenger*, a similar instant messaging program. This means you can use the same method to add *Yahoo Messenger* users to your contacts list and communicate with them. A *Yahoo ID* ends with **@yahoo.com**.

9.5 A Contact Adds You

The contact you added to your contacts list in the previous section receives a notification. If someone else adds you to his or her contacts list, you will receive a similar message.

In that case you see this window:

Do you want to add this contact?

☞ **Click** [OK]

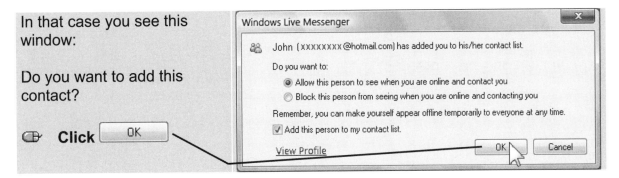

You can also avoid communicating with this person and decline this contact. In that case the person who added you will not be able to see if you are online.

You see that the person who added you to his or her contacts list, is in your list as well:

In this example this person is not online:

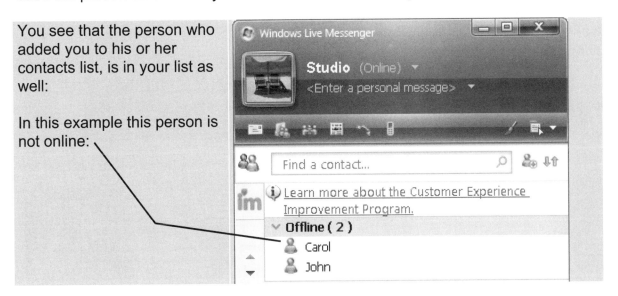

9.6 Using Windows Live Messenger

 Please note:

You can only work through the following sections if you have a contact to practice with.

To show you how *Live Messenger* works, you can read a step by step description of the process of contacting the contact Carol. The first step of this process is signing in. If you do not sign in to *Windows Live*, none of your contacts know that you are online.

In this case you are already online.
In the example the user name 'Studio' is used:

Both contacts are still Offline .
You can also tell that from the color of . The icons are grey:

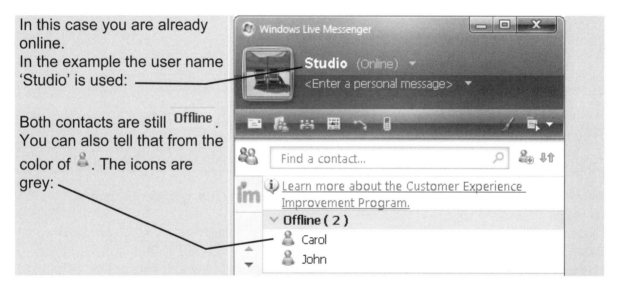

As soon as Carol signs in, you see a notification on the taskbar:

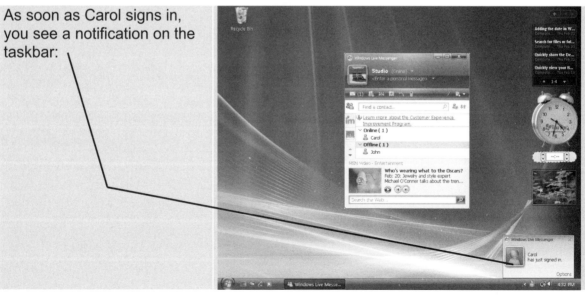

In the *Windows Live Messenger* window one contact is Online.

The icon ᐸ for this person is green:

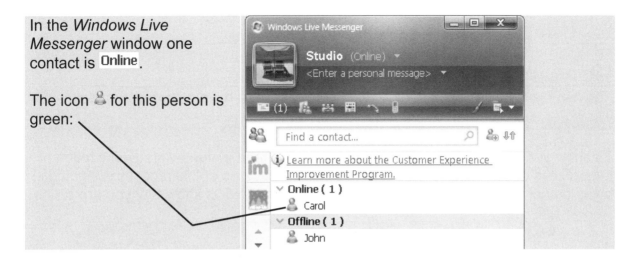

9.7 Sending Instant Messages

⇨ **Please note:**

You can only work through this section if you have a contact to practice with.

When one of your contacts is online, you can communicate with him or her by sending *Instant Messages*. You can do that like this:

☞ **Right-click the online contact**

☞ **Click**
Send an instant message

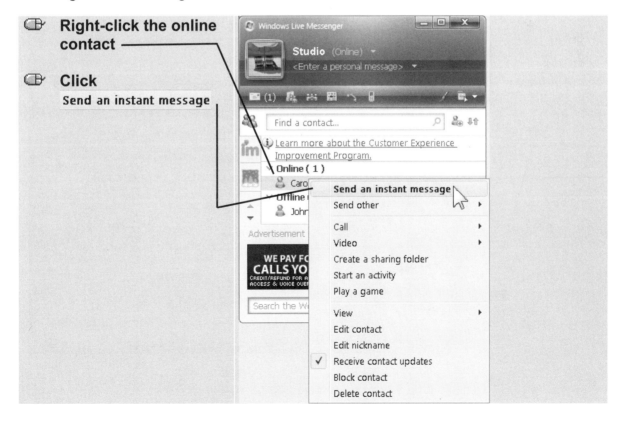

A conversation window with the name of your contact opens.

 Tip

If you double-click the name of an online contact, the conversation window is opened automatically.

You can type your message at the bottom of this window:

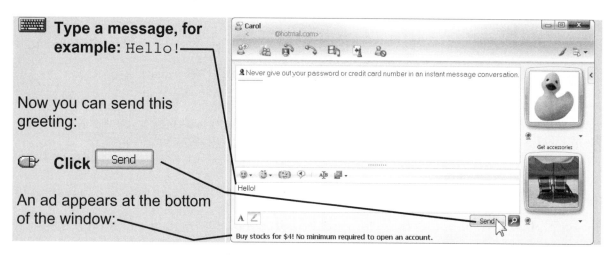

▓ **Type a message, for example:** Hello!

Now you can send this greeting:

☞ **Click** [Send]

An ad appears at the bottom of the window:

⇨ **Please note:**

You can also send your message by pressing the Enter key.
As long as you do not press the Enter key, you can adjust your message before you send it. If you want to start a new line in your message:

▓ **Press the keys** [⇧ Shift] + [Enter ↵] **at the same time**

You see your message appear at the top of the conversation window:

At the bottom of the window you see that contact Carol is writing a message:

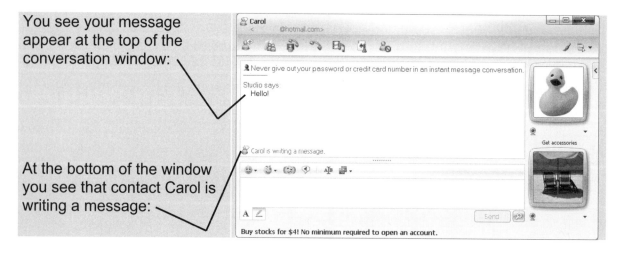

Her message will appear shortly: ———

By default, a sound is played when the message appears.

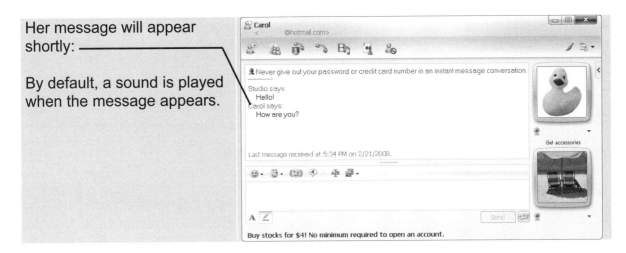

You can see how easy and fun it is to communicate directly with your contact. The interesting part is that your contact may be located on the other side of the world. This type of communication through the Internet is also known as *chatting*.

9.8 Making a Video Call

In the previous section you have learned how to send and receive instant messages. You can also use a video and sound connection to communicate with your contact in *Live Messenger*. This is called a *video call*.

⇨ **Please note:**

To be able to make a video call you need to have a webcam and a microphone connected to your computer. If you do not have these yet, you can just read through this section.
In addition to that, you need a contact that is online and also has a webcam and a microphone or headset. You can also use a webcam with a built-in microphone.
In that case you hear the sound of your contact through your computer speakers.
If you do not have anyone to practice with, you can just read through this section.

You can start the video call from the window where you send the instant messages like this:

Before you can start the video call, you need to first check the settings for your webcam, speakers and microphone. You see the window *Audio and Video Settings*:

☞ **Close all other programs that play sound or display video**

☞ **Check if your webcam, speakers and microphone or headset are plugged in**

When everything is connected correctly:

🖰 **Click** Next >

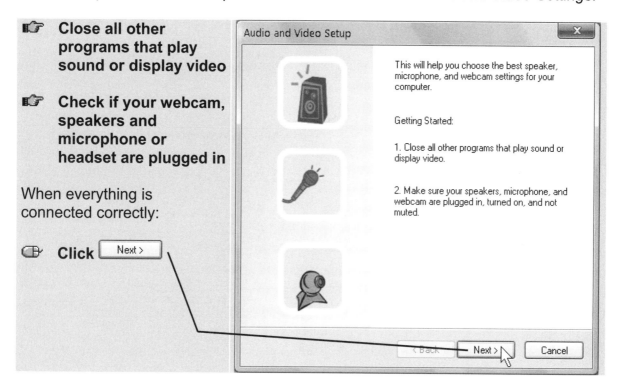

You start by setting the right volume for your speakers.

🖰 **Click** Play Sound

You hear some music. If the sound is too loud or not loud enough, you can use the volume slider ▭ to adjust the volume:

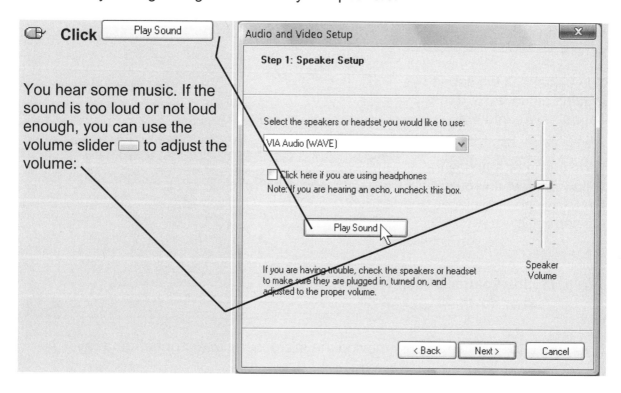

When you are satisfied with the sound:

☞ **Click** [Stop Sound]

☞ **Click** [Next >]

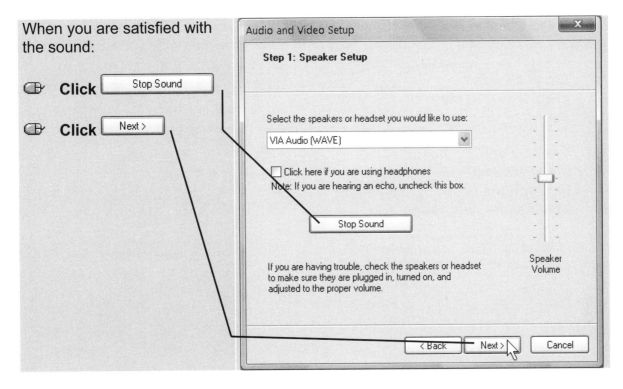

Now you can adjust the microphone settings:

If there are more microphones connected to your computer, you can choose the right microphone here: ──────

You can check the sound by reading aloud the text that appears here into the microphone: ──────

If the indicator reaches the yellow area when you speak, the microphone is placed and set correctly: ──────

If not:

☞ **Drag the volume slider up or down** ──────

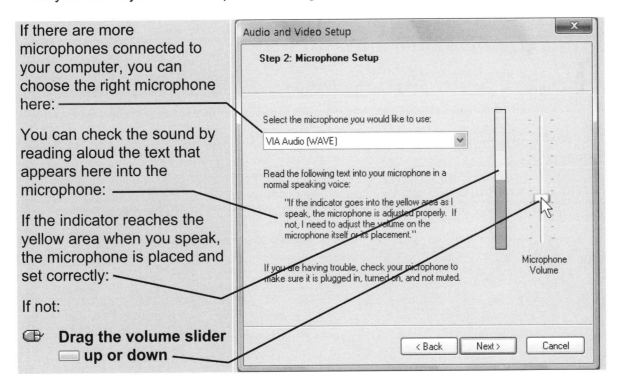

If you need to, you can also try moving the microphone closer or farther away.

When the recording volume is set correctly:

☞ **Click** Next >

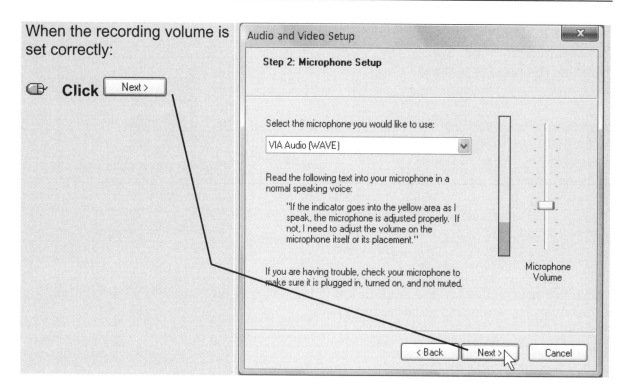

Now you can adjust the settings of your webcam.

Here you can select the webcam you want to use: —

Please note: if there is a TV tuner card installed in your computer, it may sometimes be displayed as a webcam. Make sure to click the right webcam.
You can use the Preview pane to adjust the angle and focus of the image: —

☞ **Adjust the angle and focus of your webcam until you are satisfied with the image**

☞ **Click** Finish

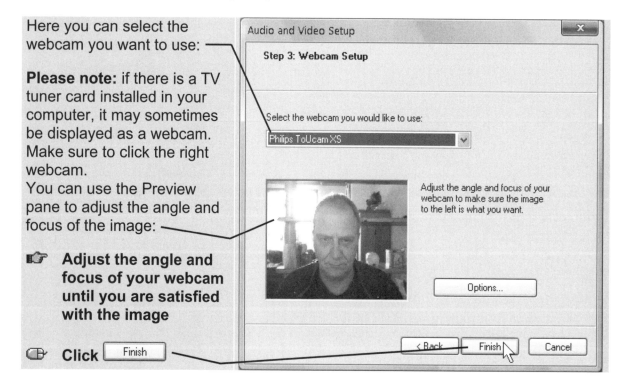

You see that the conversation window has changed. You hear the sound of a phone ringing.

As soon as your contact accepts the video call, the image of his or her webcam appears here: ——

Here you see the image of your own webcam: ——

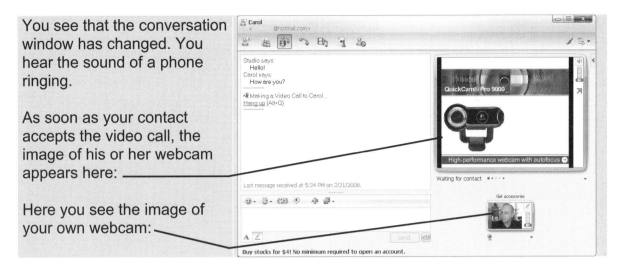

Now that your contact has accepted the video call, you can see and speak to each other over the video and sound connection.

When your conversation has finished, you can break the connection:

🖰 **Click** Hang up ——

👉 **Close the window** *&*3

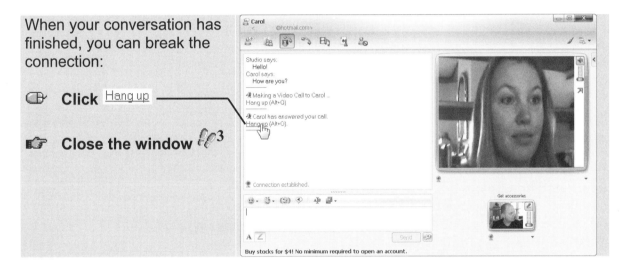

The video call is a fun and convenient way to get in touch with your friends and family. Even if they are on the opposite side of the globe, you can talk face to face!

💡 **Tip**

Full screen
During the video call you can display the image of your contact's webcam full screen. You can do that like this:

🖰 **Click** ↗ ——

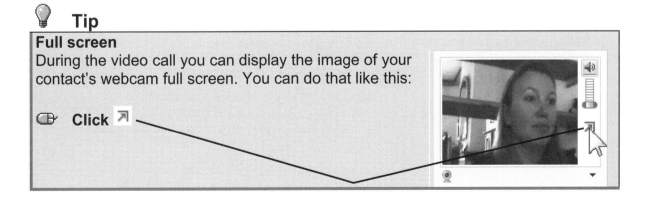

9.9 The Windows Live Messenger Settings

To understand how *Messenger* responds to your Internet connection, you can take a look at the program settings:

☞ **Click your name, for example**
Studio (Online) ▾

☞ **Click** Options...

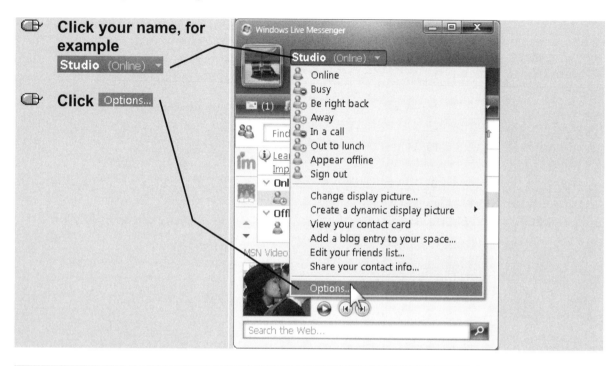

You see this window:

☞ **Read through the settings on this page**

You can adjust your screen name for example.

☞ **Click** General

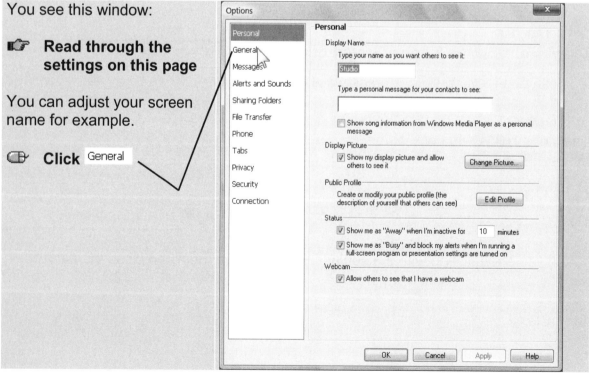

The default settings of *Messenger* assume that you have a permanent Internet connection and that you want to keep *Messenger* on at all times.

The program is started as soon as you turn on your computer:

Both the main window and *Windows Live Today* are opened:

If you do not want that, you can remove the check marks for these options.

If you want to sign in automatically when there is an Internet connection:

☞ **Click to check mark**
Allow automatic sign in when connec

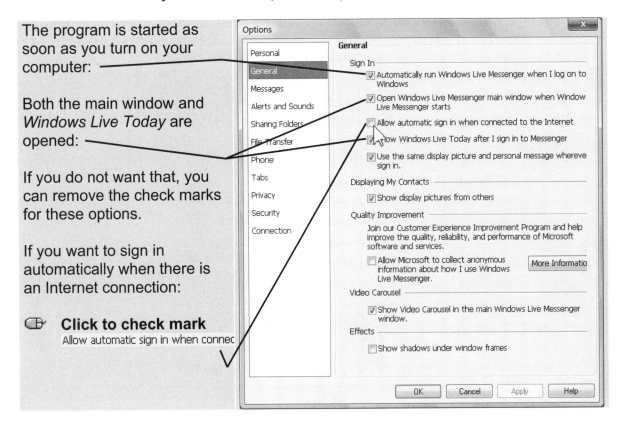

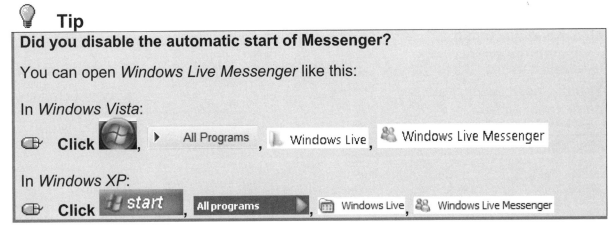

💡 **Tip**

Did you disable the automatic start of Messenger?

You can open *Windows Live Messenger* like this:

In *Windows Vista*:

☞ **Click** [Start], ▶ All Programs, 📁 Windows Live, 👥 Windows Live Messenger

In *Windows XP*:

☞ **Click** [start], All programs ▶, 🗔 Windows Live, 👥 Windows Live Messenger

When you are satisfied with the settings, you can save them and close the *Options* window:

☞ **Click** [OK]

9.10 Your status

When you are online with *Messenger,* you can show your contacts that you are ready to receive instant messages or that you are busy. This is called your *status.* You can view your possible status messages like this:

☞ **Click your name, for example**
Studio (Online) ▼

You see a list with various messages you can show to your contacts:

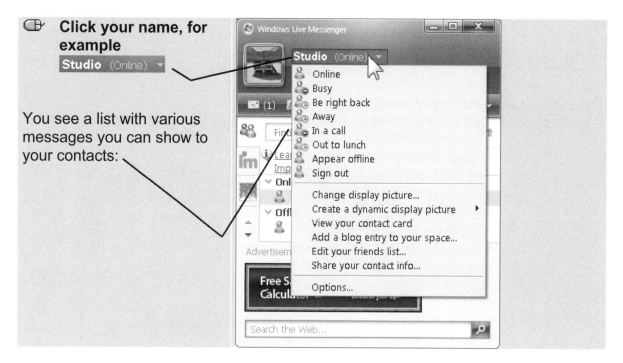

In this way you can decide for yourself if you want to make contact or not. Maybe you do not want to be disturbed because you are making a phone call. When you choose 🔵 In a call , this status appears in your contacts' window right away.

You can also give yourself the 🔵 Appear offline status, while you are still connected to the Internet. This gives you more control over your communication.

9.11 Quitting Windows Live Messenger

If you want to quit using *Windows Live Messenger*, you cannot simply close the window. This is what happens:

☞ **Click** [X]

The *Messenger* window has disappeared, but the program remains active.

The system area of the taskbar now looks like this:

The green icon indicates that *Messenger* is still active.

You can open *Windows Live Messenger* again:

☞ **Double-click**

The *Messenger* window is opened again.
In order to really quit the *Windows Live Messenger* program, you must sign out.

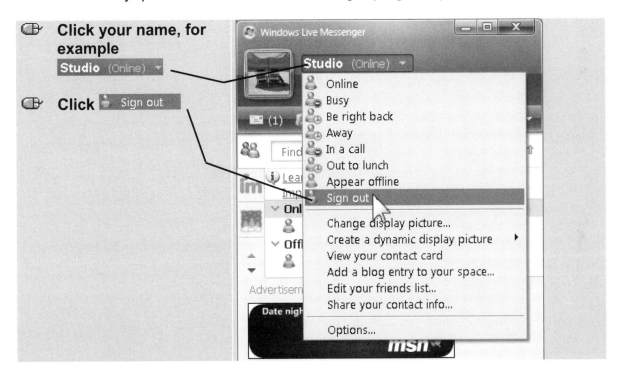

☞ **Click your name, for example**
Studio (Online)

☞ **Click** Sign out

Now you can close the *Windows Live Messenger* window:

☞ **Click** X

The program is closed and you are no longer signed in to *Messenger*.

9.12 Background Information

Glossary	
Chatting	Real-time communication between two or more people based on typed text messages that are sent using computers that are connected to the Internet at the same time.
Contact	The people that you have set up to communicate with using instant messaging in *Windows Live Messenger*.
Instant message	Abbreviated as *IM*, is a typed message you send to a contact that is online at the same time using *Windows Live Messenger*.
Status	You can use your status in *Windows Live Messenger* to show if you are available to receive instant messages or not. For example, you can select 'Busy' or 'In a call'.
Video call	Conversation with a contact over a sound and video connection.
Webcam	Small camera you can connect to the computer and use to send images over the Internet. This way you can create a video connection with a contact.
Welcome to Windows Live	Webpage containing *Windows Live* news that is opened by default when you sign in to *Messenger*.
Windows Live ID	A *Microsoft* service that enables you to use various *Microsoft* services with only one account. When you create a webmail address that ends with hotmail.com of live.com, you automatically have a *Windows Live ID* at your disposal. You can sign in to *Windows Live Messenger* using your *Windows Live ID*.
Windows Live Messenger	Program you can use to connect to your contacts over the Internet. For example by sending instant messages or making a video call.

Webcam

Webcam is short for web camera. Webcams are miniature cameras, especially designed to shoot video images that can be used in Internet applications.

The resolution of these images is low, for example 640x480 pixels – depending on the camera. This reduces the file size.

The quality of webcam images cannot be compared to that of an average digital video camera. However, the quality is sufficient enough to use on the Internet, especially when you look at the image in a small window instead of full screen.

Many webcams also have a feature that allows you to take photos. Compared to a digital photo camera the quality of these images is poor, but good enough for use on the Internet. Some webcams also have a built-in microphone.

The price of a simple webcam is about $ 25. The more expensive models may cost $ 100 or more. Make sure you choose a webcam that is compatible with the version of *Windows* running on your computer and any particular program you want to use with it.

Do you use a laptop computer? Then you can check if there is a built-in webcam above the screen:

Generally a webcam can be connected to a USB port of your computer. Here you see the USB plug of the webcam connected to the USB port at the back of the system case:

Many computers also have USB ports at the front of the system case:

A USB port can be recognized by this symbol:

10. Windows Live Spaces: Your Own Place on the Internet

Windows Live Spaces is *Microsoft's* free social networking and blogging platform where you can create a personal website. You can use this website to publish and share your photos, add text and connect to other *Windows Live Spaces* users. Over 120 million people worldwide use *Live Spaces*.

When you have your own *Space* you can write a *blog,* upload photos, create lists, add gadgets and RSS feeds. You can personalize your *Space* by designing it with your favorite colors and themes. Even the structure of your *Space* can be easily modified.

You decide for yourself who is allowed to see your *Space*. This might be everyone on the Internet or just a select group of friends.

Windows Live Spaces is a free service provided by *Microsoft*. Banner advertisements appear on the *Windows Live Spaces* website. This enables *Microsoft* to defray some of the costs of providing the service. Subscribers to premium *Windows Live* services are able to turn these advertisements off.

In this chapter you will learn how to:

- sign in to *Windows Live Spaces*;
- create a profile;
- protect your online identity;
- modify your *Space*;
- create a blog;
- share your photos;
- find people with similar interests;
- view your Friends list.

⇨ Please note:

The *Windows Live Spaces* website is frequently updated.
The screenshots you see in this chapter may look a bit different from what you see on your screen. For example, a certain button or link you need to click may have been moved or have a slightly different name. In that case, take a good look at the window to find the correct link.

10.1 Signing In to Windows Live Spaces

Windows Live Spaces is a free online service provided by *Microsoft*. To be able to use *Windows Live Spaces*, you will need a *Windows Live ID*. This is a webmail address that ends with **hotmail.com** or **live.com**. You have already created this free webmail address in *Chapter 8*. Your *Windows Live ID* gives you access to *Windows Live Spaces* where you can create your own *Space*.

 HELP! I did not create a Windows Live ID yet.

If you would like to obtain a Windows Live ID now, follow the instructions in chapter 8.

☞ **See *section 8.1 Creating a Windows Live Hotmail address***

☞ **Open *Internet Explorer* 🐾¹**

☞ **Surf to web address www.home.live.com 🐾²**

You see the *Windows Live* home page:

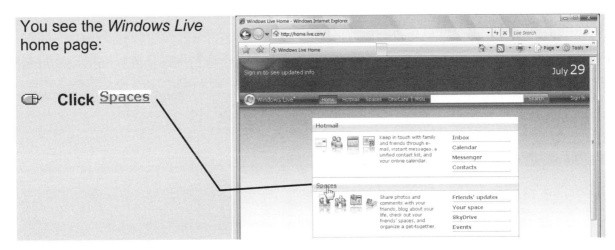

🖰 **Click Spaces**

You see the *Windows Live Spaces* home page:

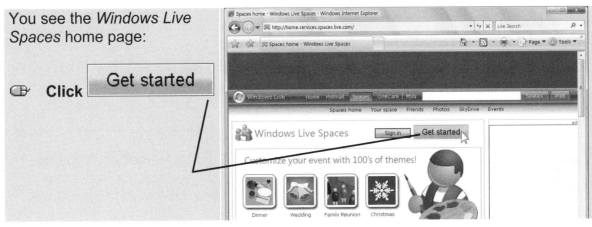

🖰 **Click Get started**

You see the *Sign in* page. Here you can enter your hotmail.com or live.com webmail address:

Type your webmail address next to
Windows Live ID:

Type your password next to Password:

Click Sign in

Now your own *Space* is created.

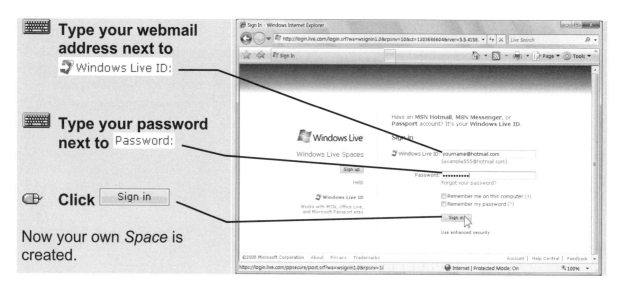

10.2 Your Profile

You are now viewing your own *Space* page. This webpage is still empty. The first thing you will do is edit your profile.

➡ **Please note:**

The layout of a new *Space* page may change once in awhile. It is possible that the page you see on your screen does not match the examples in this book. In that case you may have to search for the hyperlinks and buttons that are used in this chapter.

Click Edit profile

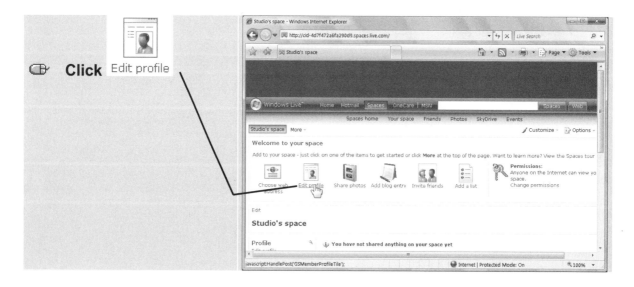

You start by entering the name you want to use on your *Space* page.

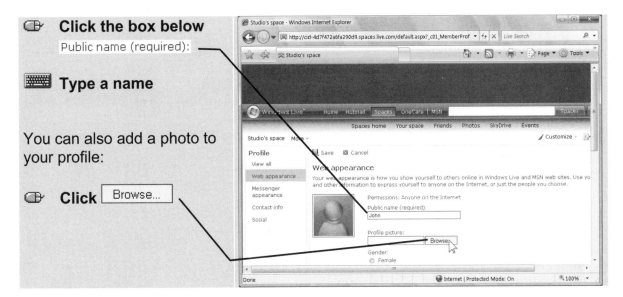

☞ **Click the box below**

Public name (required):

⌨ **Type a name**

You can also add a photo to your profile:

☞ **Click** Browse...

You see the window *Choose file*. If you use *Windows XP*, this folder looks a little bit different. This does not make a difference for the actions you need to perform.

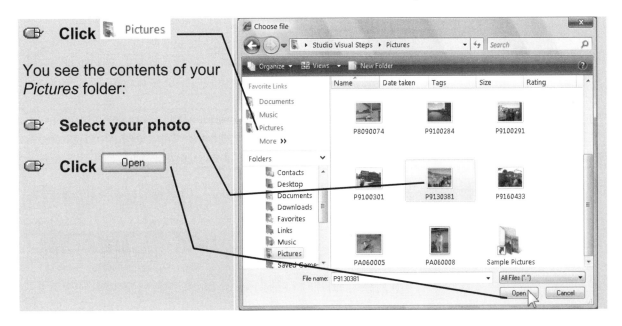

☞ **Click** 🖼 Pictures

You see the contents of your *Pictures* folder:

☞ **Select your photo**

☞ **Click** Open

The photo is not uploaded immediately. When you finish filling in the additional information and press the save button, the photo will be uploaded.

Drag the scroll bar down

Enter the requested information

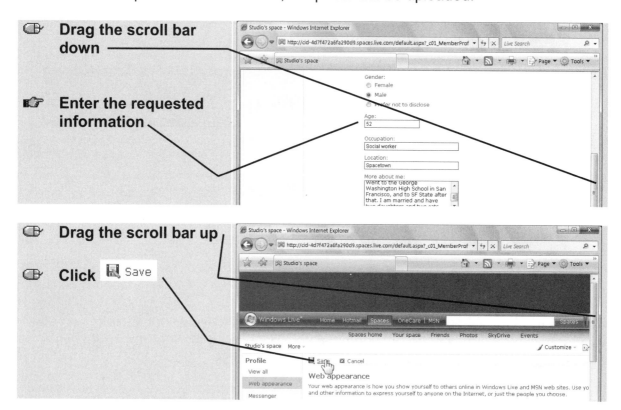

The *Contact info* page appears. Here you can add more information to your profile. This additional information is however optional. The information you enter on this page will only be visible to you and the people you allow to see this part of your profile.

Enter the requested information

Drag the scroll bar up

Click Save

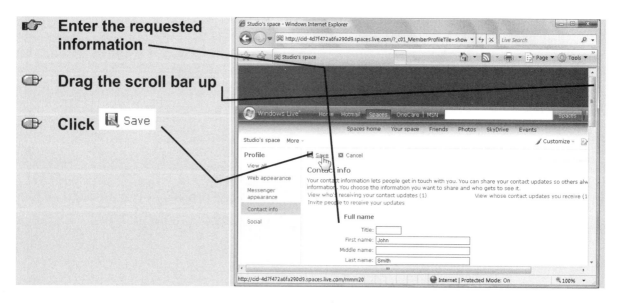

The final area of your profile information is the *Social* page. Here you can select who is allowed to see your profile:

☞ **Click** `Social`

☞ **Click**
`Anyone on the Internet`
next to `Permissions:`

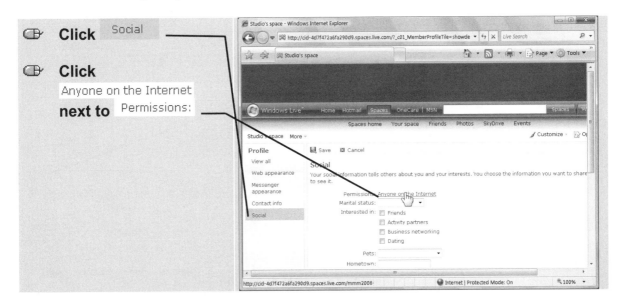

You see the form where you can select who is allowed to view your social information. You can choose between just you, anyone on the Internet, or just your *Messenger* contacts, *Spaces* friends or webmail contacts:

☞ **Drag the scroll bar down**

☞ **Click to select the permission of your choice**

☞ **Click** `Save`

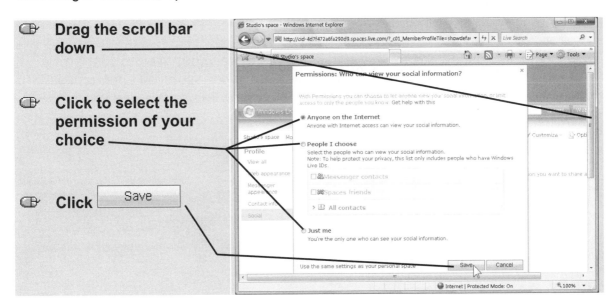

In the next window you can add more information to your profile. For example, next to `Interested in:` you can select the type of contacts you may be interested in.

It is not mandatory to enter any information on this page:

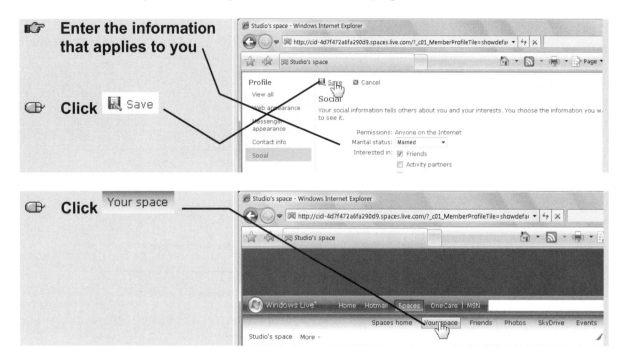

☞ **Enter the information that applies to you**

🖱 **Click** 🖫 Save

🖱 **Click** Your space

10.3 Editing Your Space

You can customize the layout of your *Space* to suit your own preferences. For example, you can change the title of your *Space* and display a blog and a photo album. You can start by editing the title:

🖱 **Click** Edit

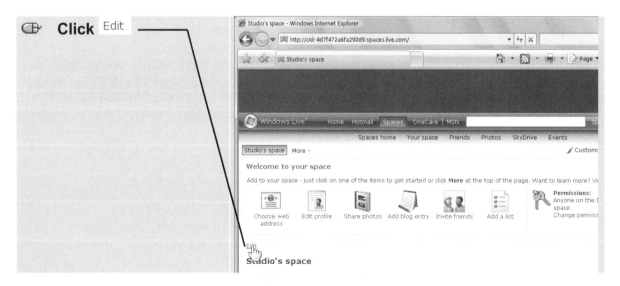

You see the window *Edit the title and tagline* where you can change the title of your *Space*. You can also change the font and the style:

Type a title next to
Text (required):

Type a tagline next to
Text:

If you want, you can choose a different font, size, style and color

Drag the scroll bar down

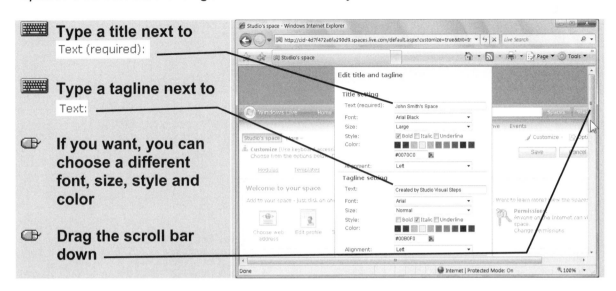

You see a preview of your new title and tagline:

Click Save

Now you can select which modules to display on your *Space*:

Click More

A menu appears:

Click Add other modules

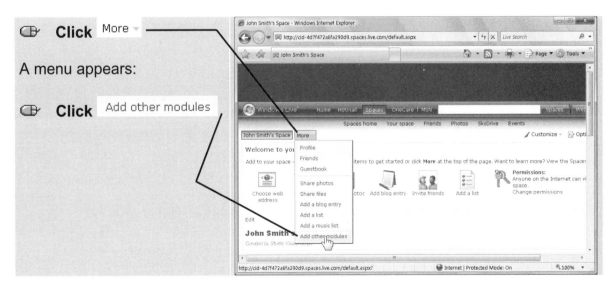

You see a tab with different modules. You can decide for yourself which modules you want to display or hide on your *Space*. You can change the default setting by clicking `Hide` or `Show` next to a module. In this example the modules ☑ Guestbook , 🖼 Photos and 📝 Blog are visible on the *Space*:

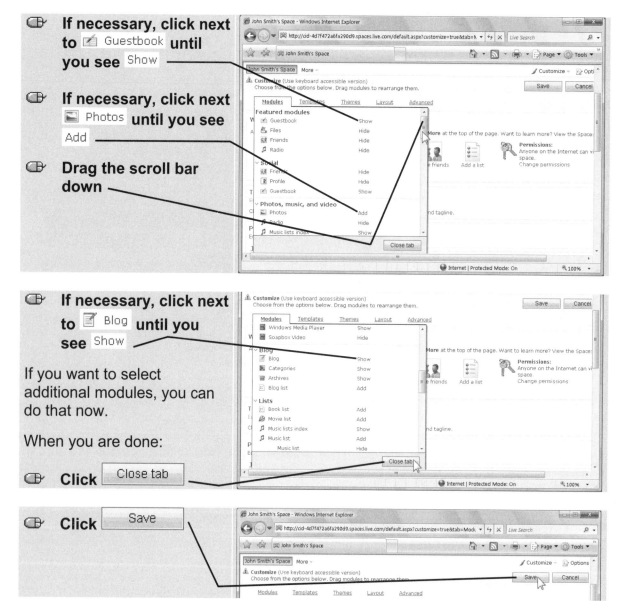

☞ **If necessary, click next to** ☑ Guestbook **until you see** `Show`

☞ **If necessary, click next** 🖼 Photos **until you see** `Add`

☞ **Drag the scroll bar down**

☞ **If necessary, click next to** 📝 Blog **until you see** `Show`

If you want to select additional modules, you can do that now.

When you are done:

☞ **Click** Close tab

☞ **Click** Save

You have used the Modules tab to display the modules *Blog, Guestbook* and *Photos* on your *Space*. You can use the tabs Templates , Themes , Layout and Advanced to change the appearance of your *Space*. You can try that yourself later.

In the next section, you will learn how to add some content to your *Space*.

10.4 Selecting a Web Address

In *Windows Live Spaces* you can choose the web address for your *Space.* You can use this web address to inform other people about your *Space.* You can choose your web address like this:

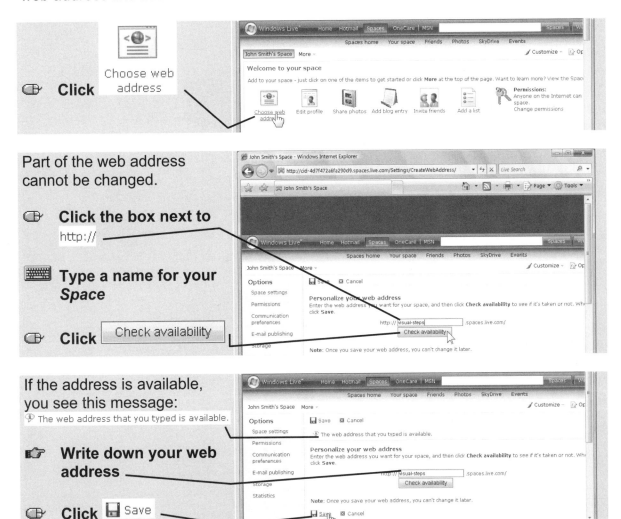

Click Choose web address

Part of the web address cannot be changed.

Click the box next to http://

Type a name for your Space

Click Check availability

If the address is available, you see this message:
The web address that you typed is available.

Write down your web address

Click 🖫 Save

 HELP! The address is not available.

If the address you typed is not available, you will need to try a different one.

Type a different name

Or

Select a web address from the list of suggested web addresses

10.5 Starting Your Blog

You can maintain a blog on your *Space*. A blog, also known as a weblog or web log is a type of online journal or diary. To add your first blog entry:

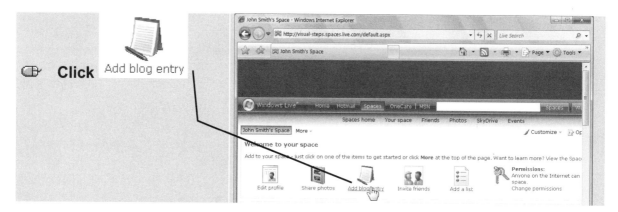

⊕ **Click** Add blog entry

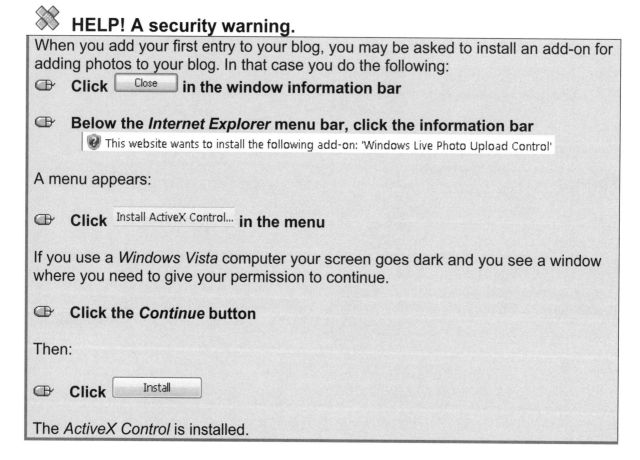

HELP! A security warning.

When you add your first entry to your blog, you may be asked to install an add-on for adding photos to your blog. In that case you do the following:

⊕ **Click** Close **in the window information bar**

⊕ **Below the *Internet Explorer* menu bar, click the information bar**

> 🛡 This website wants to install the following add-on: "Windows Live Photo Upload Control"

A menu appears:

⊕ **Click** Install ActiveX Control... **in the menu**

If you use a *Windows Vista* computer your screen goes dark and you see a window where you need to give your permission to continue.

⊕ **Click the *Continue* button**

Then:

⊕ **Click** Install

The *ActiveX Control* is installed.

You see a window with a text editor. If you are accustomed to using *Word*, you will see many familiar text editing options such as font size, font color, bold and italics:

Type a title next to
Title (required):

Type a short text in the text box

Click ✓ Publish entry

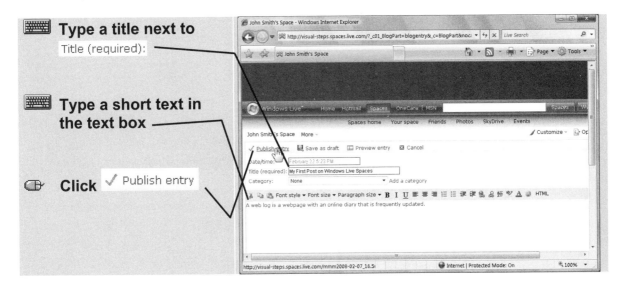

You see your own *Space* again:

Drag the scroll bar down

Here you can see the first post has been added to your blog:

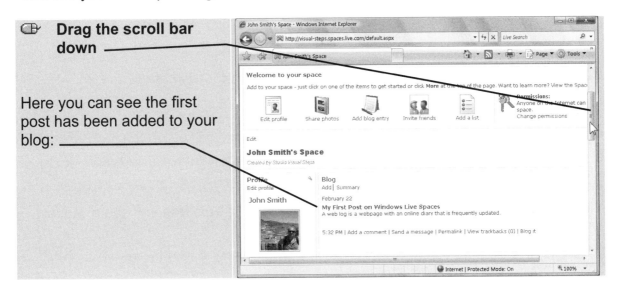

10.6 Sharing Your Photos

You can also share your photos on your *Space*. Start by bringing the top of your *Space* page into view:

Drag the scroll bar up

Click Share photos

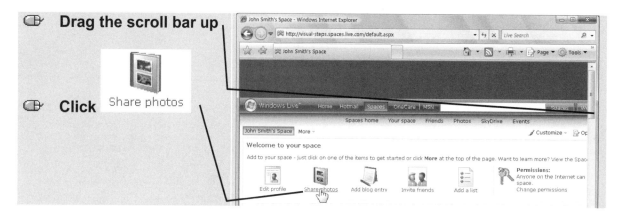

Windows Live Spaces organizes your photos in albums. To create your first album:

Click Add album

Next to Album title: you see today's date. You can change this name into something more meaningful:

Type the title of your album next to
Album title:

Click Save and close

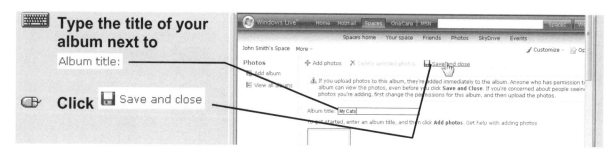

Now you can add photos to this album:

Click (0) My Cats

Click Edit album

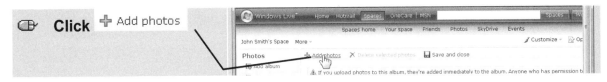

Click Add photos

The folder Pictures is opened.

You can use the sample pictures that come packaged with *Windows*, or your own photos:

Select the photos for the album

Click Upload Now

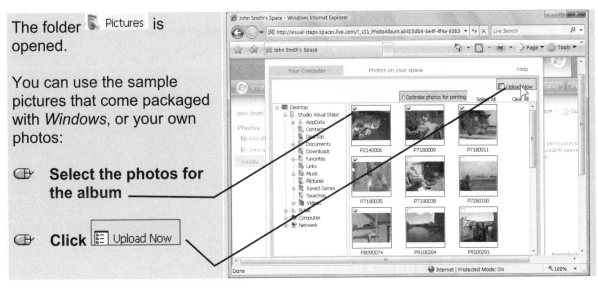

Uploading is the transferring or copying of the selected files (photos) from your computer to another computer, usually a larger system such as the one hosting the online application *Windows Live Spaces.* You can follow the upload in the window *Upload Progress.*

You see smaller versions (thumbnails) of the uploaded images appear on your *Space:*

You can also add captions to the photos, but that is not necessary now.

☞ **Click** 💾 Save and close

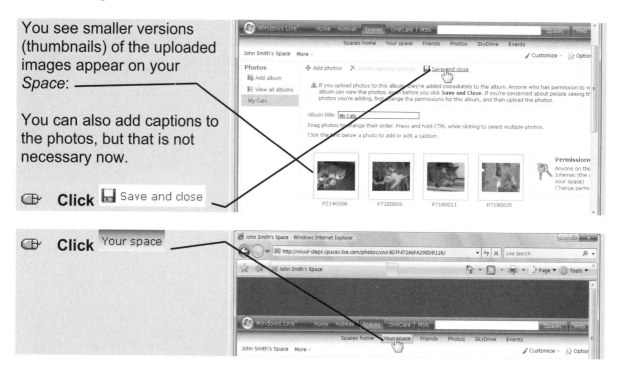

☞ **Click** Your space

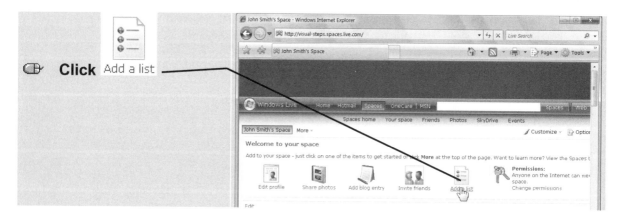

10.7 Adding a List

You can also add lists to your *Space,* for example a list of your favorite books or movies. You can do that like this:

☞ **Click** Add a list

You see the window *Add a List.* In this example you add a list of your favorite songs:

Type the name of your list next to List title:

Type a brief description of the list next to List description:

Click to select the list type

Click Add a list

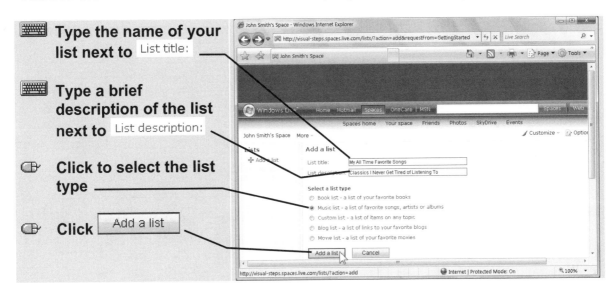

Now you can start adding entries to your list:

Click ✚ Add item

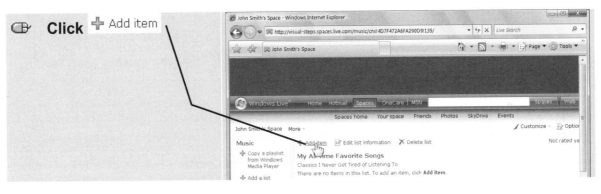

Type the information about the first song in the boxes

Drag the scroll bar down a little

Click Save

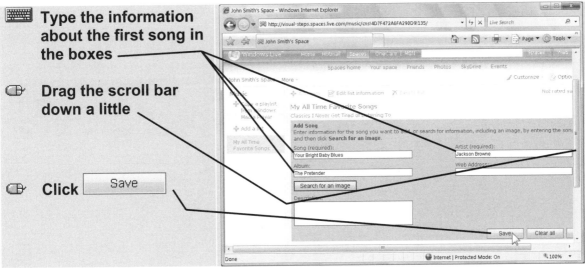

You see the information you entered in the music list. You can add more items to the list in the same way. In the example below a top 5 was created.

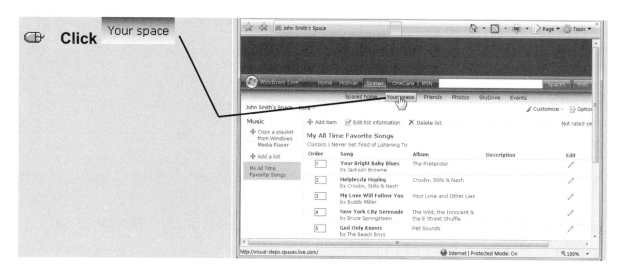

10.8 Finding People with Similar Interests

Windows Live Spaces contains a convenient search feature. You can use it to find people with similar interests:

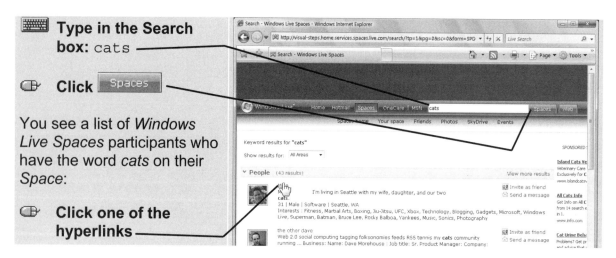

You see the *Space* of a *Windows Live Spaces* participant:

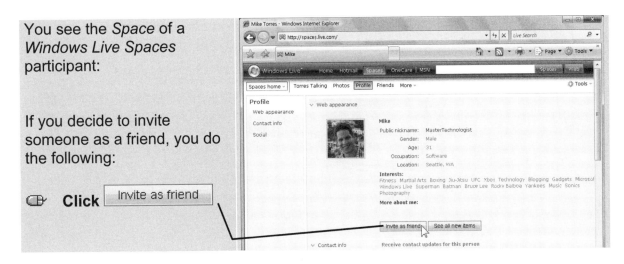

If you decide to invite someone as a friend, you do the following:

☞ **Click** [Invite as friend]

The person you just invited is added to your friends list. He or she will receive an invitation that can be accepted or declined.

You see a window where you can edit the information for this friend.

You do not need to change anything now. Save this friend to your friends list:

☞ **Click** [💾 Save]

You return again to your own *Space*.

 Tip

Returning to your own Space
When you are viewing someone else's *Space*, you can quickly return to your own *Space* like this:

☞ **Click** [Your space]

10.9 Viewing Your Friends List

In the previous example you have invited one friend. In time, your list of friends will grow. Your Friends list automatically keeps track of the people who consider themselves your friends:

 If necessary, click
Friends

 Place the mouse

pointer on the icon
of one of your friends

You see a small popup
window with a summary of
that friend's *Space*:

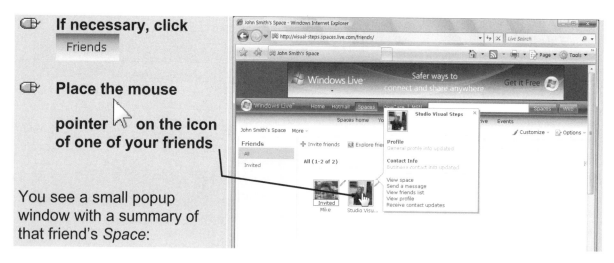

💡 Tip

Invited
The people you have invited to become your friend will be marked as | Invited | in
your friends list until they have accepted the invitation.

💡 Tip

Editing a friend
To edit the description or tags of a friend:

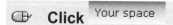 **Click the pencil icon** ✏ **next to their thumbnail image**

To return to your own *Space*:

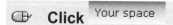 **Click** Your space

10.10 Signing Out

If you want to stop working on your *Space* you can sign out:

In the top right corner of the window:

☞ **Click** `Sign out`

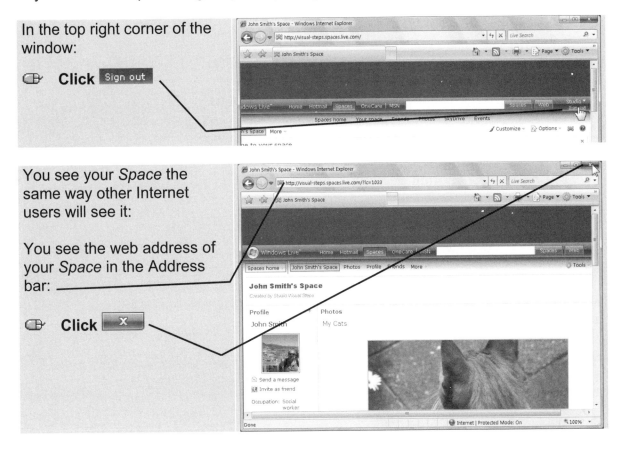

You see your *Space* the same way other Internet users will see it:

You see the web address of your *Space* in the Address bar:

☞ **Click** `X`

In this chapter you have learned how to create and manage your own *Space* on *Windows Live Spaces*.

10.11 Background Information

Glossary	
Account	An account gives the user access to a service. To be able to access *Windows Live Spaces* you need a *Windows Live ID* and a password.
ActiveX control	Technology that allows interactivity between various components or programs. These controls need to be installed in *Internet Explorer* separately.
Blog	A *blog*, also called a web log or weblog, is a webpage with content that is frequently updated by the owner. You can maintain a blog in *Windows Live Spaces*.
Hotmail	*Hotmail* is a free webmail service provided by *Microsoft*.
Profile	*Windows Live Spaces* feature that can be used to add personal information to a *Space*.
Webmail	E-mail service that is offered through a website. You can use this convenient service to read your e-mail on any computer in the world that is connected to the Internet.
Windows Live ID	A *Microsoft* service that allows you access to various online services provided by *Microsoft* with just one account. When you create a webmail address that ends with hotmail.com or live.com, you automatically have a *Windows Live ID* at your disposal. You can sign in to *Windows Live Spaces* using your *Windows Live ID*.

10.12 Tips

 Tip

Changing the appearance

You can modify the appearance of your *Space* to suit your own taste. *Windows Live Spaces* offers a number of different options for personalization:

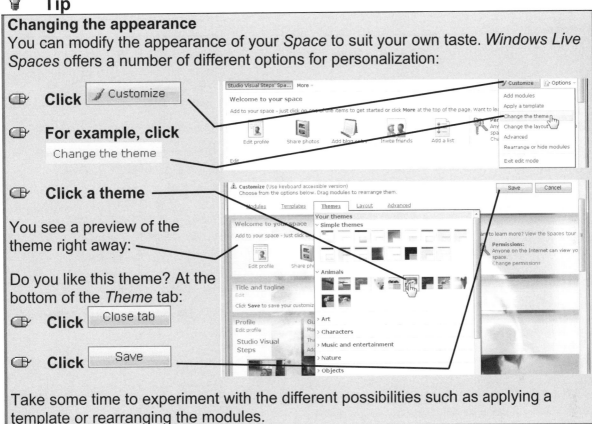

☞ **Click** ✎ Customize

☞ **For example, click** Change the theme

☞ **Click a theme** ───

You see a preview of the theme right away: ────

Do you like this theme? At the bottom of the *Theme* tab:

☞ **Click** Close tab

☞ **Click** Save

Take some time to experiment with the different possibilities such as applying a template or rearranging the modules.

 Tip

Deleting your Space

At some point you may want to remove your *Space*. In *Windows Live Spaces* this is known as 'clearing'. When you *clear* your *Space*, the contents are removed and the web address is no longer available. You can delete your *Space* like this:
Please note: if you want to keep the web address of your *Space*, it is a better option to just clear the contents of each separate module.

In the top right corner of the window:

☞ **Click** 🗒 Options

☞ **Click** Space settings

At the bottom of the window:

☞ **Click** Clear your space ✗

☞ **Click** Clear your space

11. Your Home Video on YouTube

The website *YouTube* has developed into a huge phenomenon on the Internet. *YouTube* is a free online streaming service where people can share their digital videos. The ease with which one can post a video clip and allow others to view and comment on it has made *YouTube* enormously successful. The contents of these clips can be as diverse as a vacation movie, a family pet, and people singing songs or footage of a parade or a public speech. *YouTube* has profoundly affected the ways in which we receive news and information.

YouTube was founded in February 2005. At this moment the website is owned by *Google*, the company that operates the popular search engine and other services such as *Google Earth* and *Google Maps*. *YouTube* now accounts for a third of all video viewed on the web. More than 60,000 new video clips are uploaded each day. By now, the most popular video clip has been watched at least 60 million times. Burgeoning artists have attained overnight celebrity status largely due to videos that were posted on *YouTube*.

Anyone can watch video clips on *YouTube*, but if you sign up for a *YouTube* account, you gain access to the *YouTube* community. With a membership you can rate the video clips and leave comments and you can upload your own videos.

In this chapter you will learn how to:

- find and play video clips on *YouTube*;
- sign up for a *YouTube* account;
- upload a video to *YouTube* and remove it again.

⇨ **Please note:**

In one of the exercises, you will upload the practice movie to the *YouTube* website. Later in the section, you will learn how to remove the video clip. **Make sure to remove the practice video clip!** It would be very unfortunate to saturate the *YouTube* website with thousands of the same practice movie.

Please note:

To perform the exercises in this chapter, you will need to copy the practice movie from the website of this book, **www.visualsteps.com/online**.
You can read how to do that on the website **www.visualsteps.com/online**, under the heading *Practice files*.

 Please note:

The creators of websites are constantly adding new information. The sreenshots used in this chapter may look different from what you see on your screen. This should not pose any problems; the basic features will not be removed. However, it is possible that certain features will be moved to a different location on the website.

11.1 Using YouTube

Everyone can watch videos on the *YouTube* website. You open the website like this:

☞ **Open *Internet Explorer*** 🖐¹

☞ **Surf to the web address www.youtube.com** 🖐²

You see the *YouTube* website:

Tabs for different parts of *YouTube*: —————

Searching for clips: —————

Promoted videos: —————

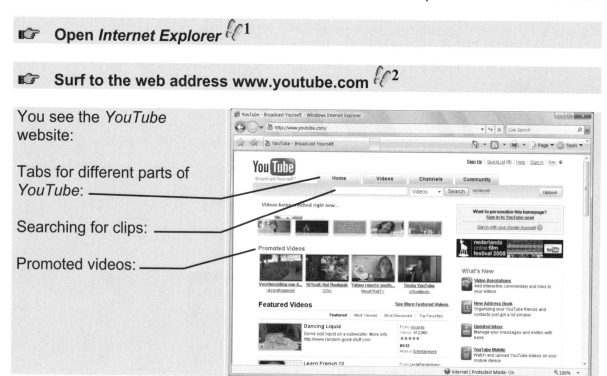

The examples used in this chapter are from the global *YouTube* website. Many countries have their own *YouTube* portal, for example the UK, Australia, Canada and New Zealand. You can switch to another site like this:

☞ **Click** Site: ● **in the top right-hand corner and select a country from the list**

11.2 Playing Video Clips on YouTube

There are several different ways for you to locate and view video clips on *YouTube*. Video clips that appear on the home page can be played right away. These video clips are either very popular or have received a high rating:

👆 **Click the first video clip below**
Featured Videos

The selected video starts playing right away in the video player:

The video you see on your screen will be different than what is shown here. New video content is added to the website regularly and the Featured Videos list is continuously updated.

👆 **Click** ⏸

HELP! I do not see the video player.

YouTube plays videos using the *Flash Player*. If you do not see a video player, you need to install the latest version of the *Flash Player*:

You see a warning:

👆 **Click**
Get the latest Flash player.

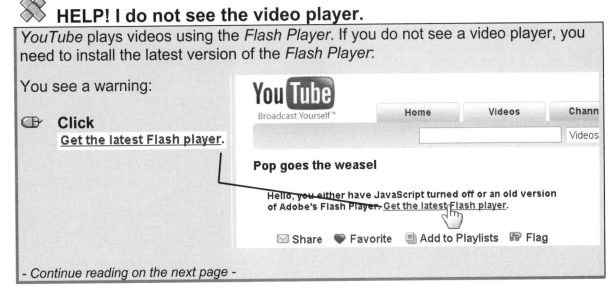

- Continue reading on the next page -

You see the *Flash Player* download page:

☞ **Click to remove the check mark for**
Free Google Toolbar

☞ **Click**

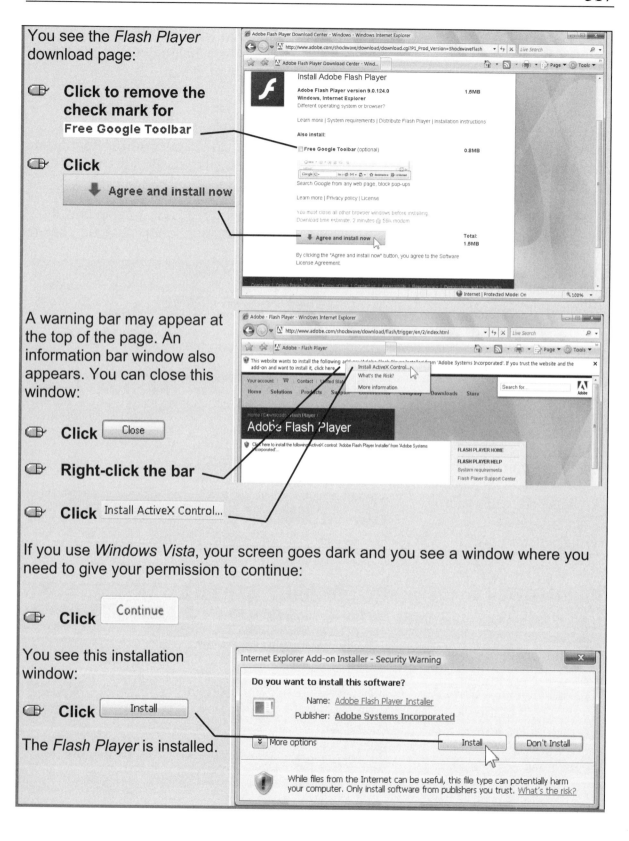

A warning bar may appear at the top of the page. An information bar window also appears. You can close this window:

☞ **Click** Close

☞ **Right-click the bar**

☞ **Click** Install ActiveX Control...

If you use *Windows Vista*, your screen goes dark and you see a window where you need to give your permission to continue:

☞ **Click** Continue

You see this installation window:

☞ **Click** Install

The *Flash Player* is installed.

When you click a video clip on *YouTube* it is *streamed* to your computer. This technology allows listening and viewing while content is still being downloaded. You do not have to wait for the entire video clip to be downloaded first.

Usually the video clips on *YouTube* are set to download faster than they play, so you can start watching the video immediately. Sometimes a short delay may occur for instance when trying to view a large sized video clip or when your Internet connection is not fast enough. In that case the video may not play continuously: it starts and stops and then starts again.

To avoid this problem you can pause the video by clicking  and waiting until the video clip has completely finished downloading. You can see that in the video player:

The red bar indicates how much of the video has been downloaded:

As soon as the video has downloaded completely you can play it again:

☞ **Click ▶**

The video starts playing at the point where you paused it earlier:

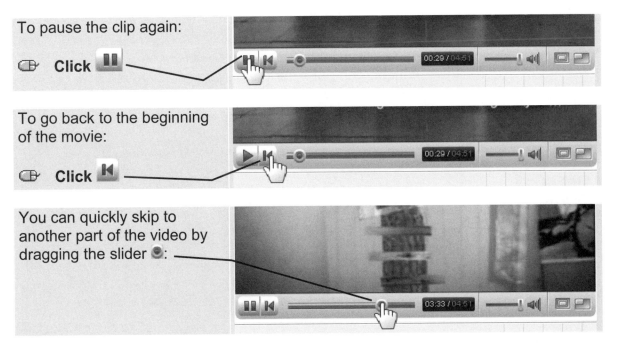

To pause the clip again:

☞ **Click ⏸**

To go back to the beginning of the movie:

☞ **Click ◀◀**

You can quickly skip to another part of the video by dragging the slider ●:

The other parts of the video player have these functions:

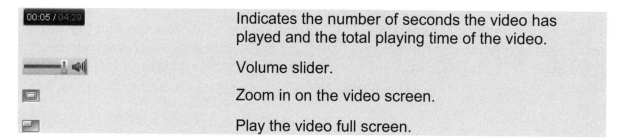

00:05 / 04:29	Indicates the number of seconds the video has played and the total playing time of the video.
Volume slider.	
Zoom in on the video screen.	
Play the video full screen.	

11.3 Finding Videos on YouTube

You can use the *YouTube* search feature to find a video by its subject or title:

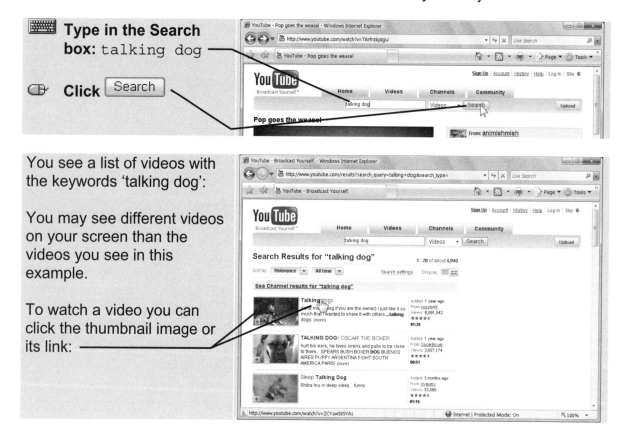

Type in the Search box: `talking dog`

☞ **Click** Search

You see a list of videos with the keywords 'talking dog':

You may see different videos on your screen than the videos you see in this example.

To watch a video you can click the thumbnail image or its link:

11.4 Signing Up for a YouTube Account

There are a number of benefits to being a *YouTube* member. You can rate the videos you watch and leave comments. You can also upload videos to *YouTube* yourself. Signing up for a *YouTube* account is relatively easy and should take only a few minutes of your time. You can sign up like this:

Click Sign Up

You see the sign up window:

Type your e-mail address next to
Email Address:

Type the password you choose yourself twice

Type a user name next to YouTube Username:

If your user name is already in use you see the message Username unavailable. Enter a different user name.

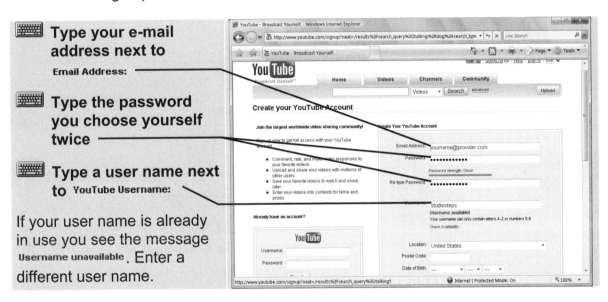

☞ **Write down your e-mail address, user name and password on a piece of paper and store it in a safe place**

Now you enter the rest of the required information:

☞ **Enter your personal information**

⌨ **Type the verification code you see in the image**

🖱 **Click to remove the check mark for**
☐ Let others find my channel on YouTube if they ha address

🖱 **Click a check mark for**
☑ I agree to the Terms of Use and Priva Policy.

🖱 **Click** Create my account

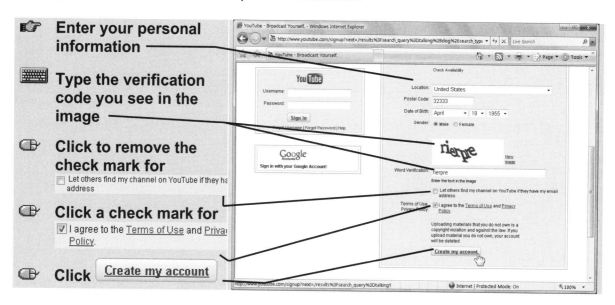

🡆 **Please note:**

If you did not type the verification code fast enough, an error message appears when you click the Create my account button. In that case you will need to type a new verification code and re-enter and confirm your password again. Also make sure to uncheck the ☐ Let others find my channel on YouTube if they have my email address option.

Your registration is processed:

You see this window:

A confirmation e-mail has been sent to your e-mail address.

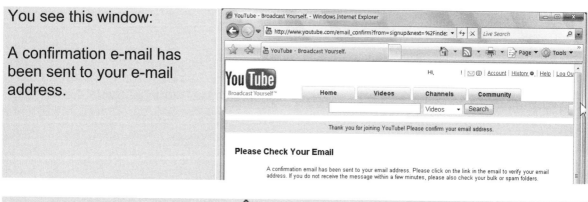

☞ **Open your e-mail program** 👣⁶

☞ **Receive your e-mail** 👣⁷

☞ **Open the new e-mail message from** *YouTube* 👣¹³

The e-mail contains a hyperlink:

☞ **Click** <u>click here</u>

Your registration is added to the *YouTube* database.

You see a new *Internet Explorer* window or tab with the confirmation of your registration: ─────

You are signed in automatically. You see your user name here: ─────

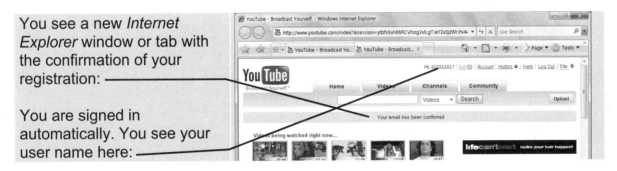

☞ **Close all windows of your e-mail program** ℓℓ3

Now you can begin to use *YouTube* as a registered member. To avoid confusion close any other open *YouTube* windows or tabs, except the one shown above:

In case of multiple tabs:

☞ **Click the first *YouTube* tab**

☞ **Click** ✕ ─────

In case of a new window:

☞ **Click** ▬✕▬ **in the previous *YouTube* window**

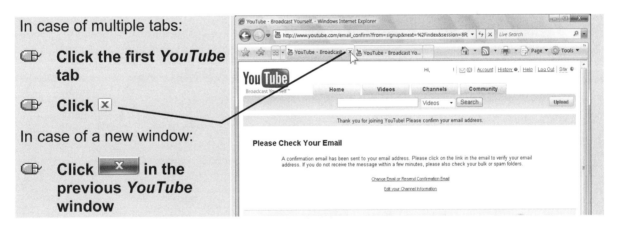

Now you only see the window that contains the text

Your email has been confirmed .

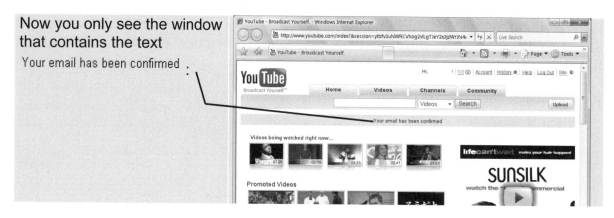

After you signed up for your *YouTube* account, a personal web space called *My Videos* was created for you. Here you can upload, edit and remove your own videos.

 Tip

Next time you visit the *YouTube* website, you are taken to your *My Videos* web space when you log in. To do so, click Log In in the top right-hand corner of the window.

11.5 Uploading a Video to YouTube

Now that you have a *YouTube* account, you can start uploading videos. To try this, you can use the practice video clip that you copied from the website of this book. It is a *Microsoft* video clip that comes packaged with some versions of the *Windows* operating system:

Click Upload

Before you can upload the video clip, you need to enter some information about it, such as title, description, tags and what category it falls under. The information about the video is divided into several segments.

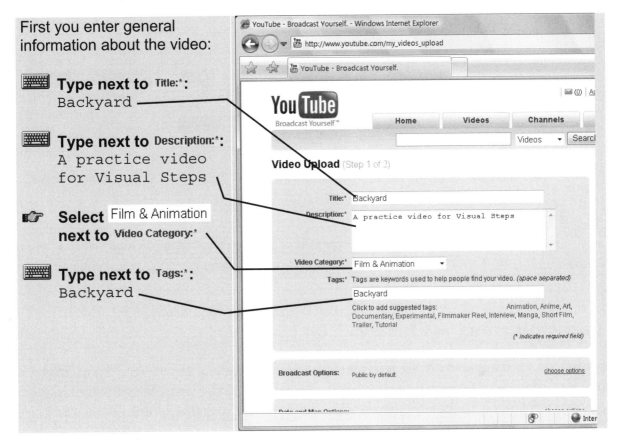

First you enter general information about the video:

⌨ **Type next to** Title:*:
Backyard

⌨ **Type next to** Description:*:
A practice video for Visual Steps

☞ **Select** Film & Animation **next to** Video Category:*

⌨ **Type next to** Tags:*:
Backyard

You can use *Broadcast Options* to select who is allowed to watch the video:

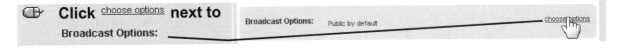

👆 **Click** choose options **next to** Broadcast Options:

You see the broadcast options:

Since this is a practice video, you can keep it private:

👆 **Click to select**
Private Viewable by you and up to 25 other

If you select the option
Public Share your video with the world!
anyone can watch the video.

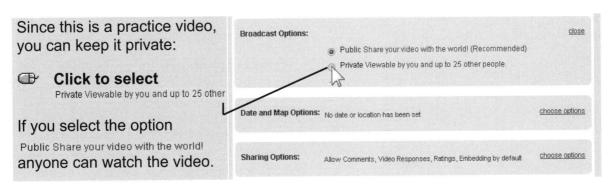

You see a box where you can view and enter your *YouTube* contacts:

If you just started using *YouTube*, this box is still empty. By clicking *Edit contact lists?* you can edit your contacts yourself:

Please note: if you click *Edit contact lists?* , the information you already added about the video is lost.

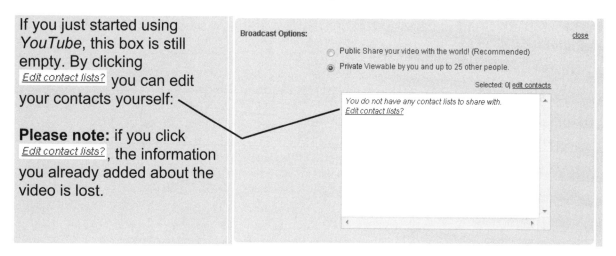

You are now the only one who can watch this video on *YouTube*.

In *Date and Map Options* you can enter information about the date and the location where the video was shot:

☞ **Click** choose options **next to**
Date and Map Options:

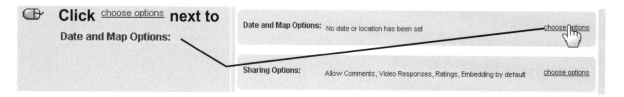

The *Date and Map Options* segment is opened:

☞ **Drag the scroll bar down**

Now you can enter the date the video was made. For this example, you can select today's date:

☞ **Click** Today

By dragging the marker ⚲ on the map, you can display the location where the video was made in *Google Maps*:

You can navigate with these buttons:

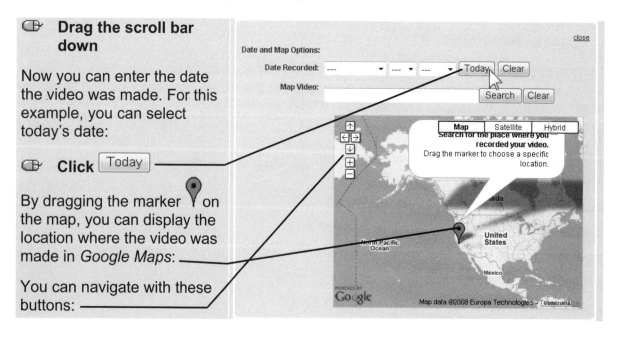

For example, you can place the marker on your home address.

In the segment *Sharing Options* you can enter if and how others are allowed to respond to your video clip:

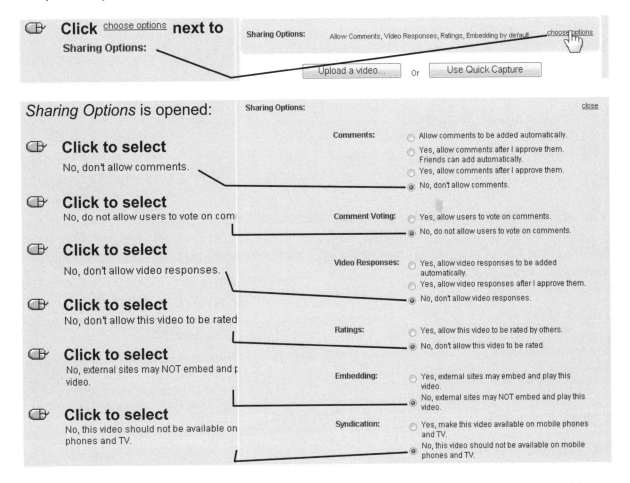

With these specific settings you have made sure that nobody can comment on this video with a text or video response, or rate it and the video cannot be played from other websites, on mobile phones or on TV.

If you upload your own video, you can determine the settings for yourself. In this example it is necessary to use these settings, because every reader of this book uses the same practice video.

Now you can go to the second step of the video upload:

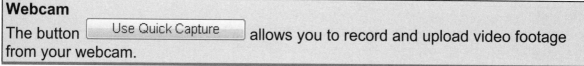

- **Click** Upload a video...

Tip

Webcam

The button Use Quick Capture allows you to record and upload video footage from your webcam.

The second step is selecting the video you want to upload:

You see this page:

- **Click** Browse...

Windows Vista users may now see a security warning:

- **Click** Allow

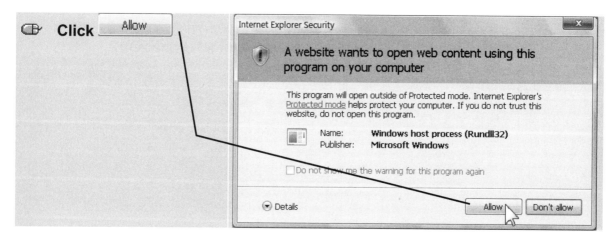

You see this window:

In *Windows Vista*:

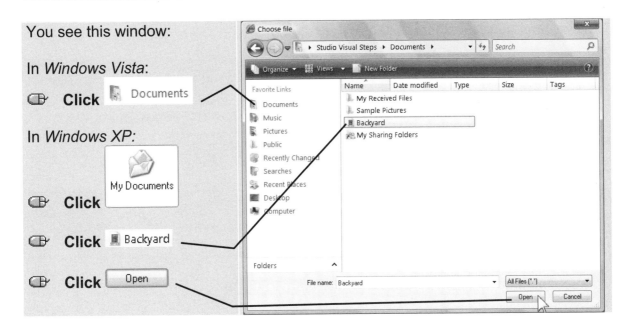

⊕ **Click** 📄 Documents

In *Windows XP*:

⊕ **Click** [My Documents icon]

⊕ **Click** 💻 Backyard

⊕ **Click** [Open]

Now you can upload the video:

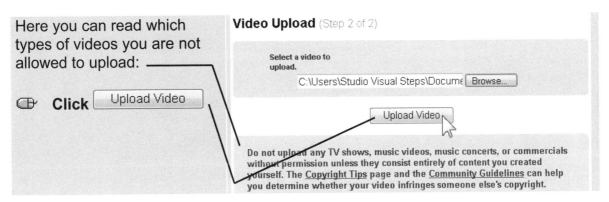

Here you can read which types of videos you are not allowed to upload:

⊕ **Click** [Upload Video]

Video Upload (Step 2 of 2)

Select a video to upload.

C:\Users\Studio Visual Steps\Docume [Browse...]

[Upload Video]

Do not upload any TV shows, music videos, music concerts, or commercials without permission unless they consist entirely of content you created yourself. The Copyright Tips page and the Community Guidelines can help you determine whether your video infringes someone else's copyright.

The practice video is uploaded from your computer to *YouTube*. This may take a couple of minutes, depending on the speed of your Internet connection:

You see this window:

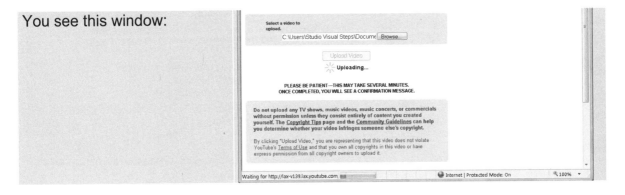

As soon as the upload is completed, you see a confirmation message:

You can use the button
Upload another video to upload
another video:

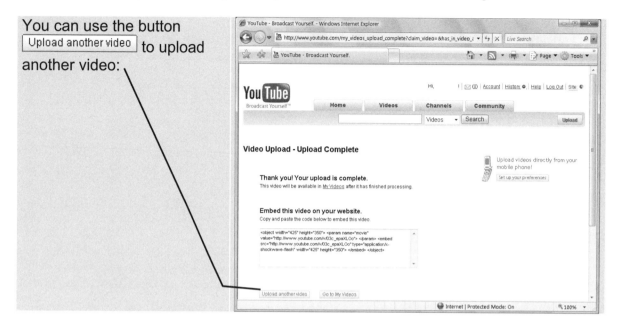

Now you can watch the video yourself on *YouTube*. To do this, go to your *My Videos* web space:

At the bottom of the window:

☞ **Click** Go to My Videos

You see your own web space on *YouTube*:

Edit video information: ———

The videos you uploaded: ———

Your favorite videos on *YouTube*: ———

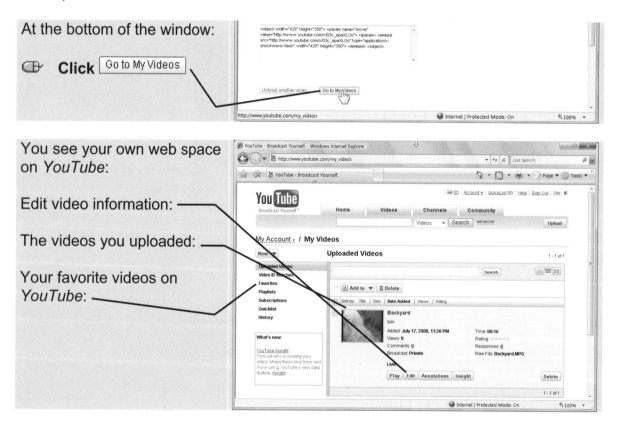

You can watch the video you uploaded:

☞ **Click** Play

If you cannot click this hyperlink, the video has not yet been placed online. This may happen if the website is very busy.
When there is a delay, you can check back later to see if the video has been added.

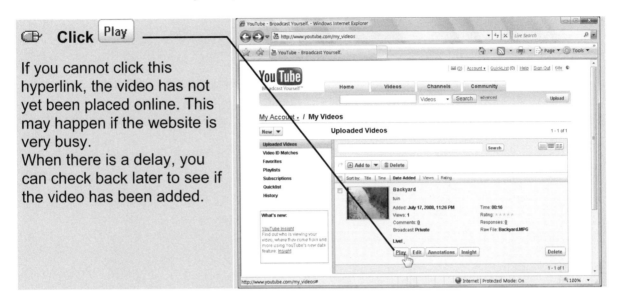

The video is played:

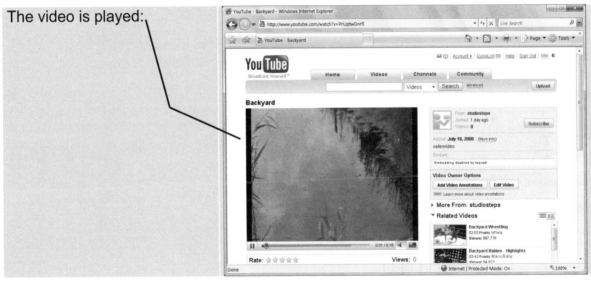

11.6 Removing a Video from YouTube

You can always remove a video you uploaded to *YouTube*. Make sure to follow the steps in this section to remove the practice movie.

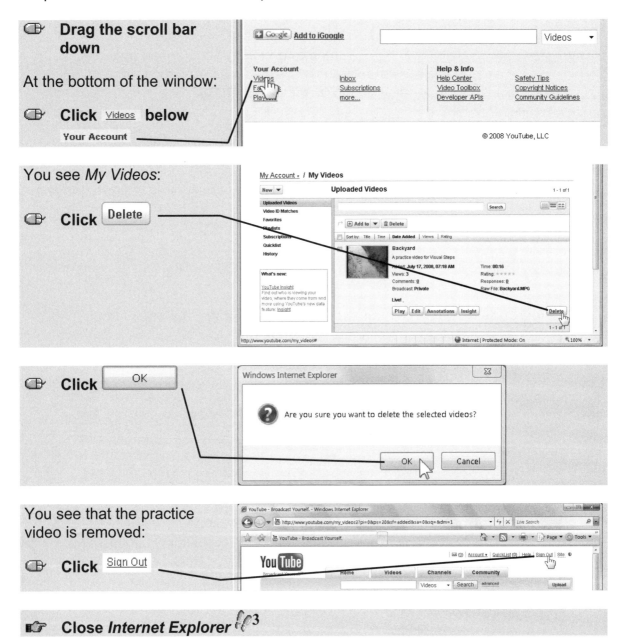

☞ Drag the scroll bar down

At the bottom of the window:

☞ Click Videos **below** Your Account

You see *My Videos*:

☞ Click Delete

☞ Click OK

You see that the practice video is removed:

☞ Click Sign Out

☞ Close *Internet Explorer* ^{3}

In this chapter you have learned how to locate and view videos on *YouTube*. You have also learned how to upload and remove a video clip. Now you can start uploading your own videos.

11.7 Background Information

Glossary

Copyright	The legal right granted to an author, composer, playwright, publisher, or distributor to exclusive publication, production, sale, or distribution of a literary, musical, dramatic, or artistic work.
Downloading	Transferring a file, for example a program, from a computer on the Internet to the hard disk of your own computer.
Flash Player	Versatile video player created by *Adobe*, often used for playing streaming video.
Streaming video	Video that can be played while it is still being downloaded.
Uploading	Transferring a file, for example a video clip, from your computer to a computer on the Internet.
Verification code	Letters or numbers hidden in an image that need to be typed before submitting a website form. Guards against programs attempting to use these forms to distribute spam.
Video player	Software that can be used to play videos.
YouTube	Website where users can view and share their home made videos.

The best video format
Various types of video formats may be uploaded to the *YouTube* website: WMV, AVI, MPG (MPEG) and MOV. For high quality results, *YouTube* suggests the following settings:
- MPEG4 (Divx, Xvid);
- a resolution of 320 x 240;
- MP3 audio;
- thirty frames per second.

12. Your Digital Photos in a Web Album on the Internet

With the onset of digital cameras, it has never been easier to share photos with friends and family. You can add photos to your e-mails, or view them in attractive slideshows. It is also becoming more and more popular to place your digital photos in web albums on the Internet. You no longer need to send huge file attachments with your e-mail correspondence. Your friends and family can view your photos on your personal photo website. They can even order their own prints from there.

You can edit a web album directly online. This is very convenient when you are traveling for example. You can add photos to your web album from any computer that is connected to the Internet. Your friends and family at home can keep abreast of all your travel experiences by visiting your web album.

You can create a free web album with an unlimited number of photos using the application *myphotoalbum.com*. The costs of this free service are covered by advertisements. This means you will see ads when you create and view web albums. If you like this application, you may want to consider joining the *MyPhotoAlbum Club* for $ 20.00 per year. Members do not see these ads and enjoy additional benefits.

In this chapter you learn how to:

- sign up for a *MyPhotoAlbum* account;
- upload photos to your album and add captions to your photos;
- select an album cover and rearrange the photos;
- play a slideshow;
- rotate photos and delete photos from your album;
- share your album with your contacts.

⇨ **Please note:**

To remain a member of *MyPhotoAlbum's* free service you are required to:
- purchase photo merchandise (including club membership, photo gifts, prints or enlargements) through the *MyPhotoAlbum Store* at least once every 365 days;
- visit your *MyPhotoAlbum* account at least once every 365 days;
- perform at least one photo or video upload and album update every 365 days.

Free or discounted offers (including the twenty free prints you receive when signing up for your account) **also** count as a purchase, even if you only pay for shipping. These requirements do not apply to *MyPhotoAlbum Club* members.

12.1 Creating a MyPhotoAlbum Account

Before you can publish your first web album on the Internet, you need to create a *MyPhotoAlbum* account first.

☞ **Open *Internet Explorer*** 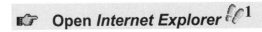¹

☞ **Surf to the website www.myphotoalbum.com** ²

⇨ **Please note:**

The creators of websites are constantly adding new information. The sreenshots used in this chapter may look different from what you see on your screen. This should not pose any problems; the basic features will not be removed. However, it is possible that certain features will be moved to a different location on the website.

You see the *MyPhotoAlbum* start window:

☞ **Click**

> **Get Started!**

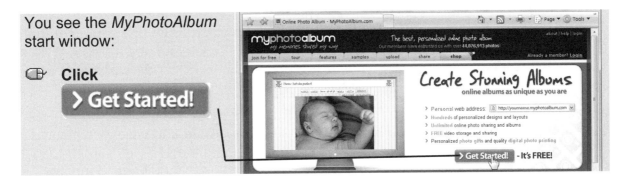

You start by creating your personal web address. This web address begins with your **user name** and ends with **.myphotoalbum.com**. You can choose the user name yourself:

⌨ **Type a user name below**
① Create your personal web ad...

⌨ **Type your e-mail address twice below**
② Enter your email addre...

☞ **Click to check mark**
I Agree to the MyPhotoAlbum Term...

☞ **Click**
> **Join Now for FREE!**

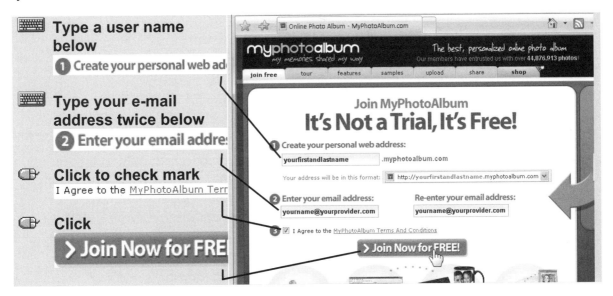

HELP! My user name is already taken.

Type a new user name in the text box

or:

Select one of the suggestions

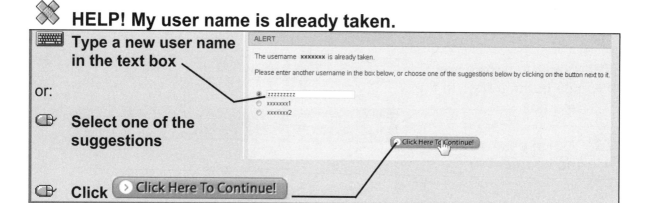

Click [Click Here To Continue!]

If your signup was successful, you see the message that you have received a confirmation e-mail:

Open your e-mail program $\ell\ell^6$ and receive your e-mail $\ell\ell^7$

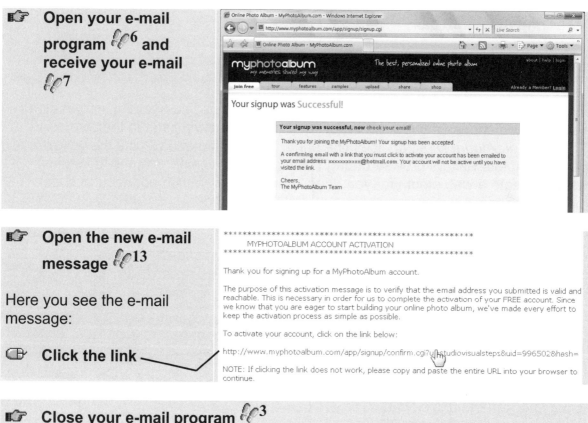

Open the new e-mail message $\ell\ell^{13}$

Here you see the e-mail message:

Click the link

Close your e-mail program $\ell\ell^3$

The *Account Confirmation* page appears in a new browser window. Here you need to enter some more information for your account:

Type the letters you see in the image in the text box ——

Type a password in the box next to Desired Password: ——

Type your password again next to Retype Password: ——

Drag the scroll bar down ——

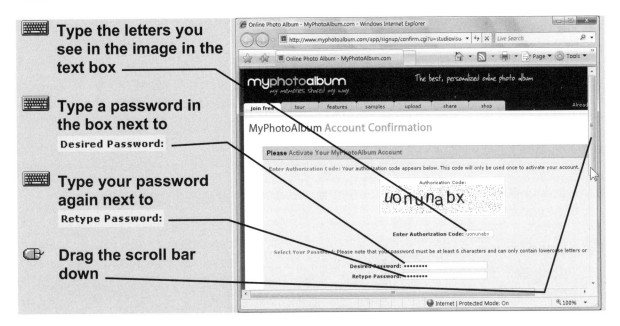

In the second half of the form you are asked to provide some personal information. You can also choose if you want to list your *MyPhotoAlbum* page in the *Directory*. The *MyPhotoAlbum Directory* is online photo album 'phonebook' (like the yellow pages) that lets visitors browse through categories of member albums. If you just want to create a web album for your friends and family, you do not need to check mark this option.

Type the requested information below Account Information: ——

It is not required to enter your household income.

In this example the option List your MyPhotoAlbum in the directory is not check marked. You can decide for yourself if you want to be listed.

Click Activate Now!

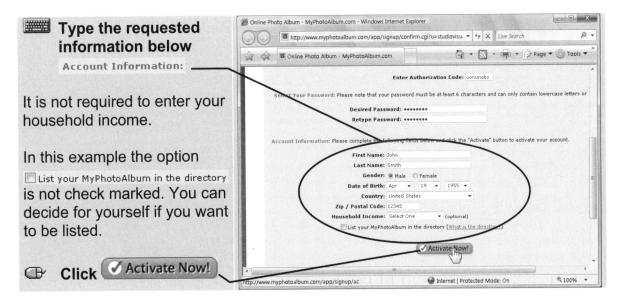

You see a congratulations message, with an overview of your account information.

☞ **Write down your personal web address, user name and password on a piece of paper and store it in a safe place**

⊞ **Click**
> **Click Here To Continue!**

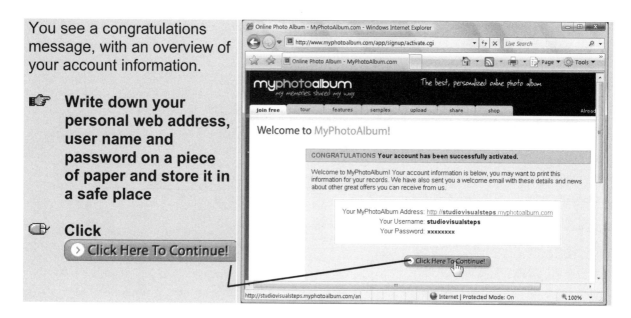

12.2 Adding Photos to Your Album

You can start adding photos to your web album right away:

⊞ **Click**
> **Start Adding Photos**

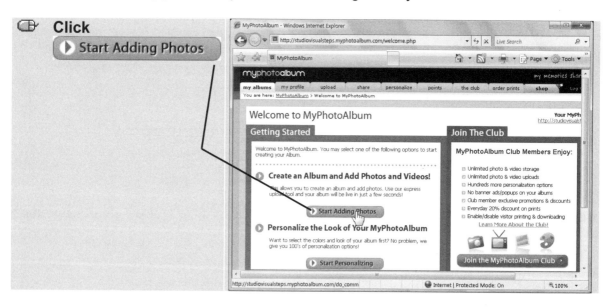

You can organize your photos in separate albums on your *MyPhotoAlbum* webpage. For example, you can separate your holiday photos from the ones you took at a recent family gathering. This makes it easier for people who visit your *MyPhotoAlbum* webpage to quickly find the photos they want to see.

You are going to add photos to your first album.

At the top of the page you see `You are here:`
`MyPhotoAlbum > Add to Untitled Album` :
This means the photos you add will be placed in an album called `Untitled Album` on your *MyPhotoAlbum* page. You can add a name for this album later.

Click
▶ Add Photos to Album

MyPhotoAlbum checks your computer to see if your computer is capable of running the *Easy Upload Tool*. You can read more about this tool in the next section. You are first going to try the basic ● One-by-One Upload Tool :

Click
Other Upload Software

Click One-by-one Upload Tool

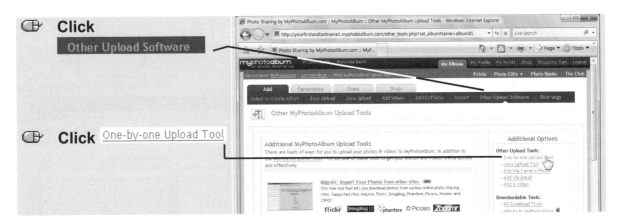

Depending on the settings of your computer, the *One-by-One Upload Tool* is opened in a new tab or a new browser window:

On this page you can select up to sixteen photos, one at a time:

Click Browse...

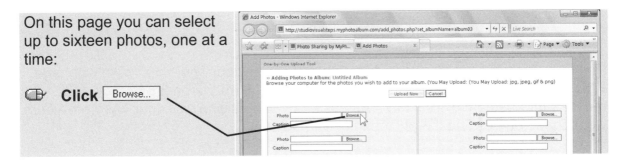

You see the *Choose file* window:

This *Choose file* window looks a little different in *Windows XP*. The ability to move in and out of your folders to find the photo you want remains the same.

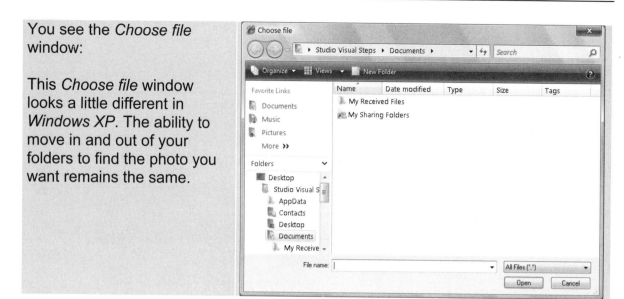

It does not matter which photos you use for this practice web album. You can use your own photos. You can also use the *Windows* sample photos. In this example the *Windows* sample photos are used:

☞ **Open the folder with the photos you want to use**

You see the contents of the selected folder:

Depending on the settings of your computer, the files may be displayed differently than what is shown in this window.

🖰 **Click the first photo**

🖰 **Click** Open

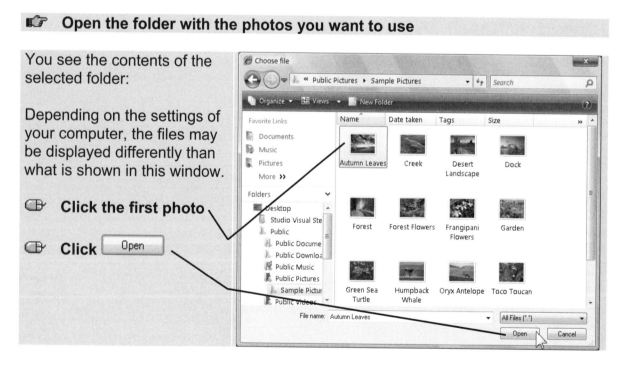

The full path to the photo on your computer (its actual location) is shown in the box:

☞ **Click the next button**

Browse...

☞ **Click another photo**

☞ **Click** Open

You have selected two photos for your album.

If you want, you can also add a caption for each photo in the text box next to Caption:

You can edit or remove this caption later.

☞ **Click** Upload Now

The photos are uploaded:

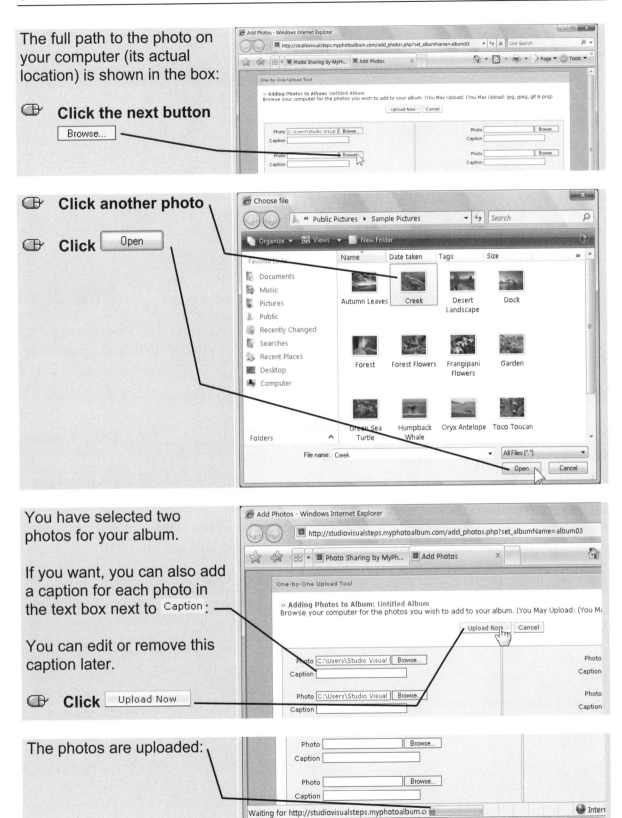

As soon as the upload is complete, you see a confirmation:

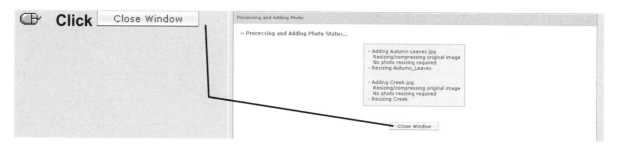

You may see a yellow bar with the message

Pop-up blocked.

In that case you need to allow pop-ups:

Click the bar

Pop-up blocked.

A menu appears:

Click

Always Allow Pop-ups from This S

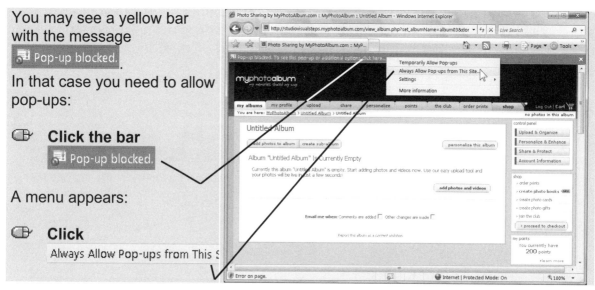

You need to confirm this:

Click Yes

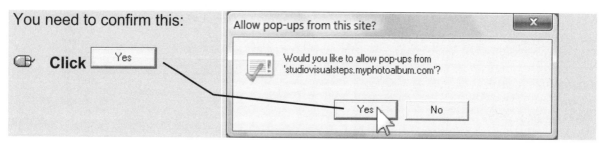

The two photos have been added to your web album:

Please note:

Always make sure to retain a copy of the photos you upload to your web album, either on your own computer or on an external storage device, such as a USB stick, CD or DVD. This guards against any errors made or photos getting lost somehow in the upload process.

12.3 Using the Easy Upload Tool

You can use the *Easy Upload Tool* to add a large number of photos to your web album all at once. You need an *add-on* for that. An add-on is a small program that adds a feature to another program. In this case the add-on is added to *Internet Explorer*.

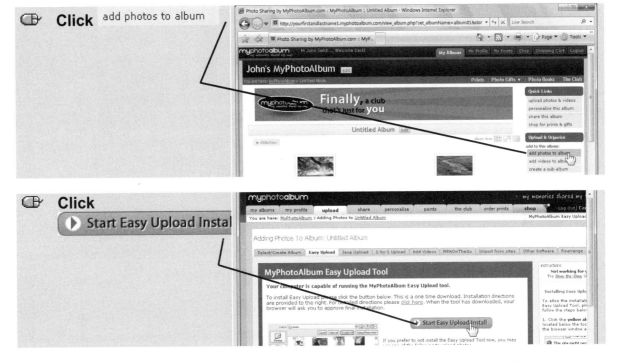

Depending on your *Internet Explorer* security settings, you may see the following window with information about the information bar:

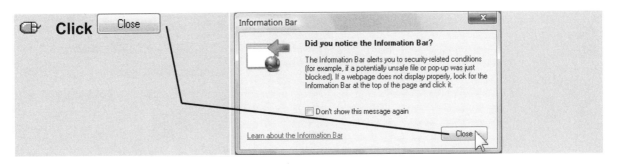

Click

🔲 This website wants to install the following add-on and want to install it, click here...

A menu appears:

Click

Install ActiveX Control...

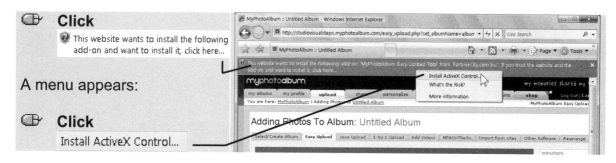

If you use a *Windows Vista* computer your screen goes dark. You see a window where you need to give your permission to continue.

Click Continue

Click Install

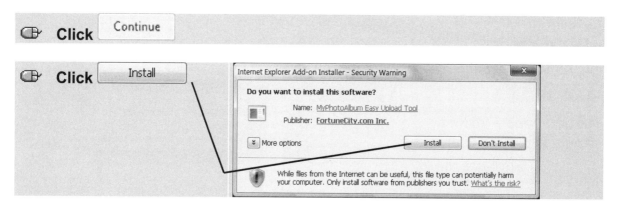

Now that it is installed, you need to give your permission to run the add-on:

You see this window again:

Click Close

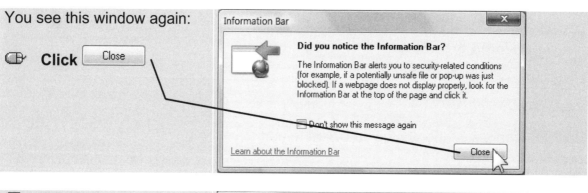

Click

🔲 This website wants to install the fo

A menu appears:

Click Run ActiveX Control

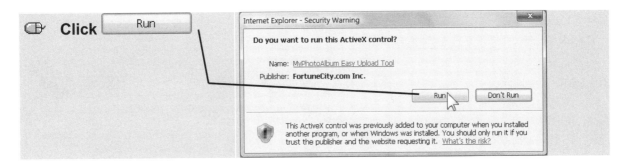

☞ **Click** Run

Now you see a *Windows XP* style pane in your browser window. By default, the contents of the *My Pictures* folder are displayed. In *Windows Vista* this folder is called *Pictures*.

On the left you see buttons that represent folders on the hard disk of your computer:

You can open a folder by clicking its button:

You can double-click a folder icon to display its contents:

☞ **Open the folder containing the photos you want to upload**

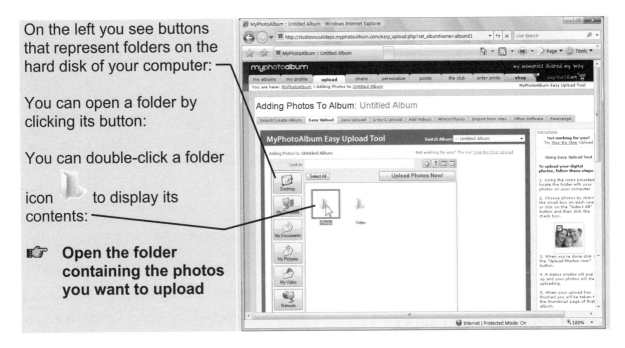

Now you can select the photos you want to add to your album:

☞ **Click to check mark the photo**

The photo is selected ☑.

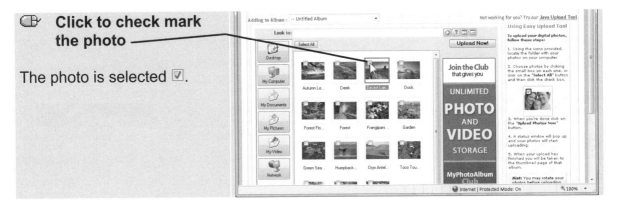

👉 **Select four more photos**

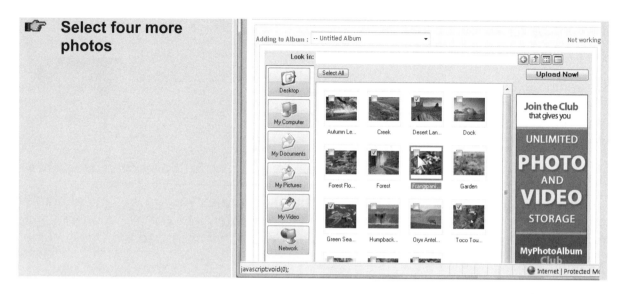

You can also remove photos from the selection:

👆 **Click to remove the check mark for a selected photo**

Now the photo is no longer selected ☐.

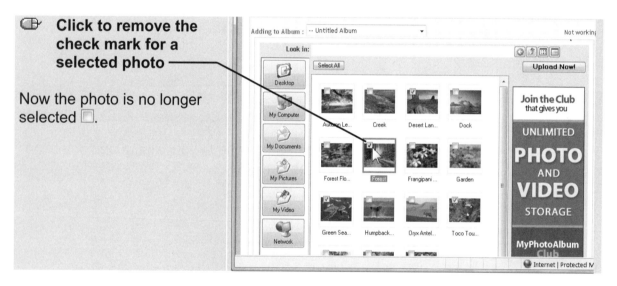

You can upload the selected photos at once:

👆 **Click** [**Upload Now!**]

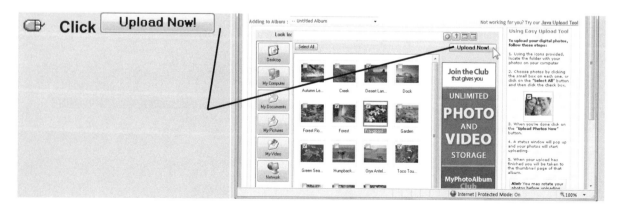

The photos are uploaded to your album on the Internet.

Uploading a large batch of photos will take some time. You see the estimated time needed for the upload here:

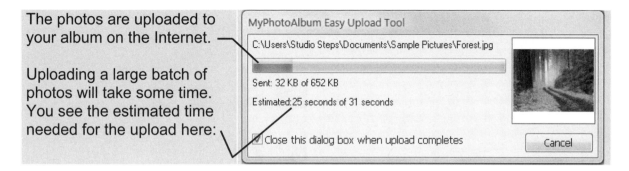

You can use this *Easy Upload Tool* for adding photos when you are working at home on your computer. When you are using a public computer, for example when you are traveling, you may not be able to install the add-on. In that case, use the *One-by-One Upload Tool*.

As soon as the upload is finished, you see this message:

☞ **Click** OK

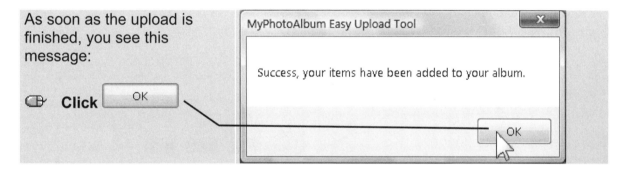

You are taken to the webpage where you can add a title to your album and select an album theme. You can try this in the next section.

12.4 Personalizing Your Album

The fun thing about *MyPhotoAlbum* is that you can personalize each album with a different look. To make it easier for visitors to find the photos they want to see, you can give each album a distinctive title and a description.

☞ **Click** edit album title

Now you can select a theme for this album. A theme is a combination of a color scheme and a layout. Using the free *MyPhotoAlbum* account, you can choose from 25 different themes. Members of the *MyPhotoAlbum Club* have more themes at their disposal, including special themes for Christmas, babies, weddings, sports etcetera.

You can preview a theme like this:

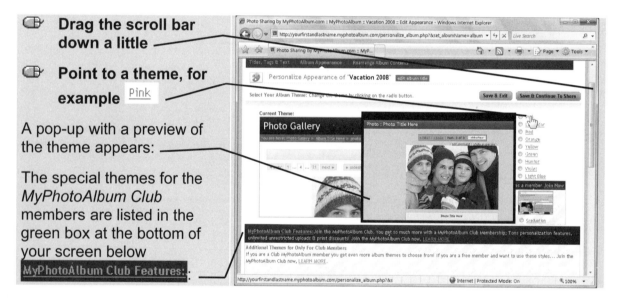

You can choose the theme you like best.

Click ○ to select a theme

The next step in personalizing your album is editing the captions that appear below each photo:

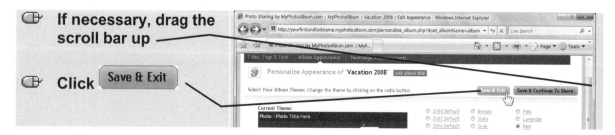

For each photo you can add a title, a description, and tags. Tags are keywords you can add to describe your photo. If you add tags to all the photos in your web album, visitors can search for photos based on the tags. For example, if they see a photo with the tag 'boat', they can click this tag to quickly display all photos that have the same tag. This only works well if you diligently tag all of your photos. In this example only titles are added to the photos.

Click `caption all album items`

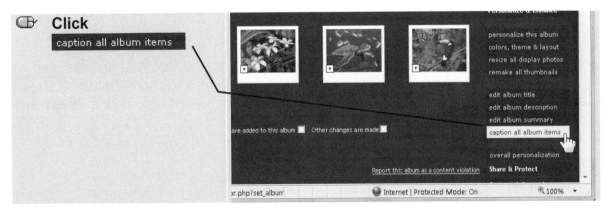

Drag the scroll bar down a little

You see the first picture:

Type a title next to `Title :`

Drag the scroll bar down

Add titles to the other photos as well

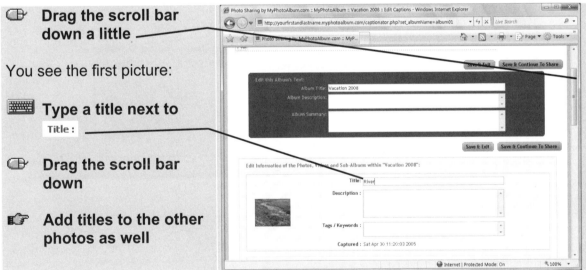

When you are done you can save the captions:

Click `Save & Exit`

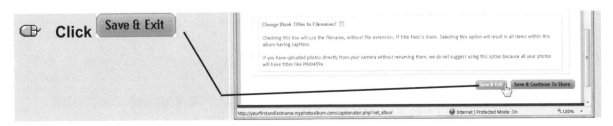

You see your album in the
selected style:

The titles have been added
below each photo:

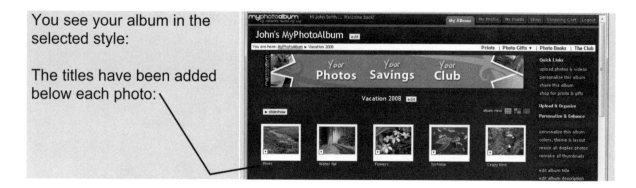

12.5 Rotating Photos

In *MyPhotoAlbum* you can also rotate photos that are displayed sideways or upside
down. You can try that with a random photo:

☞ **Point to** ▼ **below a photo**

A menu appears:

☞ **Click** rotate photo

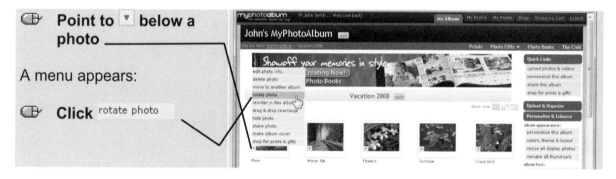

Depending on the settings of your computer, the *Rotate Photo* tool appears in a new
window or a new tab:

☞ **Click**

The photo rotates clockwise.

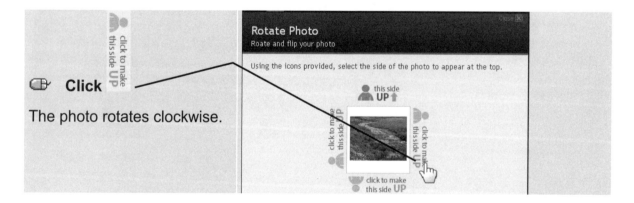

To go back to the original orientation of the photo:

☞ **Point to** ▼ **below the photo**

A menu appears:

☞ **Click** rotate photo

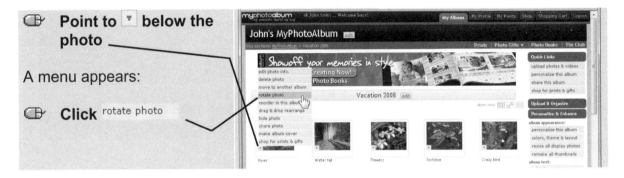

The photo rotates clockwise.

☞ **Click**

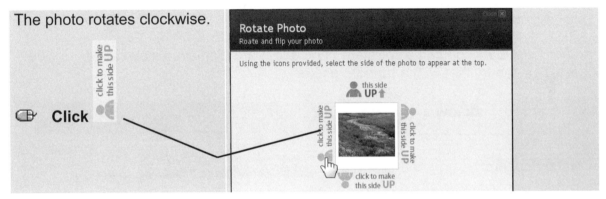

12.6 Selecting an Album Cover

You can select one of the pictures as the cover for the album. Like this:

☞ **Point to** ▼ **below a photo**

A menu appears:

☞ **Click** make album cover

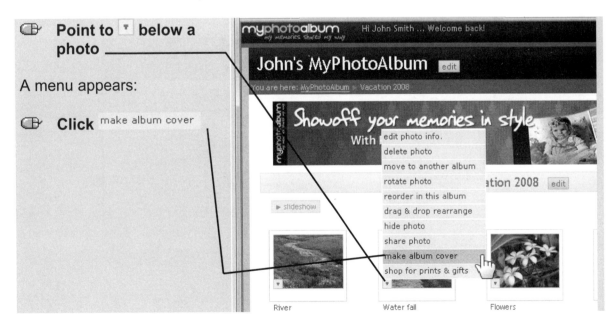

To see the effect, you go to your main *MyPhotoAlbum* page:

Click MyPhotoAlbum

You see your main *MyPhotoAlbum* page. The album you created is represented by a stack of photos. The cover you selected is on top of the stacks. When you create more albums, they will be added below this one.

Visitors to your
MyPhotoAlbum page can
open the album by clicking
the cover:

Click the cover photo

12.7 Playing a Slideshow

You can play a slideshow of the photos in your album:

Click slideshow

You see the slideshow. Every
few seconds you see a
different photo:

The slideshow controls have these functions:

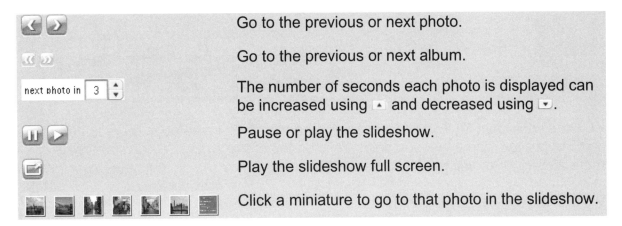

	Go to the previous or next photo.
	Go to the previous or next album.
	The number of seconds each photo is displayed can be increased using ▲ and decreased using ▼.
	Pause or play the slideshow.
	Play the slideshow full screen.
	Click a miniature to go to that photo in the slideshow.

At the end of the slideshow you see this slide:

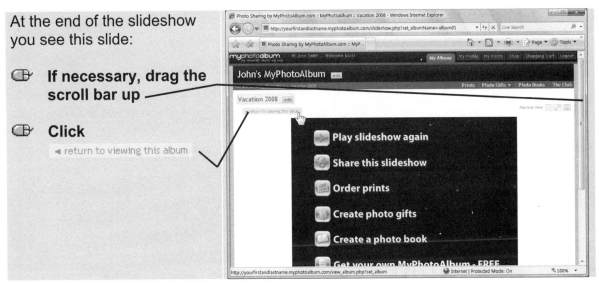

☞ **If necessary, drag the scroll bar up**

☞ **Click**

◄ return to viewing this album

You see the album again.

12.8 Rearranging the Photos

Your photos may be in the wrong order after you uploaded them to your album. You can quickly rearrange them like this:

☞ **Click**

Upload & Organize

A list containing menu options expands:

☞ **Click**

drag & drop rearrange

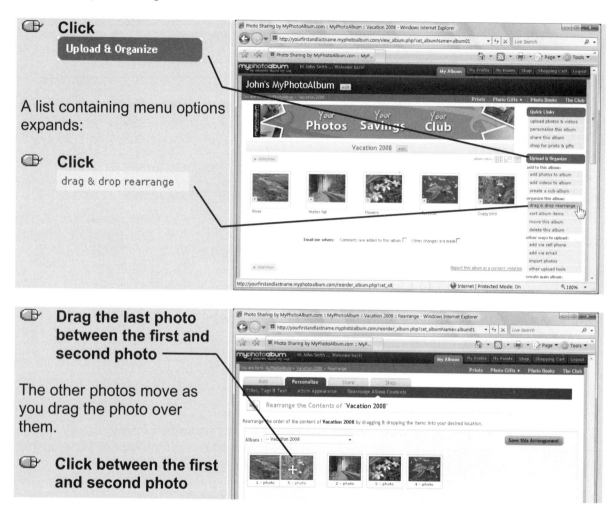

☞ **Drag the last photo between the first and second photo**

The other photos move as you drag the photo over them.

☞ **Click between the first and second photo**

When you are done rearranging the photos you can save the new arrangement:

☞ **Click**

Save this Arrangement

You are taken back to the album.

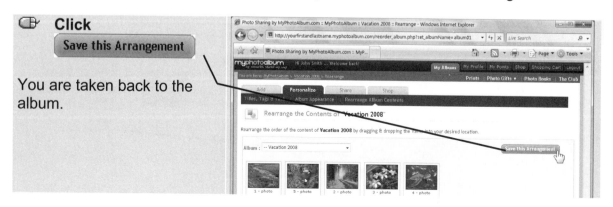

12.9 Deleting Photos

You can delete photos from your web album like this:

Point to ⏷ **below a photo**

A menu appears:

Click delete photo

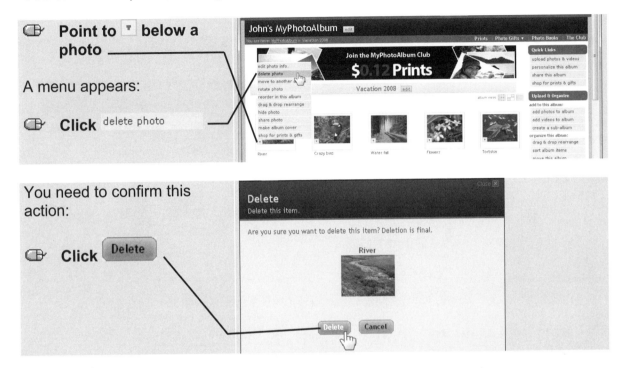

You need to confirm this action:

Click Delete

12.10 Adding Contacts

The main goal of creating a web album is sharing it with your friends and family. You can let them know about your album by sending them an e-mail invitation. First you add your e-mail contacts to your *MyPhotoAlbum* address book:

Click Upload & Organize

The list is collapsed again.

Click Account Information

Click my address book

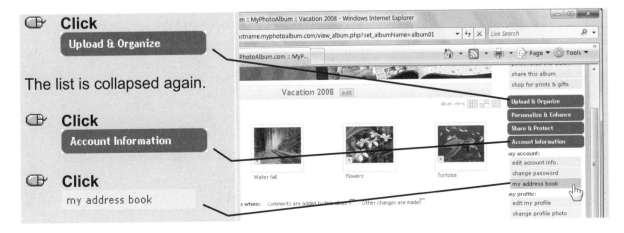

You see the address book:

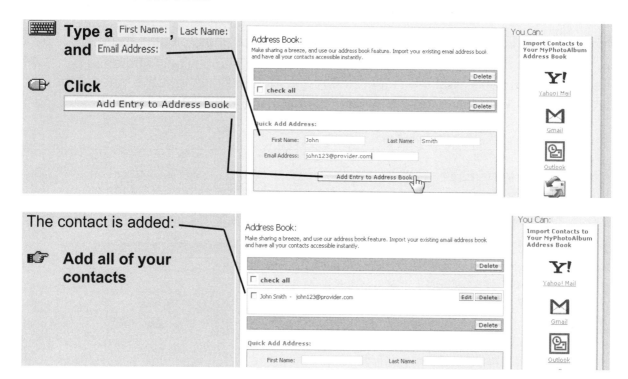

Type a First Name:, Last Name: **and** Email Address:

Click
Add Entry to Address Book

The contact is added:

 Add all of your contacts

💡 **Tip**

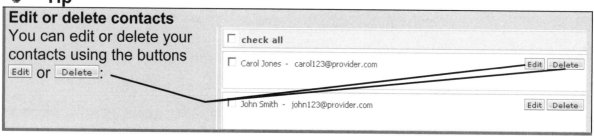

Edit or delete contacts
You can edit or delete your contacts using the buttons Edit or Delete :

12.11 Sharing Your Album

Now you can invite your contacts to take a look at your photo album. There are two options: `share album slideshow` and `share this album`. The obvious difference between these two is that the first invitation links to the slideshow, the other to the album. But all visitors can surf from the slideshow to the album, and vice versa.

You can send the e-mail invitations like this:

If necessary, click `Share & Protect` **at the right side of the window**

Click `Share Slideshow`

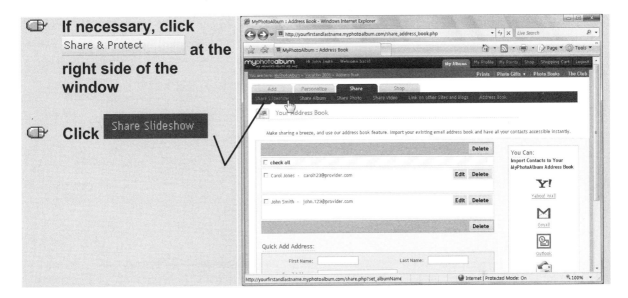

First you go to the address book to select the contacts you want to invite:

Click `» Add from Address Book`

If you have more than one album, you can select another album here

`Or, select another album:`
`-- Vacation 2008`

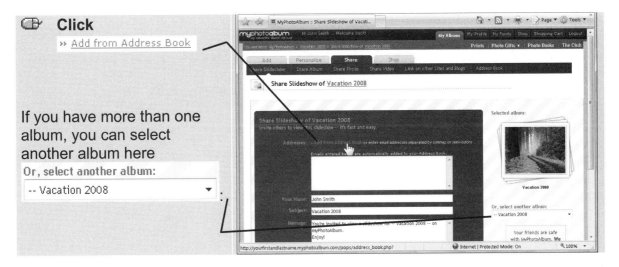

Depending on the settings of your computer, the address book opens in a new tab or a new browser window. Here you can select the contacts you want to invite:

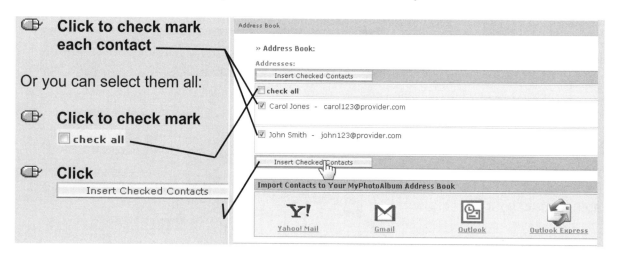

Click to check mark each contact

Or you can select them all:

Click to check mark
☐ check all

Click
[Insert Checked Contacts]

The address book does not close automatically:

☞ **Close the address book window or tab**

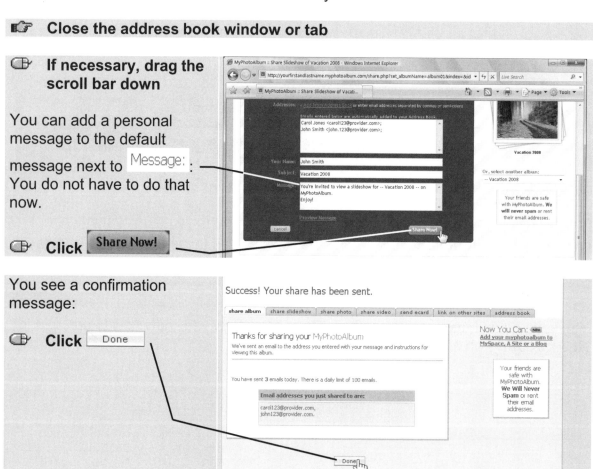

If necessary, drag the scroll bar down

You can add a personal message to the default message next to Message: . You do not have to do that now.

Click [Share Now!]

You see a confirmation message:

Click [Done]

💡 **Tip**

E-mail

The contacts you have invited will receive this e-mail message.
They can view the slideshow by clicking `Vacation 2008` or the button

▶ **View My Slideshow** :

Your contacts do not need to sign up for their own *MyPhotoAlbum* account to be able to view your slideshow.

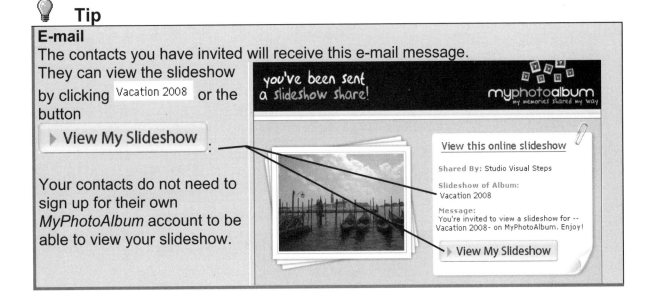

You can log out now:

☞ **In the top right corner, click** `Log Out`

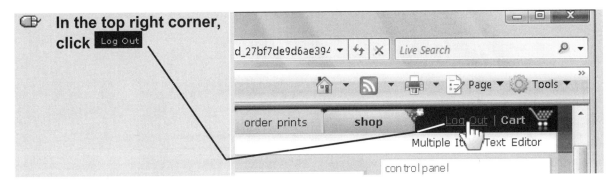

The next time you want to add photos to your web album, you must first log in to **www.myphotoalbum.com** by clicking the link `Login` in the upper right-hand corner.

📖 **Close** *Internet Explorer* 👣³

You have been introduced to myphotoalbum.com. Now you know how to create and edit your own web album.

12.12 Background Information

Glossary	
Add-on	A program that adds functionality to a web browser. Examples of add-ons are extra toolbars, animated mouse pointers and interactive web content. Add-ons are also known as *ActiveX controls*, plug-ins, browser extensions or Browser Helper Objects.
Contact	Name and e-mail address of the persons that are allowed to view your album or receive an e-card.
Downloading	Copying and transferring files from the Internet to the hard disk of your computer.
E-card	Digital version of a greeting card.
Resolution	The number of pixels in a photo or another digital image. The higher the resolution, the sharper the photo will be. But a higher resolution also means a larger file that will take longer to download or upload.
Uploading	Transferring (copies of) files from the hard disk of your computer to a computer that is connected to the Internet.
Web album	Photo collection on the Internet.

Privacy

In this chapter you have created a public web album. Anyone who knows your personal *MyPhotoAlbum* web address can view all your albums and add comments to the photos.

It is possible to limit the visibility of your albums by giving specific users a user name and password. You can create different privacy settings for each separate album. In the Tip at the end of this chapter you can read how to do that.

12.13 Tips

  Tip

Password protect albums

In order to protect a web album with a password, you have to start by defining the users that you want to allow to view one or more of your albums. You can define users like this:

👆 **Click** `Account Information` , `manage album users`

The user named `admin` in your Friends list is you:

👆 **Click** `Create User`

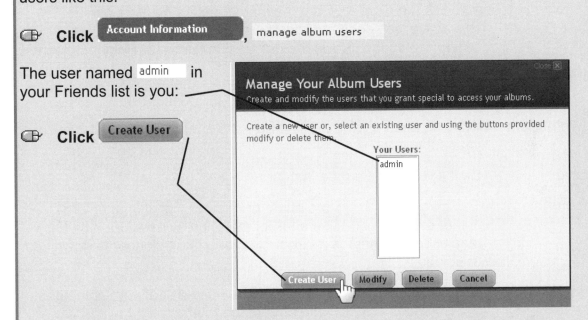

You type a user name and a temporary password for this friend. You can also decide if this friend is allowed to create new albums within your album. By default, this new user will receive an e-mail with a link to create his or her new password.

👉 **Enter the required information**

👉 **Select if you want to allow this user to create albums or not**

👆 **Click** `Create User`

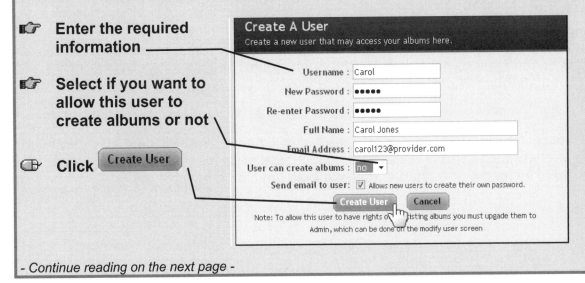

- Continue reading on the next page -

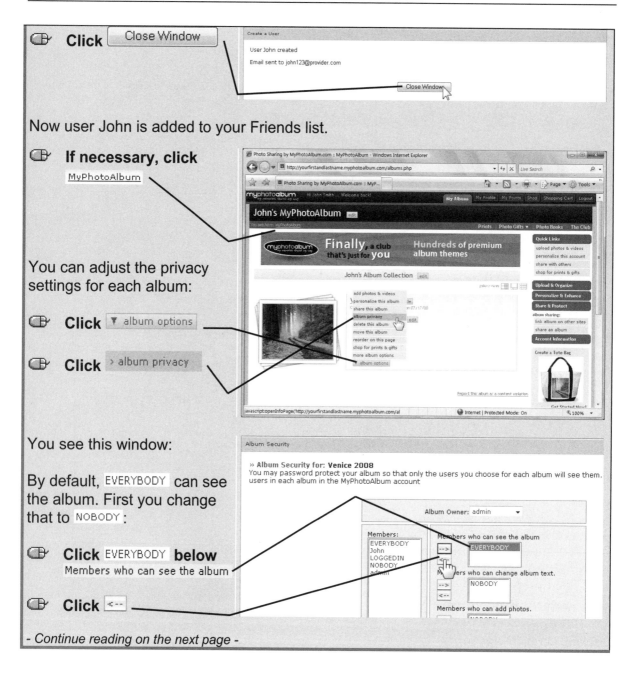

☞ **Click** [Close Window]

Now user John is added to your Friends list.

☞ **If necessary, click**
   MyPhotoAlbum

You can adjust the privacy settings for each album:

☞ **Click** [▼ album options]

☞ **Click** [› album privacy]

You see this window:

By default, EVERYBODY can see the album. First you change that to NOBODY :

☞ **Click** EVERYBODY **below**
   Members who can see the album

☞ **Click** [‹--]

- Continue reading on the next page -

Now you add the members that are allowed to view the album, only you and Carol in this example:

☞ **Click** admin

☞ **Click** -->

☞ **Click** Carol

☞ **Click** -->

By default, NOBODY can change album text, add photos or modify photos:

☞ **Drag the scroll bar down**

Also, NOBODY can delete photos or create sub-albums.

But EVERYBODY (in this case admin and Carol) can view the original images, add and read comments.

☞ **Adjust these settings if necessary**

☞ **Click** Save

Now only Carol and you can access the album.

☞ **Click** Done

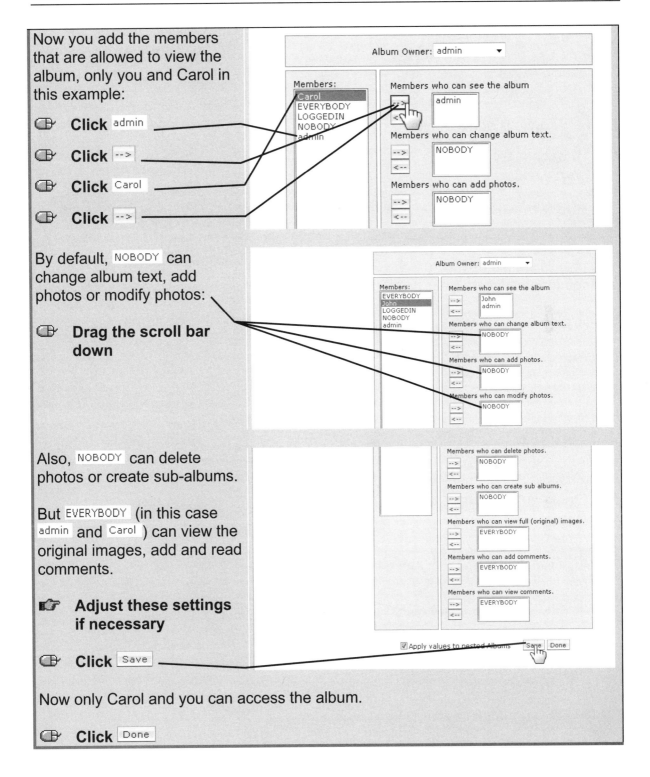

13. Interesting Online Reference Sites

A vast amount of information is available on the Internet. This information is divided over millions of websites. It is not always easy to find. Luckily there are websites that specialize in offering specific types of information. You can regard these websites as online reference books. One advantage of these reference sites is that they almost always include a useful search feature.

One of the most reputable online reference sites is *Wikipedia*: an online encyclopedia containing information on a wide range of subjects.

Dictionaries can also be found online, like the well-known *Merriam-Webster* dictionary where you can look up the meaning of a word. You can also find specialized translation sites. The new *Translator* site by *Microsoft* is a good example.

If you are interested in old photos, maps and documents, you can take a look at the many online archives containing historical material.

Finally, many websites offer comprehensive medical information, for example about health conditions, symptoms and prescription drugs.

In this chapter you learn the following:

- using *Wikipedia*;
- using an online dictionary;
- translating text online;
- finding historical material;
- finding health information.

⇨ **Please note:**

The creators of websites are constantly adding new information. The sreenshots used in this chapter may look different from what you see on your screen. This should not pose any problems; the basic features will not be removed. However, it is possible that certain features will be moved to a different location on the website.

13.1 Wikipedia

Wikipedia is an online encyclopedia that consists of millions of articles in various languages about a wide range of subjects. It looks a lot like a regular encyclopedia. The main difference is that, under certain conditions, anyone can modify or add to the articles listed on *Wikipedia.*

It may seem that this makes the information on *Wikipedia* less reliable, but editors monitor all content that is either added or modified. Information that is not correct will sooner or later be removed.

You go to the *Wikipedia* site like this:

☞   **Open *Internet Explorer*** 🖰[1]

☞   **Surf to the web address en.wikipedia.org** 🖰[2]

Please note that you do not have to type www in the web address.

You see the *Wikipedia* start page:

Article:

Navigation pane:

Information and Help:

Search box:

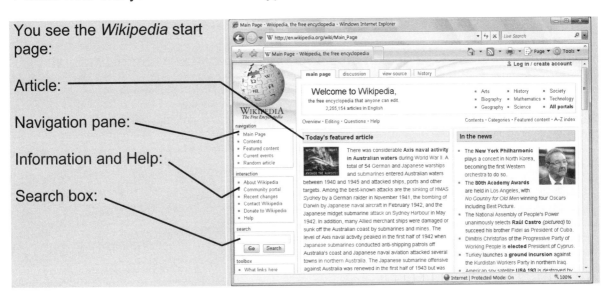

13.2 Searching in Wikipedia

Wikipedia consists of hundreds of thousands of pages. This makes it very difficult to browse to the information you need, like you would do in a regular alphabetized paper encyclopedia. But the convenient search feature makes it easy to quickly find information about a certain subject. If you are not sure you are using the correct search term, you can display a list with matching subjects first:

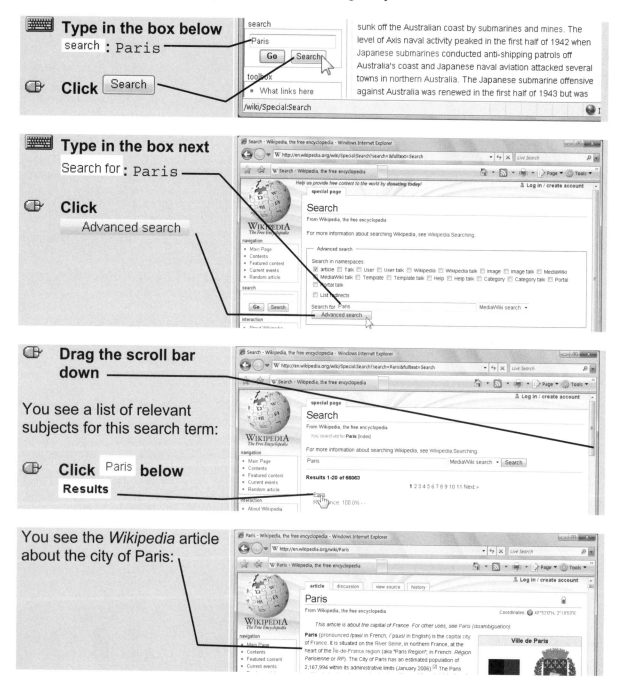

You can try to find an article even faster by using a specific search term and [Go]:

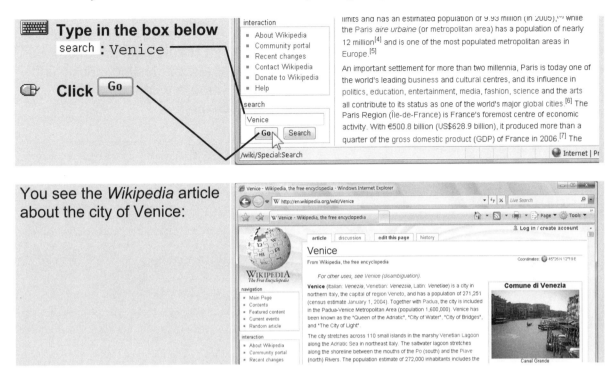

You see the *Wikipedia* article about the city of Venice:

Wikipedia lets you display information about other subjects just as fast and easy. Simply click any of the blue hyperlinks that appear in the text:

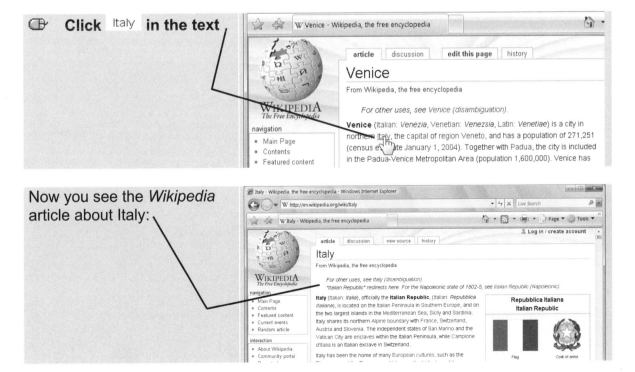

Now you see the *Wikipedia* article about Italy:

13.3 Using an Online Dictionary

A good dictionary is an indispensable reference when you are reading or writing. There are many excellent dictionaries available online, for example the *Merriam-Webster Dictionary*:

☞ **Surf to the web address www.merriam-webster.com** 👣²

You see the home page of the *Merriam-Webster* online dictionary:

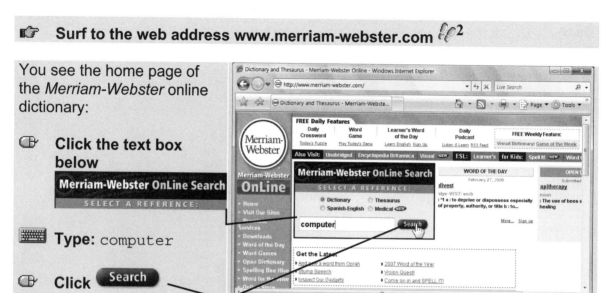

🖱️ **Click the text box below**

Merriam-Webster OnLine Search
SELECT A REFERENCE:

⌨️ **Type:** computer

🖱️ **Click** ⬤ **Search**

✋ **HELP! I see a message about the information bar.**

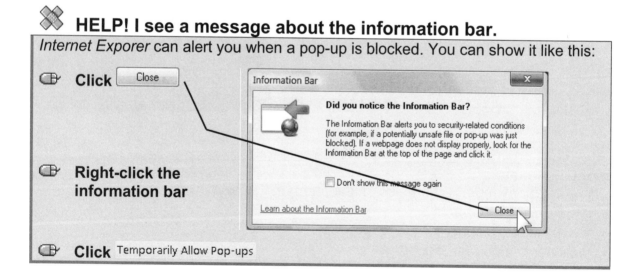

Internet Exporer can alert you when a pop-up is blocked. You can show it like this:

🖱️ **Click** Close

🖱️ **Right-click the information bar**

🖱️ **Click** Temporarily Allow Pop-ups

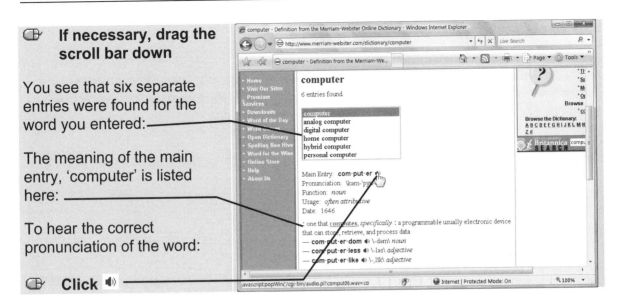

⊕ **If necessary, drag the scroll bar down**

You see that six separate entries were found for the word you entered:———

The meaning of the main entry, 'computer' is listed here: ————

To hear the correct pronunciation of the word:

⊕ **Click** 🔊 ———

Depending on the settings of your computer, a new window or a new tab opens.

☞ **Check if the computer speakers are on**

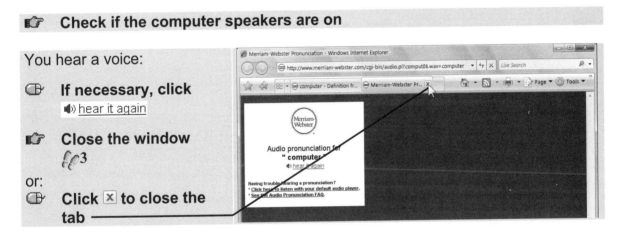

You hear a voice:

⊕ **If necessary, click**
    🔊 hear it again

☞ **Close the window**
    ³

or:

⊕ **Click** ☒ **to close the tab** ————

💡 **Tip**

More dictionaries
There are many more dictionaries on the Internet. For example:
- www.dictionary.com
- www.askoxford.com
- dictionary.cambridge.org

13.4 Translating Text

Microsoft offers an online automatic translation service that you can use to translate text from English to a foreign language, or the other way around.

⇨ **Please note:**

Automatic translation enables you to understand the gist of a foreign language word, text or website, but is no substitute for a professional human translator if complete accuracy is required.

☞ **Go to the web address translator.live.com** ⬿²

You see the *Translator* website:

First you enter the languages:

🖙 **Click ▾ next to**
Translation Languages

🖙 **Click** English - Spanish

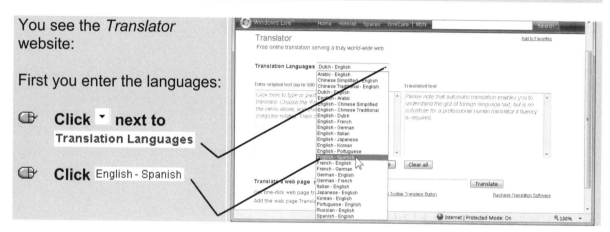

Now you can enter the text you want to translate from English to Spanish. You can enter up to 500 words:

⌨ **Type in the box below**
Enter original text :

I am typing on my keyboard.

🖙 **Click** Translate

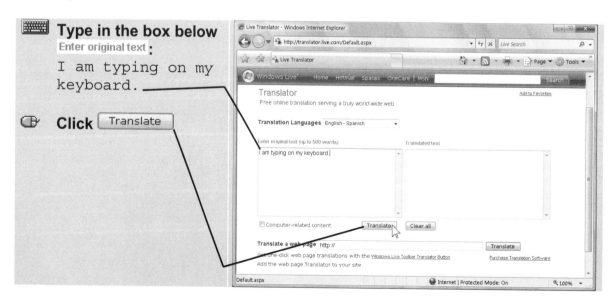

You see the Spanish
translation:——————————

This service works best when you are translating single words or short phrases. With
longer sentences, the translation becomes less accurate. You will notice this if you try
to translate the text on a foreign website.

As an example you can try to translate the Dutch Visual Steps website:

Click ⌄ next to
Translation Languages

Click Dutch - English

Type in the box next to
Translate a web page:
www.visualsteps.
nl ————————

Click Translate

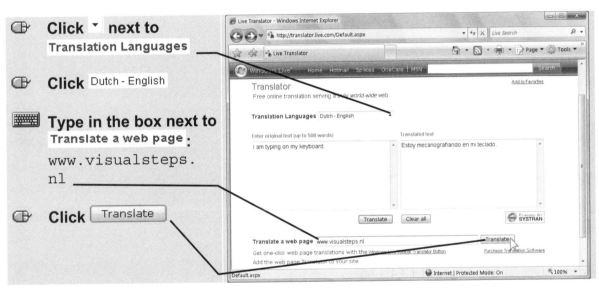

You see the English
translation of the
www.visualsteps.nl
webpage: ——————————

As you can see, the English
translation is far from fluent.
Also, hyperlinks, buttons and
unknown words are not
translated. But the translation
is good enough to let you
understand the gist of this
foreign language website.

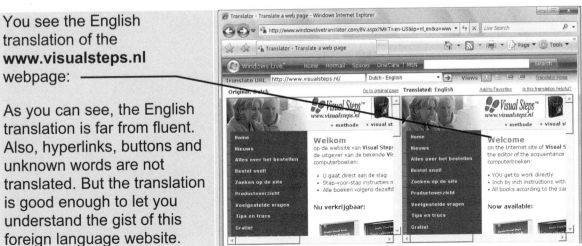

Tip

More translation websites

To translate single words to and from French, Spanish, Dutch, German and Swedish:
- www.interglot.com

To translate text to and from French, Spanish, German, Italian, Russian, Portuguese and Chinese:
- www.reverso.net/text_translation.asp?lang=EN

Links to the largest set of dictionaries (from Abenaki to Zulu), grammars, and other language resources on the web:
- www.yourdictionary.com/languages.html

13.5 Finding Historical Material

You can find a large amount of historical material on the Internet. A great source is the extensive digital collection placed online by the *Library of Congress*. This collection is called *American Memory*.

American Memory offers multimedia collections of digitized documents, maps, photographs, recorded sound, motion pictures, and text from the American historical collections of the *Library* and other institutions. *American Memory* now offers more than 7.5 million digital items from more than 100 historical collections.

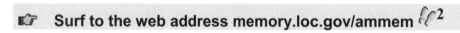 **Surf to the web address memory.loc.gov/ammem**

You see the *American Memory* index page:

You can search the collections by keyword here:

You can also browse through the collections by topic:

Click **Sports, Recreation**

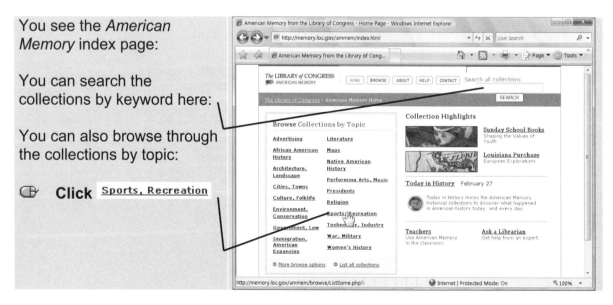

You see a list of collections:

👉 **Click**

   Baseball Guides and Spalding ~ 188

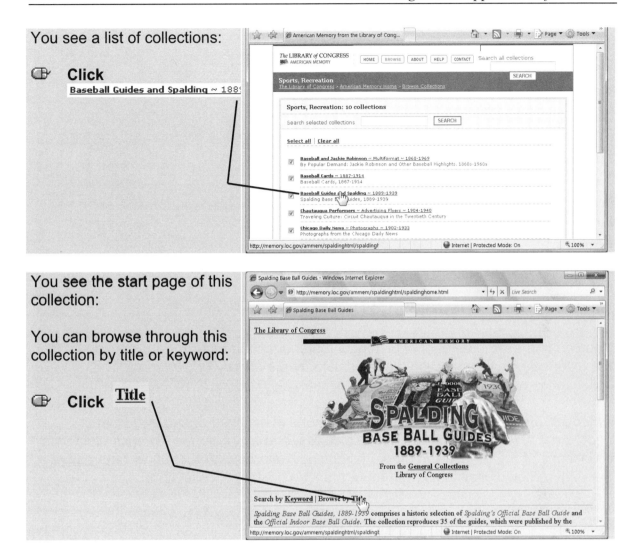

You **see the start page of this** collection:

You can browse through this collection by title or keyword:

👉 **Click** **Title**

You see a list of the titles that are available in this collection:

👉 **Click the first title**

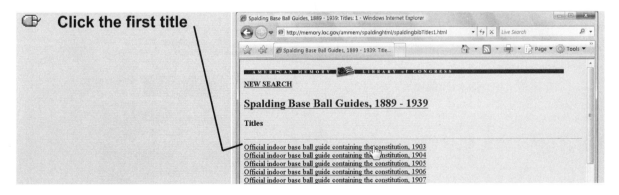

You can view the text or the scanned page images:

☞ **Click on the picture**

You see the cover of the guide:

You can browse through the guide by clicking **NEXT IMAGE** :

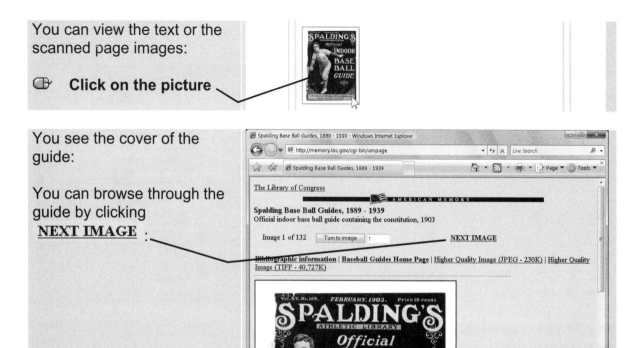

American Memory contains an enormous amount of digital material. Each collection contains links you can click to browse through the collection.

Genealogists and family historians may want to take a look at the *National Archives* website. Here you may find documents that may provide clues to your family's history. For example military service records, census records, immigration records (ship passenger lists), naturalization records and land records.

☞ **Surf to the web address www.archives.gov** ✎²

You see the *National Archives* website:

Here you see links to the most requested documents:

☞ **Click** • Genealogists/Family Historians **below** ARCHIVES.GOV FOR...

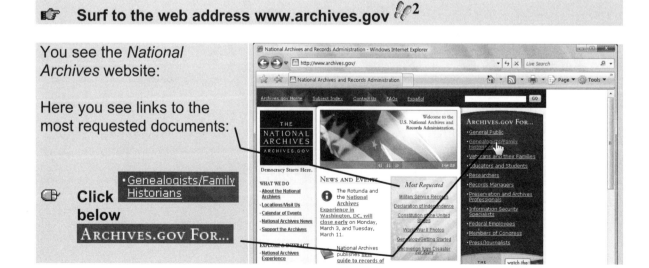

You see the webpage with information for genealogists and family historians:

 Click

    Starting Your Genealogy Research

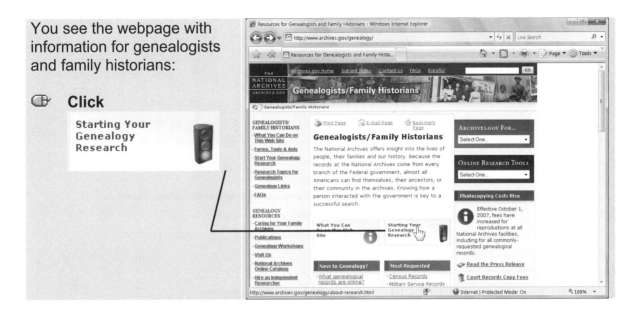

The links on this page can help you start your own family history research using the records from the *National Archives*.

Please note: many records are not yet available online or can only be ordered if you pay a fee. For example, a copy of a passenger arrival list will cost $ 25.00.

💡 **Tip**

More websites containing historical material
For example:
* www.picturehistory.com   Large digital image collection.
* memory.loc.gov/ammem/gmdhtml   Historical map collections of the Library of Congress.

13.6 Medical Reference Sites

There are many websites containing medical and health information. You may want to consult one of these sites from time to time. Even if you have a minor complaint you may find useful information, such as what to do when you get a blister from a new pair of shoes or suffer an insect bite or get sunburned.

☞ **Surf to the web address www.mayoclinic.com** 🖐²

You see the *Mayo Clinic* website:

You can Look up a disease or condition or Look up a symptom :

You can also consult the first-aid guide:

👉 **Click First-Aid Guide**

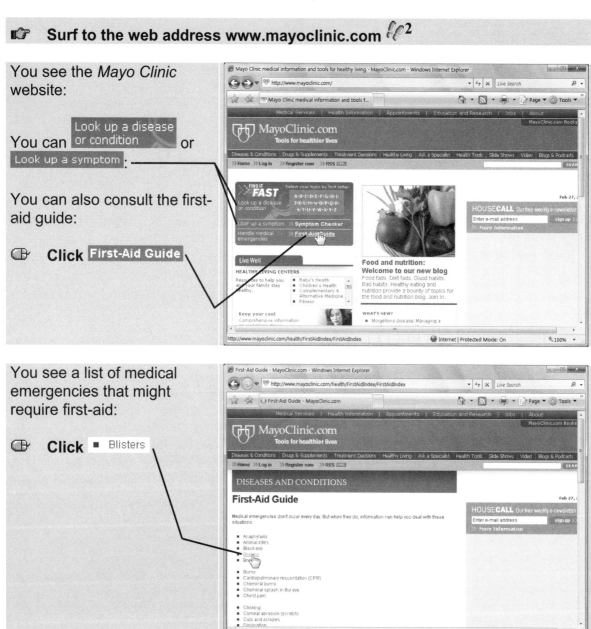

You see a list of medical emergencies that might require first-aid:

👉 **Click ■ Blisters**

You can read the information
on this page:

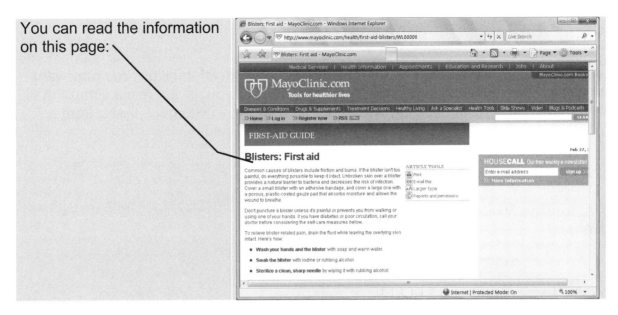

 Tip

More websites containing medical information
For example:

• www.nlm.nih.gov/medlineplus/ druginformation.html	Information about drugs from the U.S. National Library of Medicine.
• www.intelihealth.com	Consumer medical information from Harvard Medical School.
• www.aarp.org/health	Health information from AARP.

In this chapter you have been introduced to some useful reference sites on the Internet. You can find more sites like this when you search using www.google.com for example.

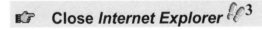 **Close** *Internet Explorer* $\ell\ell^3$

13.7 Background Information

Glossary

Database   Organized collection of data or files such as photos.

Encyclopedia   A work that contains articles on many different subjects, events and people.

Wikipedia   A multilingual, web-based free content encyclopedia project. *Wikipedia* is written collaboratively by volunteers, its articles can be edited by anyone with access to the website.

Useful links to interesting reference sites

In addition to the websites mentioned in this chapter, you can also take a look at these online reference sites:

Nature and Science

www.nationalgeographic.com	Information about geography, archaeology and natural science.
www.si.edu	Very rich website of the Smithsonian Institute, with many subsites.
www.nasa.gov	A treasure trove for all things to do with space exploration from NASA.

Movies, TV and Music

www.imdb.com	The world's largest movie database with information about movies, actors and characters.
www.allmusic.com	Large music database with information about artists, albums and songs.
www.tv.com	Database with information about current and discontinued TV series and shows.

Encyclopedias

www.encyclopedia.com	Encyclopedia and article search engine.
www.britannica.com	The online version of the famous Encyclopedia Britannica. Paid membership required to access all features.

- Continue reading on the next page -

Art

www.hermitagemuseum.com	Information about the history and collections of the famous Hermitage Museum in St. Petersburg.
www.britishmuseum.org	Extensive website of the British Museum.
www.rijksmuseum.nl	Website of the large Rijksmuseum (Dutch National Museum) in Amsterdam.
www3.vangoghmuseum.nl	Website of the Van Gogh Museum, Amsterdam
www.louvre.fr/llv/commun/ home.jsp?bmLocale=en	Website of the Louvre Museum, Paris
mv.vatican.va/3_EN/pages/MV _Home.html	Website of the Vatican Museums, Vatican City
www.metmuseum.org	The Metropolitan Museum of Art, New York

Royalty

www.royal.gov.uk	The official website of the British Monarchy, plus a great deal of historical information, timelines, etcetera.

Government

www.usa.gov	Information of the US Government on a large number of government-related subjects.
www.whitehouse.gov	Information about current affairs as well as historical information.
www.fbi.gov	FBI website that includes current as well as historical information.
www.cia.gov	CIA website with information about current affairs and an interactive historical timeline.

Presidents

www.whitehouse.gov/history/ presidents/chronological	Information about the current and previous presidents. Contains links to the websites of presidential libraries of former presidents, for example:
www.nixonlibraryfoundation.org	Website of the Nixon Library and Birthplace.
www.jimmycarterlibrary.org	Website of the Jimmy Carter Library and Museum.
www.jfklibrary.org	Website of the John F. Kennedy Presidential Library and Museum.

Appendices

A. Removing a Program

You may have programs installed on your computer that you no longer use. You can remove a program from your computer by going through the following steps:

In Windows Vista

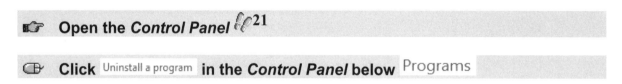

☞ Open the *Control Panel* ℓℓ21

☞ Click Uninstall a program in the *Control Panel* below Programs

You see the list of programs that can be uninstalled.

In this example the program *Adobe Reader* will be removed:

☞ Click
Adobe Reader 8.1.2

☞ Click Uninstall

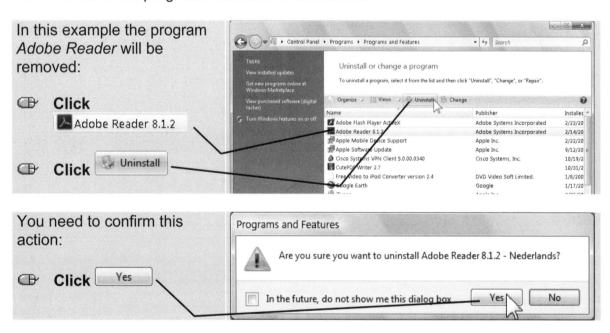

You need to confirm this action:

☞ Click Yes

Now the program removal is prepared. Your screen goes dark and you **see a** window where you need to allow a program to access your computer.

☞ Click → Allow

You can watch the progress of the program removal in the next window.

The program has been uninstalled. In some cases you will need to restart the computer after removing a program. If that is the case, you will see an alert message.

In Windows XP

☞ **Open the *Control Panel*** ℓℓ**21**

🖱 **Click** 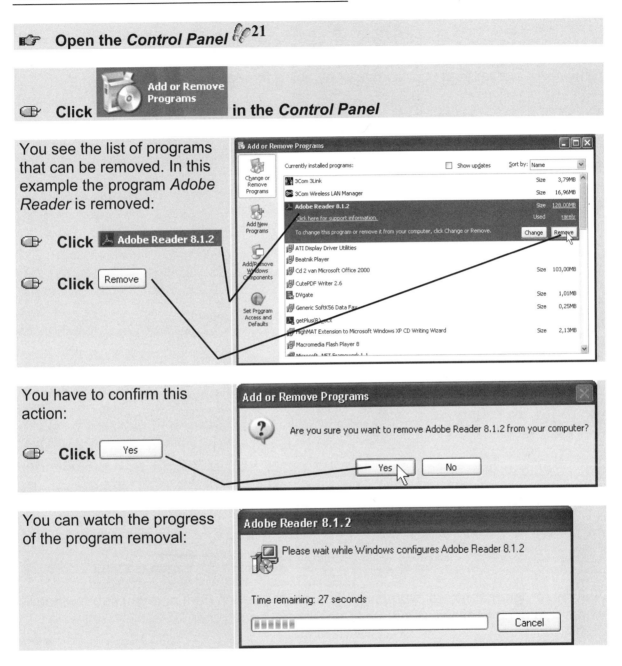 **in the *Control Panel***

You see the list of programs that can be removed. In this example the program *Adobe Reader* is removed:

🖱 **Click** Adobe Reader 8.1.2

🖱 **Click** Remove

You have to confirm this action:

🖱 **Click** Yes

You can watch the progress of the program removal:

The program has been uninstalled. In some cases you will need to restart the computer after removing a program. If that is the case, you will see an alert message.

B. How Do I Do That Again?

In this book some actions are marked with footsteps: 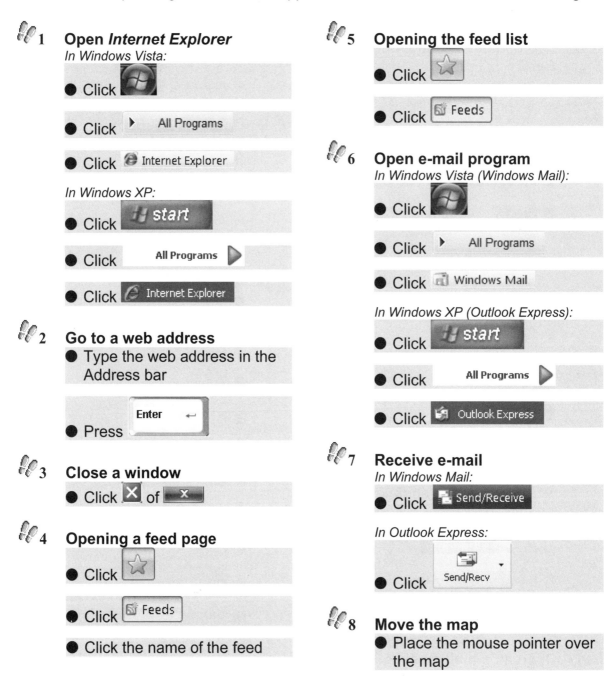[1]
Find the corresponding number in the appendix below to see how to do something.

1 Open *Internet Explorer*
In Windows Vista:
- Click [Windows logo]
- Click ▸ All Programs
- Click 🔹 Internet Explorer

In Windows XP:
- Click 🏁 start
- Click All Programs ▶
- Click 🔹 Internet Explorer

2 Go to a web address
- Type the web address in the Address bar
- Press Enter ↵

3 Close a window
- Click ✖ of ✖

4 Opening a feed page
- Click ☆
- Click ⭐ Feeds
- Click the name of the feed

5 Opening the feed list
- Click ☆
- Click ⭐ Feeds

6 Open e-mail program
In Windows Vista (Windows Mail):
- Click [Windows logo]
- Click ▸ All Programs
- Click 📧 Windows Mail

In Windows XP (Outlook Express):
- Click 🏁 start
- Click All Programs ▶
- Click 📧 Outlook Express

7 Receive e-mail
In Windows Mail:
- Click 📨 Send/Receive

In Outlook Express:
- Click 📨 Send/Recv ▾

8 Move the map
- Place the mouse pointer over the map

- Click and press the mouse button down. Hold it pressed down.

- Drag the mouse pointer

- Release the mouse button

9 Zoom in and out in *Google Earth*
- Click ⊖ or ⊕

10 Moving the photo
- Place the mouse pointer on ✋

- Press the left mouse button

- Drag ✋ in the desired direction

- Release the mouse button

11 Opening *My eBay*
- Click My eBay

12 Sign in to *eBay*
In the eBay window:
- Click Sign in

- Type your user ID next to User ID

- Type your password next to Password

- Click Sign in

- If you see the *AutoComplete Passwords* window, click No

13 Open an e-mail message
- Double-click the e-mail message

14 Enlarge the window
- Place the mouse pointer on the edge of the window's frame

- Press the left mouse button

- Drag the window's frame down

- Release the mouse button

15 Open the *Dashboard*
When you are signed in / from the blog:
- Click Customize

- Click Dashboard

From the Pick new template tab:
- Click Dashboard

16 Add a new post
- If necessary: sign in to *Blogger*

- Click ✚ New Post

- Type the message

- Click PUBLISH POST

17 Add a photo to a message
- Sign in to *Blogger*

- Click Posts next to ✿ Manage:

- Click Edit

- Click 🖼

- Click Browse...

- Select a photo

- Click Open

- Click **UPLOAD IMAGE**
- Click **DONE**
- Click **PUBLISH POST**

18 **Sign out of** *Blogger*
- Click Sign out

19 **Surf to a blog**
- Type the web address of the blog in the Address bar
- Press Enter ←

20 **Sign in to** *Blogger*
- Surf to www.blogger.com
- Type your e-mail address next to Username (Email):
- Type your password next to Password:
- Click **SIGN IN**

21 **Opening the** *Control Panel*
In Windows Vista:
- Click
- Click Control Panel

In Windows XP:
- Click **start**
- Click Control Panel

22 **Open your** *Facebook* **home page**
- Click home

23 **Sign out of** *eBay*
- Click Sign out

24 **Open** *Windows Live Messenger*
In Windows Vista:
- Click
- Click ▶ All Programs
- Click Windows Live
- Click Windows Live Messenger

In Windows XP:
- Click **start**
- Click All Programs ▶
- Click Windows Live
- Click Windows Live Messenger

C. Index

Interesting Online Applications for SENIORS